D1000555

AMERICAN LOBOTOMY

CoRpoRealities: Discourses of Disability

American Lobotomy

A RHETORICAL HISTORY

Jenell Johnson

University of Michigan Press

Ann Arbor

Copyright © by the University of Michigan 2014
All rights reserved

This book may not be reproduced, in whole or in part, including illustrations, in any form
(beyond that copying permitted by Sections 107 and 108 of the U.S. Copyright Law and
except by reviewers for the public press), without written permission from the publisher.

Published in the United States of America by
The University of Michigan Press
Manufactured in the United States of America
♾ Printed on acid-free paper

2017   2016   2015   2014   4   3   2   1

A CIP catalog record for this book is available from the British Library.

ISBN 978-0-472-11944-8 (hardcover : alk. paper)
ISBN 978-0-472-12058-1 (e-book)

For my parents, James and Joy Johnson

You think the guy telling this is ranting and raving my *God*; you think this is too horrible to have really happened, this is too awful to be the truth! But, please. It's still hard for me to have a clear mind thinking on it. But it's the truth even if it didn't happen.

—KEN KESEY, *ONE FLEW OVER THE CUCKOO'S NEST* (1962)

ACKNOWLEDGMENTS

Tracing the line of where this book begins and ends is difficult, and drawing the boundaries of my gratitude is nearly impossible. Thanks first to the teachers and professors whose imprint can be seen in my work: John Archer, Robin Brown, Dan Chicos, Loren Dunham, Stephanie Foote, Keith Gilyard, Gail Hawisher, Richard Leppert, Mark Micale, Peter Mortensen, Jeff Nealon, Elaine "Dr. E" Richardson, Jack Selzer, and Paula Treichler. Special thanks to Debbie Hawhee, a mentor from the day I began graduate school. Thank you to Michael Bérubé, whose feedback was invaluable in the construction of chapters 3 and 4, even though he spoiled the ending of *Terminal Man*. Thank you to Stephen Browne, who encouraged me to think deeply about memory and the *vita contemplativa*. Deep thanks to Rosa Eberly, who reminds me of the necessity to periodically *Howl* in public. Finally, my immeasurable gratitude and affection to Susan Squier. As an advisor, Susan's wise direction shaped this book in its infancy. As a scholar, Susan's commitment to interdisciplinary inquiry has been inspirational.

I have presented portions of this work in a number of venues and to a variety of audiences. Thanks to Steve Schiff and the Penn State College of Medicine's Neurosurgery and Psychiatry departments; the Rhetoric Society of America; the Penn State Conference on Rhetoric and Composition; the Rhetoric Society of America's Medical Rhetoric Summer Institute (especially Susan Wells, Ellen Barton, and Scott Graham); the University of Wisconsin's Life Sciences Communication Department; the Society for Literature, Science, and the Arts; Nikolas Rose, Giovanni Frazzetto, Klaus-Peter Lesch, the European Neuroscience and Society Network, and my fellow 2010 Neuroschool rebels; and Louise Whiteley, Adam Bencard, Thomas Söderqvist, Morten Bülow, Jesper Vaczy Kragh, and the staff of Copenhagen's Medical Museion.

An early version of chapter 1 appeared as "Thinking with the Thalamus: Lobotomy and the Rhetoric of Emotional Impairment," in *Journal of Literary and Cultural Disability Studies* 5, no. 2 (2011): 185–200; and a version of chapter

5 appeared as "A Dark History: Memories of Lobotomy in the New Era of Psychosurgery," in *Medicine Studies* 1, no. 4 (2009): 367–378. Thank you to Springer and Liverpool University Press for allowing me to reprint them here. The book's epigraph is from *One Flew over the Cuckoo's Nest* by Ken Kesey, copyright © 1962, renewed © 1990 by Ken Kesey. Used by permission of Viking Penguin, a division of Penguin Group (USA) Inc.

Thank you to my broad circle of academic fellow travelers and friends: Abram Anders, Jesse Ballenger, Sarah Birge, Kevin Browne, Tony Ceraso, Suzanne Cerrato, Amy Clukey, Melissa Girard, Scott Herring, Jordynn Jack, Elizabeth Mazzolini, Carrie Neerland, Andrew Pilsch, Jeff Pruchnic, Spencer Schaffner, Marika Siegel, Michelle Smith, Robyn Thoren-Smith, Shannon Walters, Angela Ward, Joshua Weiss, and Megan Zuelsdorff. Special thanks to Melissa Littlefield, who in addition to serving as my sounding board, coauthor, and collaborator in neurothings, is also directly responsible for pointing me toward the University of Michigan Press.

My sincere thanks to the wonderful folks at the University of Michigan Press, particularly my two editors: Tom Dwyer, who supported this project from the day I pitched the idea to him over Indian food during the Society for Literature, Science, and the Arts Conference, and LeAnn Fields, who took the reins after Tom's departure. Christopher Dreyer, Marcia LaBrenz, and Carol Sickman-Garner: thank you making such a beautiful book. My gratitude as well to David Mitchell and Sharon Snyder, for including this book in the pathbreaking Corporealities series, and to Margaret Price for being a rhetorical catalyst.

Thank you to the people of Louisiana and Wisconsin for their support of the two great public universities that have allowed me to finish this project. At Louisiana State University, thank you to my friends, colleagues, and students, especially: Steve Bickmore, Jim Catano, Brannon Costello, Gina Costello, Stephanie Houston Grey, Rachel Hall, Dustin Howes, Cara Jones, Laura Jones, Michelle Massé, Anna Nardo, Dan Novak, Lisi Oliver, Irv Peckham, Rick Popp, Shannon Popp, Brooke Rollins, April Weber, Chris Weber, and Sue Weinstein. Many, many thanks to Lilly Bridwell-Bowles, my fabulous mentor, always-elegant lunch date, and Louisiana tour guide. At the University of Wisconsin, my thanks to Rob Asen, Dominique Brossard, Jim Brown, Karma Chávez, Jonathan Gray, Linda Hogle, Rob Howard, Vance Kepley, Eunjung Kim, Linda Lucey, Steve Lucas, Sara McKinnon, Logan Middleton, J. J. Murphy, Lynn Nyhart, Christa Olson, Ellen Samuels, Walt Schalick, Dietram Scheufele, Sue Zaeske, and the faculty, staff, and students of the Communication Arts Department. Thank you to George Hamel and Pamela Hamel for their generous support of faculty research. Thanks to my writing partners for keeping me on track: Monica Grant, Eunjung Kim, Lori Kido Lopez, Christa Olson, Ellen Samuels, and Catalina Toma. Thank you also to Amanda Swenson and Jennifer Ellis West for their research assistance when it was most needed, and to Liz Barr, for helping me to wrap up the loose ends.

A number of friends and colleagues have provided feedback on this work in different forms: Steve Bickmore, Lilly Bridwell-Bowles, Kevin Browne, Elizabeth Donaldson, Rachel Hall, Christa Olson, Rick Popp, Catherine Prendergast, Brooke Rollins, Ellen Samuels, Mike Xenos, and the two anonymous reviewers: thank you from the bottom of my heart.

Thank you to the archivists and staff members of George Washington University's Gelman Library, whose warm welcome and assistance were invaluable in the early stages of this project. Thank you the guides of the Trans-Allegheny Lunatic Asylum, particularly Greg "Copperhead" Graham. Mike Xenos drove with me for sixteen hours to West Virginia, walked through an abandoned asylum all day and part of the night, and helped me document the experience: is "thank you" enough for that?

And finally, thank you to my family. My huge extended family. My grandparents Leonard Johnson, Bernice Johnson, and Annabelle Chervestad. My grandpa Juell Chervestad, who was one of the most inquisitive and quietly brilliant people I've ever known. He would have read every word of this book, and I miss him dearly. My incredible sisters, Jodi Carreon and Jenna Clay, who became friends at some ineffable point. My brothers-in-law, Kevin Clay and Ryan Carreon. My parents, James and Joy Johnson, who were the best teachers anyone could have asked for. And finally, Max, my partner in everything: *Do you know*?

CONTENTS

Introduction

Marvelous History

> Marvels are meanings out of control.
>
> —IAN HACKING, *REWRITING THE SOUL: MULTIPLE PERSONALITY AND THE SCIENCES OF MEMORY* (1995)

When people discover I am writing a book about lobotomy, they have many questions. Did doctors really use an ice pick? Was there really a plan to lobotomize criminals? Have I heard the joke *I'd rather have a bottle in front of me than a frontal lobotomy*? Did the United States/Russia/China use lobotomy for mind control? Did Jeffrey Dahmer lobotomize his victims before he killed them? Wasn't Tennessee Williams's sister/Allen Ginsberg's mother/John F. Kennedy's sister lobotomized? And invariably, someone whispers, *do they still do that?*

People have a lot of questions about lobotomy. But in the six years I have been working on this book, nobody has asked what seems to be the most obvious question of all: *What is a lobotomy*? Most people are not medical historians, most have never held a scalpel, and most have had no personal or family experiences with lobotomy. Yet most people in the United States know something about this operation, and what they know appears to be drawn entirely from its representation in public culture.[1] Lobotomy has been the subject of conspiracy theories, political propaganda, radio and television documentaries, autobiographies, biographies, paintings, t-shirts, jokes, and congressional hearings. The operation features in novels like Robert Penn Warren's *All the King's Men* (1946) and Bernard Wolfe's *Limbo* (1950); plays like Tennessee Williams's *Suddenly, Last Summer* (1958); poems like Allen Ginsberg's "Howl" (1955); songs like the Ramones' "Teenage Lobotomy" (1977); and films like *A Fine Madness* (1966), *Planet of the Apes* (1968), *One Flew over the Cuckoo's Nest* (1975), *Frances* (1982), *Repo Man* (1984), *A Hole in One* (2004), and *Asylum*

(2008). Lobotomy has become something of a national landmark in American cultural geography.

First used in 1935 by Portuguese neurologist Antonio Caetano de Abreu Freire "Egas" Moniz, lobotomy was imported in 1936 to the United States, where it remained part of the psychiatric armamentarium for nearly twenty years.[2] The operation was used to "bleach" or "blunt" strong emotion in people diagnosed with certain mental illnesses and, to a lesser extent, to ameliorate chronic pain.[3] Most patients underwent prefrontal lobotomy, an invasive form of neurosurgery that severed fibers connecting the thalamus and the frontal lobes. Others received a variation called transorbital lobotomy, in which an instrument resembling an icepick was hammered through the orbital plate (eye socket) and swung back and forth to damage the same area of the brain. In the United States alone, tens of thousands of women, men, and even children were subjected to some form of lobotomy.[4]

Although lobotomy has been consigned to the trash heap of medical treatments now considered bizarre and barbaric, the operation was once in the mainstream of modern medicine, heralded as evidence of the "golden era of discovery and healing," as one newspaper story put it ("Medicine's Golden Era" 1944). While lobotomists now populate the ranks of medicine's most infamous, Walter Freeman, often called "America's dean of lobotomy," was a respected neurologist who lectured in teaching hospitals and wrote a column for the *American Journal of Psychiatry* for nearly fifteen years. Lobotomy was not on the margins of medicine, practiced in dark corners by unlicensed quacks. Rather, it was—at least for a time—perched within medicine's "pantheon," a fact best illustrated by the fact that in 1949 Egas Moniz was awarded the Nobel Prize for Medicine (J. Pressman 1999, 5; Valenstein 1986, 4).

People are often shocked to discover that lobotomy was honored with the Nobel Prize and find it difficult to reconcile the fact that one the most reviled events in the history of medicine was once among its most revered. This surprise stems from the fact that in American public culture, lobotomy has emerged as "our most visible icon for everything that is dangerous and bad about uncontrolled medical science" (J. Pressman 1999, 3). Yet lobotomy is not only an icon of bad medicine. Representations of lobotomy, particularly films like *One Flew over the Cuckoo's Nest*, *Planet of the Apes*, and *Frances*, also carry strong social and political overtones. Although lobotomy largely disappeared from American medicine by the late 1950s, the operation lives on in public culture as an authoritarian mode of behavioral control: a surgical means to

Fig. 1. Egas Moniz gives Walter Freeman an award, 1948. (Courtesy of the Special Collections Research Center, The George Washington University.)

suppress dissent, force obedience, and extinguish the individual personality. In the American imagination, lobotomy looms as perhaps the ultimate threat to the individualism and liberalism at the mythic core of the nation.

Jack Pressman's award-winning history *Last Resort: Psychosurgery and the Limits of Medicine* (1999) positions itself in direct contrast to the image of lobotomy I have described above.[5] The tales we have told about lobotomy, Pressman argues, have distorted our understanding of lobotomy's medical history, and have led to the contemporary opinion—including the opinion of many doctors and historians—that lobotomy was a worthless, unscientific therapy practiced by unscrupulous physicians at the edge of the profession (403, 441). Representations of lobotomy in American public culture, which transform the operation into mad science and lobotomists into monsters, are particularly vexing to Pressman. These texts "make for great polemics and for spine-tingling science fiction," he writes, "but as history they are often just plain wrong" (4).

I have no quarrel with Pressman's claim that representations of lobotomy in public culture are often wrong. There is no evidence that Soviet agents posing as psychiatrists ever planned to use psychosurgery to orchestrate a takeover of the United States, as one story I discuss in chapter 3 claims. Actress Frances Farmer almost certainly did not receive a lobotomy, as the biography *Shadowland* (Arnold [1978] 1982) and the biopic *Frances* (1982) suggest. And it is unlikely that Walter Freeman's ghost is haunting the halls of the Trans-Allegheny Lunatic Asylum in West Virginia, or at least not in the way that the paranormal investigators from *Ghost Adventures* (2009) would like you to believe. Pressman is right that stories like these often do not match up with what happened in doctors' offices, operating rooms, professional conferences, and medical journals— those texts and spaces that comprise contemporary medicine as well as its traditional archive. Nevertheless, they ought not be discarded simply because they are "wrong." These stories *are* histories. To be sure, they are not histories of medicine in the sense that Pressman's *Last Resort* is a history of medicine. They are histories of something else: they are documents of the meaning of lobotomy in American culture. If lobotomy has become our "most visible icon" for bad medicine, as Pressman suggests, then that iconicity has a history too.

No matter how dutifully they are policed, the boundaries between fact and fiction, medicine and culture, and even benevolence and malevolence are permeable, sometimes uncomfortably so. After all, "it requires only a small shift in our credibility for the surgeon to become the slasher" (Boss 1986, 21). Take the horror film *Asylum* (2008), for example. In it, six college freshmen discover that their newly renovated dormitory was once a private mental hospital. "It was supposed to be a safe refuge for patients," explains one student in the conspiratorial tone of campfire ghost stories,

> but it really turned out to be their worst nightmare. Around 1935, the asylum got taken over by a psychiatrist. His name was Dr. Magnus Burke. And what he did was he got rid of all the patients except teenagers. Burke thought that he somehow could cure mental illness caused by childhood pain if he treated it quick enough. But I'm telling you guys, nobody—not the parents, not the patients, not even the authorities had any idea about what these supposedly disturbed kids were going to be subjected to.

A montage of gruesome images flashes in rapid succession: a convulsing boy strapped to a bed, a girl chained to a wall, wearing a straitjacket of barbed wire. The student continues:

> Up until Burke, people would do lobotomies by hand-drilling holes into heads . . . but Burke found another way. Burke would drive lobotomy picks into both eyes at once to simultaneously destroy tissue in the frontal lobes.

The film cuts to a computer screen with an image of a man's unmistakably hirsute forearm positioning an icepick in a young boy's eye socket and then to a flashback in which Dr. Burke reassures his squirming young patient that he will make "all the bad things go away." "Eventually," our narrator concludes,

> Burke's lobotomies were seen for what they were: another brutal form of restraint. He was discredited and ostracized as a new generation of drugs took the place of his procedures. With a damaged reputation, he suffered a psychotic breakdown, and began to murder the teens. One day in 1939, the patients led a rebellion and killed the doctor. Nobody ever found his body. And some people think he's still here, roaming the asylum.

Naturally, Dr. Burke returns to pick off the six students one by one, finding terrible new uses for his surgical instruments.

Even though *Asylum* and its murderous M.D. are clearly works of fiction, the film manages to get a surprising number of details about Dr. Burke's operation correct. Walter Freeman, clearly the inspiration for Magnus Burke, popularized the transorbital lobotomy in the late 1940s. Ordinary surgeon's blades were too flimsy to perforate the thick bone of the orbital plate, so Freeman turned to an instrument "ideally suited" to the procedure: the "humble" ice pick (Freeman 1950, 53). Although the ice pick was replaced by the transorbital leucotome, an instrument specially developed for the surgery, the ghastly image led the American press to christen transorbital lobotomy the "ice pick surgery." Freeman, who prided himself on his ambidexterity, did on occasion drive leucotomes through both eye sockets at the same time (El-Hai 2005, 245).

What is more, the photograph in *Asylum* depicts not the fictional Magnus Burke, but the real Walter Freeman, and the boy he is operating on is not "William," but Howard Dully, who received a transorbital lobotomy at the age of twelve. In 2005, National Public Radio broadcast Howard Dully's story "My Lobotomy," which reconstructed his family and medical history in an effort to answer why his parents had authorized the surgery that changed his life. The story begins with Dully's rich baritone:

> In 1960, when I was twelve, I was lobotomized by . . . Dr. Walter Freeman. Until this moment I haven't shared this fact with anyone, except my wife and a few close friends. Now, I'm sharing it with you. . . . If you saw me, you'd never know I had a lobotomy. The only thing you'd notice is that I'm very tall and weigh about 350 pounds. But I've always felt different, wondered if something's missing from my soul. I have no memory of the operation and never had the courage to ask my family about it. So two years ago I set out on a journey to learn everything I could about my lobotomy. ("My Lobotomy" 2005)

Audience response to the twenty-two-minute broadcast was literally overwhelming. Immediately after the story aired, listeners generated such heavy email traffic that NPR's server crashed for the first time in its history.

Until he began to work with producers David Isay and Piya Kochar, Howard Dully had shared information about his lobotomy with very few people. In fact, when first approached by the producers, Dully refused to let them use his last name or otherwise identify him (Dully and Fleming 2007, 212). In a 2005 interview, he explains why:

> There's a stigma that's attached to brain operations and mental conditions that is really overwhelming to anyone that . . . has had one or has had to deal with it. . . . Not only the lobotomy, but being housed in a state mental institution. . . . . The

fear of coming out of the closet, so to speak, was what kept me there. . . . I wasn't
sure I was willing to face . . . the possibility of ridicule. (Dully 2005)

The stigma Dully describes is more pronounced today than it was when lobotomy
was in use in American medicine. In 2010, for instance, Florida's Busch Gardens
amusement park featured the character "Lobotomy Larry," a "half-witted hulk
of a man with the mind of a deranged 2-year-old—and upchucked spaghetti
O's on his bib," who menaced visitors as they entered a Halloween attraction
(Cabrera 2010). The fear of being associated with images like this led Howard
Dully to suppress information about his past from nearly everyone in his life.
He worried:

> Would people think I was a freak? Would they treat me like I was a freak? After
> all, when you hear that someone has had knitting needles stuck in their head
> and egg-beaten around for ten minutes, you might assume that they're going
> to be some drooling Frankenstein monster. I was afraid I might be treated that
> way. (Dully and Fleming 2007, 240)

Yet images like Lobotomy Larry provoked more than just fear and shame in
Howard Dully. Confronted by the ubiquity of these images, he writes, "I began
to ask myself whether I had really been given a lobotomy. I wondered why I
wasn't a vegetable [and] if what I knew about lobotomies was true" (Dully and
Fleming 2007, 212). The image of lobotomy in American public culture was so
powerful and so persuasive, in other words, it led Howard Dully to question his
own memory.

Narratives like *Asylum* might be wrong as faithful accounts of what
happened in doctors' offices and operating rooms, and there is no question
that caricatures like Lobotomy Larry violently misrepresent real people's lives.
However, as Howard Dully's example demonstrates, stories—even wrong
stories—are formidable cultural forces, and they thus are well worth our
critical attention. Wrong stories, that is to say, those narratives stricken from
the archive as fictive, unverifiable, unreliable, invented, polemical, mythical,
erroneous, imaginative, or symbolic, are valuable for what they reveal about the
culture that created them, and they ultimately "lead us beyond facts to their
meanings" (Portelli 1991, 2, cited in Reverby 2001, 23). Howard Dully's story is
a story of American medical history, but it is also a story about the meaning of
medicine in American culture. I contend in this book that those two stories are

inextricably linked, and each has shaped, and continues to shape, the meaning of the other. If we are to fully understand lobotomy's life, its death, and its ghost in American medicine, it is essential to understand the many meanings of lobotomy in American culture.

Engaging Medicine

In the last twenty years, there has been much hand-wringing by scientists, doctors, and politicians about the public understanding, or more accurately, the public's *lack* of understanding, about science and medicine. Academic inquiry into the matter initially took shape under the aegis of the "public understanding of science," an approach that envisions communication between science and the public as a one-way flow of information from experts (who know) to nonexperts (who do not). In recent years, however, this "deficit model" has been radically reconceived, as science communication scholars have reframed public understanding as public engagement (S. Miller 2001). The American Association for the Advancement of Science (AAAS), for example, has created the Center for Public Engagement in response to what "too often has been seen as a paternalistic stance" with regard to the relationship between scientists and the public. To correct this perception, AAAS chief Alan Leshner (2003) has proposed "a more open and honest bidirectional dialogue about science and technology and their products, including not only their benefits but also their limits, perils, and pitfalls" (977). In 2007, an editorial in the journal *Public Understanding of Science* all but pronounced the deficit model dead, declaring that "we have moved from the old days of the deficit frame and thinking of publics as monolithic to viewing publics as active, knowledgeable, playing multiple roles, receiving as well as shaping science" (Einsiedel 2007, 5).

One of the primary laments of deficit model proponents is that the public does not consume enough information about science and medicine. However, perhaps a better way to sum up their critique is that the public doesn't consume the *right kind* of information. After all, we engage with science and medicine nearly every day. We wear necklaces with dangling silver serotonin molecules; we buy postage stamps that celebrate scientists and scientific achievements (e.g., R. Jones 2004); we read superhero comics featuring genetics, evolution, and biomedical ethics (e.g., S. Locke 2005); we read novels and watch films about the dangers of deregulated scientific research (*Jurassic Park*; *Splice*). We read books about how to cure autism with gluten-free diets; we are inspired by patient pathographies and surgeons' biographies; and we sob through movies about patients, celebrating their triumphs and grieving their pain and loss. On television, we find medical comedies, dramas, soap operas, reality shows, talk shows (Dr. Oz for the body, Dr. Phil for the mind), and even entire networks devoted to health and healing. We clearly are interested in science, and we are fascinated by medicine, which, "it seems, has replaced baseball as our national pastime" (Friedman 2004, 1–2).

A select few medical objects provoke especially intense fascination. Viagra, for example, appears to have shifted from the technical to the public sphere (Goodnight 1982) accompanied by a readymade collection of jokes and feminist criticism. Likewise, face transplantation, in vitro fertilization, electroconvulsive therapy, Botox, anabolic steroids, Prozac, cosmetic surgery, psychoanalysis, abortion, and lobotomy are more than just medical objects that seamlessly translate into cultural objects. Each is a "knot of knowledge making practices, industry and commerce, popular culture, social struggles, psychoanalytic formations, bodily histories, human and nonhuman actions, local and global flows, inherited narratives, new stories, syncretic technical/cultural processes, and more" (Haraway 1997, 129). Because of the powerful public fascination with these medical objects, because of their power to arrest our attention and incite our imagination, and because of the affective, historical, cultural, social, ideological, technical, and political contexts in which their meanings take shape, it is impossible to fully understand medical objects of public fascination, which I call *medical marvels*, strictly from within the domain of medicine.

Marvelous Medicine

It might seem odd to call lobotomy a medical marvel, particularly since "marvel" is typically employed as an honorific. As I will show in the early chapters of this book, this positive sense of "marvel" correctly describes lobotomy's public image in the 1930s and 1940s. However, I use the term for other reasons. An Internet search for "medical marvel" turns up predictable references to stem cells and penicillin but also returns many stories and countless images of individuals with rare bodily differences, such as conjoined twins.[6] To describe bodily difference as *marvelous* reflects the intense symbolism applied to extraordinary bodies since antiquity, and "marvel" is often uttered in the same breath as "miracle" and "monster."[7] One easily imagines "medical marvel" flying on a hand-painted banner above the freak show, where curious spectators are invited to stare at the bodies on stage.

Staring is more than just looking. Writes Rosemarie Garland-Thomson (2009):

> We stare when ordinary seeing fails, when we want to know more. So staring is an interrogative gesture that asks what's going on and demands the story. The eyes hang on, working to recognize what seems illegible, order what seems unruly, know what seems strange. Staring begins as an impulse that curiosity can carry forward into engagement. (3)

As Garland-Thomson contends, people stare in an effort to answer the question that the extraordinary body, overwritten with centuries of symbolic residue, appears to pose. To classify people with bodily or mental difference as *medical marvels*, then, hints at a symbolism so intense it stretches the limits of biomedical knowledge.

In his book *Rewriting the Soul* (1995) Ian Hacking uses this sense of *marvel* to examine the anxieties provoked when scientists confront polysemy. Marvels are "meanings out of control" (144). Scientists tend to avoid marvels, Hacking maintains, "not because marvels are vacuous, empty of meaning, but because they are too full of meaning, of hints, of feeling" (143).[8] Science does not disavow marvels like multiple personality disorder, extrasensory perception, or extraterrestrial life because they have no scientific value. If science "abhors" the marvel (143), it is because the marvel is contaminated by its unfettered circulation within public culture and the multiple meanings that accrue as a result. Science casts the marvel aside as an improper object (Butler 1994) as a way to maintain its identity, which, charged by the logical principle of noncontradiction, is tied to a singular account of the world. This "boundary work" (Gieryn 1983; Taylor 1996) may be constitutive of scientific self-recognition, but it also produces misrecognition by suppressing the imaginative and cultural realms in which much scientific invention and medical innovation takes place (see, e.g., Bachelard [1934] 1984; Waldby 1996; Squier 2004).

Avery Gordon (2008) has observed similar boundary work in sociology, which abolishes the fictive in order to shore up its disciplinary identity:

> By the fictive I mean not simply literature but . . . the ensemble of cultural imaginings, affective experiences, animated objects, marginal voices, narrative

densities, and eccentric traces of power's presence. For sociology, the fictive
is our constitutive horizon of error; it is what has been and must be exiled to
ordain the authority of the discipline and truthful knowledge sociology can
claim to produce. As a mode of storytelling, sociology distinguishes itself from
literature by its now historical claim to find and report the facts expertly. The
maintenance of the disciplinary object, social reality, that meets something akin
to the juridical strict scrutiny test is predicated upon a clear distinction between
what is (socially) real and what is fictional. (25–26)

Gordon writes these words in a book entitled *Ghostly Matters,* which is as much
a meditation about disciplinary boundaries as it is an ethereally beautiful book
about haunting. Although Gordon uses haunting as a trope, the marvel also
haunts her pages. "Ghosts are a somewhat unusual topic of inquiry for a social
analyst (much less a degreed sociologist)," Gordon admits, yet quickly adds that
her interest is not in the "occult" or the "paranormal" (7–8). Simply speaking, the
academy stigmatizes marvels like ghosts, which makes them a rather risky topic
of inquiry—even as a trope. As the eminent neuroscientist Antonio Damasio
(1999) writes about his work with consciousness, a marvel in neuroscience for
many years, this line of inquiry "was simply not the thing to do before you made
tenure, and even after you did it was looked upon with suspicion" (7). The stigma
of the marvelous may be contagious.[9]

When the marvel is taken up as a proper object of scholarly inquiry, it
is usually by looking it in the "face," as Hacking notes (244). This unmasking
tendency is perhaps best observed in historians. Although history may have a
higher tolerance for ambiguity and polysemy than the natural or social sciences,
its scholarly value is largely wedded to the fidelity of its narratives with past
events (Jenkins 2003, 13). Historical narratives that aim to correct the historical
record by unmasking the marvelous seem to be accorded particular value, it
seems. A familiar strategy in both academic and popular history is to take a
familiar person, object, or event and to peel away the layers of marvel in order
to reveal the true story concealed beneath. This is precisely Jack Pressman's
strategy with lobotomy in *Last Resort*. The marvel is often more fiction than
fact—and for many historians, the boundaries between these two realms must
be strictly maintained. This is no mere wrangling over method: as Gordon
points out, disciplinary identity may also be at stake. In history, as in science, to
confront the marvel is to remove the mask in order to look the past in the face.
But what might we see if we keep our eyes fixed on the mask?

There is a fascinating tale to tell about the origin and the impact of the marvelous, and it is a story I believe is best told with a rhetorical perspective, which allows us to suspend the unmasking reflex characteristic of so much scholarly inquiry (Sedgwick 2003, 8; Segal 2005, 5). The relation of rhetoric to history is a contentious one, and rhetoricians and historians alike have accused the rhetorical historian of stepping into unauthorized territory. Why, asks rhetorician David Zarefsky (2003), summing up this critique, "should rhetoricians do history, especially when there is also a history department?" (31). Rhetorical historians reply that there is no shortage of material from the past, and as feminist, queer, social, and labor historians know very well, there is no shortage of ways to make sense of that past. "There is no fundamentally correct 'text' of which other interpretations are just variations," writes historian Keith Jenkins (2003); "variations are all there are" (14). What characterizes the rhetorical historian then, is "not subject matter but perspective" (Zarefsky, 30).

The historian is "primarily concerned with 'truth,'" writes historian Keith Hopkins (1993), a disciplinary convention so prevalent it "hardly needs authentication" (3 f.1). The conventional historian sifts through documents in order to construct a historical narrative that at least asymptotically approaches an accurate account of what really happened.[10] In contrast, for the rhetorical historian, "accuracy is only one rather minor and elusive consideration; the power of . . . stories and images as symbolic constructions of reality for their publics is precisely the stuff of the rhetorical historian" (Turner 2003, 5). This does not mean that rhetoricians are sloppy scholars or that we are unconcerned with what really happened, despite the fact that our field has been encumbered with a Platonic curse in which "rhetoric" is frequently employed as the antonym of "reality."

For rhetoricians, to use an example I often use with my students, there is no outside Plato's allegorical cave—the cave, its shadows constructed by symbols, is all we have to work with. A rhetorical perspective adjusts our focus away from the divine glare of universal truth and toward symbols in all their messy earthly contingency: images framed by history; language bound by culture and convention; signs with unstable referents; narratives written, spoken, repeated, translated, and understood by someone, somewhere, sometime. Rhetoric investigates the power of language, often understood as persuasion, and as a discipline, rhetorical studies seeks to understand that power in action, particularly the power of meaning. "Something of the rhetorical motive comes to lurk in every 'meaning,'" writes Kenneth Burke (1969) in a famous definition, for "wherever there is persuasion, there is rhetoric. And wherever there is 'meaning,' there is 'persuasion'" (172).

I want to emphasize here that rhetorical history does not necessarily provide a better or more accurate account than other forms of history. "Rather than reject one historical account or another," writes Leah Ceccarelli (2001), "and rather than introduce a new reading that conflicts with all the rest, rhetorical inquiry takes its cue from the theory of interdisciplinarity" (179). A rhetorician is but "one voice in a dialogue. Put several such voices together, with each voicing its own special assertion, let them act upon one another in cooperative competition, and you get a dialectic that, properly developed, can lead to a view transcending the limitations of each" (Burke 1951, 203).

When confronted with a marvel, then, a thick knot of meanings emerging from a snarl of cultural contexts, the rhetorical historian's role is that of untangler rather than unmasker.[11] She might theorize why a marvel emerged at a particular place and time; hunt for the origins of its polysemic tendrils in cultural narratives, social structures, and political events; and track how a marvel is transformed when transmitted, repeated, and bounced "across bodies of discourse and across bodies" (Doyle 1997, 5). Despite its Platonic baggage, rhetoric is not opposed to reality. Rather, rhetoric is a species of reality that can be observed in the material effects and virtual traces of images, symbols, tropes, and narratives, which are best understood within the social, cultural, ideological, and political environments in which they develop meaning and in which those meanings are received, interpreted, and contested (see, e.g., Stuart Hall 1999).

If I were to write a biography of Helen Keller, for example—conventional historical fare—I would be interested in her family's history, her birth, her early illness, her famed relationship with teacher Anne Sullivan, and her later career as a public figure and political activist, and I would arrange these events to form a diachronic narrative. If I were to investigate what we might call the *rhetorical life* of Helen Keller, instead of stopping at the boundary of her biography, I might also investigate how "Helen Keller" came to represent disability education and how Helen Keller's life has been mobilized as the archetypal narrative of the "heroic overcomer," a person who overcomes long odds to achieve great things and whose story is often presented as an inspiration for nondisabled people.[12]

The rhetorical Helen Keller is an excellent example of what S. Paige Baty (1995) has described as a "representative character," a "cultural figure through whom the character of political life is articulated" (8).[13] American culture is rife with representative characters, from Helen Keller to Martin Luther King Jr. to Marilyn Monroe, the subject of Baty's study. The lives of representative characters, she writes, "are made to chart various cultural courses":

The representative character embodies and expresses achievement, success, failure, genius, struggle, triumph, and other human possibilities: one representative character's story may be written as a cautionary tale, while another's may be erected as a monument to human achievement. The influence and expression of the representative characters are not limited to their immediate lifetimes: these figures become sites of recollection after their deaths. (9)

The unmasking reflex of conventional history strips away "Marilyn Monroe" to reveal the Norma Jeanne Baker underneath. And yet Marilyn Monroe is much more than the biographical Norma Jeanne: she is also "victim, heroine, queen bitch, unattainable sex object, frigid sex symbol, dumb blonde, feminist, communist, political pawn, communist spy, photographic object, biographical subject, material object, material girl, and media manipulator" (22). Although she does not use the term, Baty writes a marvelous history rather than a conventional biography, and the product is a fascinating account of the emergence of "Marilyn Monroe" as a site where culture and politics mingle.

As the case of Marilyn Monroe suggests, while publicity is a necessary condition for the marvel, it is not a sufficient condition. Or to put it another way, there is a difference between being public and being famous, which might best be described as the intensification of publicity, in the sense that indigo is a more intense shade of blue (e.g., Nealon 2008). The marvel is more than just public. It is *saturated* with publicity. Thus, the marvel might be characterized by the density of the cultural networks that enfold it in layers of meaning. In a basic sense, this saturation can be understood as wide circulation. And yet another more crucial aspect of the marvel's circulation is its translation between various discourses and cultural fields, and particularly the bidirectional translation between fact and fiction. "Once medical images leave the strictly regulated contexts of the scientific media," explains Catherine Waldby (2000), "their debt to the imaginary, the speculative, to desire, the fictive, to particular cultural genres and stock narratives, becomes less readily ignored. The intertextuality of scientific images is more evident at these points of popularization, and this intertextuality implies that the interpretation of images by different nonscientific audiences can lead off in a number of directions and is open to various orders of appropriation" (138–139). The small inked "Prozac" stamped by Eli Lilly on a green and yellow pill of fluoxetine enters the *American Journal of Psychiatry*, where it is analyzed in articles and featured in advertisements, read by doctors, and written on prescriptions and bottles; Prozac enters memoir, is adapted into film, distilled into joke, screamed in punk rock lyrics; Prozac is reported in magazines, read by patients, spoken in a hopeful request to doctors; Prozac is named in lawsuits, written in history books, used as metaphor, subject to criticism. Translated and appropriated by a wide variety of discourses and counterdiscourses that flow, shift, and intensify meaning: this is how a green and yellow pill of fluoxetine becomes a medical marvel.

These appropriations depend on social and historical contexts for meaning, as do the affective responses that charge their reception, interpretation, and contestation. "To *marvel*. . . is to be filled with awe, surprise, admiration, or astonishment. Clearly the phenomena that will stimulate such responses will vary from age to age, region to region, and person to person" (T. Jones and Sprunger 2002, xii, original emphasis). A medical marvel at one time or place (blood transfusion, organ transplantation, or in vitro fertilization) may fail to elicit wonder—and may even provoke horror—in another. A marvel is something that a historically, geographically, and culturally specific *we* marvel *at,* and in this sense "marvel" might be better understood as a transitive verb than a noun. A medical marvel offers a glimpse into the affective, social, and political contours of a culture's relationship with medicine: our fervent hopes and trenchant fears about medicine's power to alter our bodies and psychiatry's power to change our minds.

Indeed, psychiatry may well be the most marvelous of the many medical objects that become objects of public fascination. "Psychiatry is a deeply controversial aspect of our modern, secular world of knowledge. It raises questions about the very nature of the Self, about the relations of body and mind, about our emotions and our sexuality, about the individual and the expert, about the nature of disease and illness, about the status and limits of applied science, and about compulsion and state power" (Micale and Porter 1994, 26). A cigar may be just a cigar for Dr. Freud, but in public culture, psychiatry is never just psychiatry, and Dr. Freud is never just Dr. Freud. The psychiatrist is a recurring object of public fascination: the protagonist with special insight into human nature (*The Prince of Tides*; *The Sopranos*) or the antagonist who, knowing a little something about human nature, makes an ideal sociopath (*The Silence of the Lambs*; *American Horror Story*). As June Bingham, self-described member of the lay public, advised psychiatrists in the *American Journal of Psychiatry* in 1951:

> What we think of psychiatry is largely what we think of psychiatrists. For we learn about you and your field less from *your* books than from *ours;* less from

"Psychopathology of Every Day Life" than from "The Snake Pit"; and in these novels, detective stories, plays, movies, and radio programs of ours, psychiatry appears not in the form of theory, but in the form of a person, a character, The Psychiatrist." (600–601, original emphasis)

Bingham tells her audience that the public sees them equally as "gods" and "devils," adding, "there doesn't seem to be any ceiling on what we're willing to believe about you" (600).

As psychiatrists have grown ever more marvelous in American public culture, so have their tools. Converse, for example, recently released "The Straightjacket," a shoe line covered in straps. The Internet game World of Warcraft features the power of "electroshock," which players can use to stun opponents into submission. Lithium, Prozac, and Thorazine have all been adopted as band names. Representations like these, argues Jonathan Metzl (2003), should not be thought of as

> products of science polluted by popular culture or distortions of the true concepts of psychopharmacology. Rather, they also represent psychopharmacology as the product of multiple, interrelated discourses, each of which comes to inform the other. Genetics, neurochemistry, and pharmacology might claim to uncover universal facts. But these facts are interpreted only through cultural moments in which they are given meaning, mediated through the particulars of specific time periods, philosophies, aesthetics, and other broad contexts into which pharmaceuticals come to circulate. (18)

Like Metzl observes about psychopharmacology, lobotomy emerged, developed, declined, and is remembered in particular cultural moments. At different points in its history, lobotomy has meant miracle cure, punishment, therapeutic courage, brainwashing, control, torture, castration, gag, conformity, biomedical progress, biomedical ignorance, homicide, suicide, rehabilitation, communist plot, misogynist plot, racist plot, joke, lesson, horror, and freedom. Each of these meanings emerges out of lobotomy's circulation within and between scientific, medical, social, cultural, and political discourses in which the operation came to mean much more than a type of brain surgery for mental illness.

In the chapters that follow, I explore how the meanings of lobotomy emerged, accrued, and transformed as they circulated between medicine and public culture. Like conventional histories, rhetorical histories may be organized diachronically (as this book roughly is); however, rhetorical history also relishes the synchronic view, pausing to dart sideways and slantways, in order to examine the interplay of particular texts and contexts in sometimes-microscopic detail (e.g., McGee 1980). The language of motion above reflects an important element of this book's approach: a rhetorical perspective examines particular artifacts to discover what they *do* rather than to offer commentary on what they *are* (Bryant 1973). As such, I tend to focus attention on moments of intertextual resonance—the movement, echoing, and inevitable refraction of terms, concepts, and discursive fragments—rather than offering a succession of close readings of discrete texts like one would find in many literary or cultural histories.

Chapter 1 focuses on early medical meanings of lobotomy by exploring its use to "blunt" strong emotion in people diagnosed with mental illness. Using information from medical literature and transcripts of conference proceedings, chapter 1 shows how the therapeutic objective of lobotomy—the flattening of affect—was mirrored in professional regulation of emotional discourse about its use and value. Arguments about lobotomy's value were not limited to the medical community, however. Returning to 1936, the moment when lobotomy first entered the pages of newspapers and magazines, chapter 2 traces the shifting claims about the operation's therapeutic value in medical journalism by examining how patient case histories were used as evidence of lobotomy's social value. As arguments began to shift from the praise of lobotomy to its condemnation in the late 1940s and early 1950s, two related shifts also took place: the subjects of case histories used to support arguments about lobotomy overwhelmingly switched gender from women to men, and the interpretation of the operation's effects shifted from positive to negative.

But *why* did the stories about lobotomy shift tone in the early 1950s? After its introduction to America in 1936, the number of lobotomies steadily rose throughout the 1930s and 1940s and peaked right after Egas Moniz was awarded the Nobel Prize in 1949 (Sterling 1978). Shortly thereafter, lobotomies in the United States began to rapidly decrease, a phenomenon that historians have uniformly attributed to the development of psychopharmacology in the mid-1950s. Chapter 3 complicates this conventional explanation for lobotomy's medical decline by exploring a diverse set of texts in which the American public worried about lobotomy's political value as a mode of personality change in the early years of the Cold War. The image of the psychiatric profession that emerged from these texts gripped the American imagination so thoroughly that many of the nation's psychiatrists were forced to grapple with its impact, citing the wildest of conspiracy theories in their professional journals and preparing and distributing public rebuttals of their critics. The vivid connection of lobotomy with authoritarianism and fear of the vulnerable American personality, I suggest, contributed to a hostile environment for the operation at the moment when it began to decline in medical practice, and also marks the beginning of psychiatry's "lobotomy problem" with the public (Gelman 1999, 12).

Psychiatry's "lobotomy problem" is both historical and rhetorical: it suggests the encroachment of a marvelous past upon the present that shapes a particular future. It is thus by considering the effects of the past where rhetorical history makes itself distinct from other forms of history writing. To consider artifacts for what they do is to follow their rhetorical life into a kind of afterlife and exploring how the past haunts the present. Rhetorical history is comfortable with—indeed, seeks—cultural moments when time is "out of joint" in order to examine how pasts, presents, and futures are recursively shaped (Ballif 2013). The remaining chapters mark points at which lobotomy's marvelous history shapes the present—even when, as in the case of chapter 4, the present is in the past.

Chapter 4 explores the impact of the lobotomy problem in debates over the resurgence of psychosurgery in the early 1970s. In this chapter, I analyze psychiatrist Peter Breggin's campaign against psychosurgery, which culminated in his testimony in front of the Senate Subcommittee on Health in 1973. These hearings were convened in response to public concern about the "return" of lobotomy sparked by fiction like Michael Crichton's *Terminal Man* (1972), films like *A Clockwork Orange* (1971), and Breggin's frequent interviews with the press, including his claims that psychosurgery might be used on political dissidents and people of color. These fears were not unfounded.

In recent years, lobotomy has rhetorically surfaced once again in arguments about new forms of psychosurgery like deep brain stimulation (DBS), a procedure that has been heralded as a promising "last resort" treatment for otherwise treatment-resistant depression. Using arguments from the new generation of psychosurgeons in medical journals and their interviews with the popular press, chapter 5 shows how advocates for DBS manage memories of lobotomy in order to sever the new era of psychosurgery from its "dark history" (Mashour, Walker, and Martuza 2004). Psychiatry's lobotomy problem is a rhetorical problem; as such, it has a rhetorical solution. Deep brain stimulation is not lobotomy. What these arguments illustrate, however, is the power of lobotomy's marvelous history to shape contemporary biomedical research and clinical practice.

In chapter 6, I look at how the meaning of lobotomy has settled in the American imagination as an object of fear and why the lobotomist haunts that imagination as a monster. In this chapter, I take readers on a genealogical tour of the Trans-Allegheny Lunatic Asylum in Weston, West Virginia. After Weston Hospital closed its doors in 1994, the crumbling buildings, in various stages of entropy, were purchased by a private investor and partially renovated. In 2008, Weston Hospital reopened as the Trans-Allegheny Lunatic Asylum, a tourist attraction that holds paranormal tours and an annual haunted house on the premises. The Trans-Allegheny Lunatic Asylum is a site of marvelous history where past and present, malevolence and benevolence, and fact and fiction comingle in a deeply affective environment. In this chapter, I explore lobotomy's role in the hospital's history and the performance of that history on medical and paranormal tours in order to understand the cultural function of lobotomy's meaning as a monstrous practice.

In closing, with a nod to Donna Haraway (1988), who champions the value of "partial perspective," I want to acknowledge the limits of this book's vision. This is not a disclaimer, but a point of order. I do not aim to write a universal history of psychosurgery. What this book offers is a situated account of lobotomy as it intersected with American culture at different points in its history. Although this is clearly an ethnocentric approach, it is necessarily so. Lobotomy has a different rhetorical history in the United States than it does in the United Kingdom, Norway, Brazil, or Japan. I leave those histories to others, such as Jesper Vaczy Kragh (2010), who offers a compelling account of the use of lobotomy in Denmark. In the same vein, although lobotomy was practiced by a number of surgeons across the country, Walter Freeman takes a prominent role in many of these chapters. Although focusing on one doctor may seem limited in scope for a conventional history, it is necessary for the kind of rhetorical history I undertake here. It is fitting that Freeman's biography is entitled *The Lobotomist* (El-Hai 2005) rather than *A Lobotomist*. Walter Freeman was the public face of lobotomy in the United States. He was its most vocal spokesman, its most prolific practitioner and chronicler, and its last holdout, and he remains its most prominent ghost. Famous and infamous, good doctor and brutal slasher, a representative character in both history books and horror films—Walter Freeman is himself a medical marvel.

CHAPTER 1

Thinking with the Thalamus

The Rhetoric of Emotional Impairment

> He said he did not seem to be able to worry about things.
> It made him worry because he didn't seem to be able to worry.
>
> —WALTER FREEMAN AND JAMES WATTS, *PSYCHOSURGERY IN THE*
> *TREATMENT OF MENTAL DISORDERS AND INTRACTABLE PAIN* (1950)

In 1936, Alice Hammatt received the first prefrontal lobotomy in the United States.[1] Diagnosed with "agitated" depression, sixty-three-year-old Alice "complained of nervousness, insomnia, depression of spirits, anxiety, and apprehension" and often "laughed and wept hysterically" (Freeman and Watts 1950, xviii). When she was referred to Walter Freeman, Alice and her husband were told that her condition had deteriorated to the point where they had only two choices left: operation or institutionalization. Although Alice was willing to try surgery, at the last minute she "withdrew her permission because it was explained to her that the scalp would have to be shaved, and she didn't want to lose those curls." Her doctors "got around her objection" by promising to save her hair, even though they knew it was impossible (Freeman 1970, 14–3).[2] On September 14, 1936, Walter Freeman and James Watts performed a prefrontal lobotomy in an effort to remove the "emotional nucleus" of Alice Hammatt's distress (Freeman and Watts 1942, i).

Before surgery, Alice was in a state of severe anxiety. When the anesthetist arrived, write Freeman and Watts,

> she became panicky: "Who is that man? What does he want here? What's he going to do to me? Tell him to go away. Oh, I don't want to see him." Then she cried out, writhing about in bed so that the nurse was scarcely able to control her sufficiently to administer the avertin. (Freeman and Watts 1950, xviii)

The operation took about four hours. When Alice awoke, her doctors reported that she wore a "placid expression" and that by evening she "manifested no anxiety or apprehension." The next day Alice said she couldn't remember what she had been afraid of, adding, "It doesn't seem important now." When the anesthetist later returned to check on her, "she smiled at him, gave him her hand, and greeted him pleasantly without any fear." She did not mention the loss of her beloved curly hair. Alice Hammatt lived at home until her death in 1941 from pneumonia. Her husband later wrote Walter Freeman to thank him, describing those five years as the "happiest of her life" (Freeman and Watts 1950, xix).

Lobotomy's primary objective was to "blunt" strong emotions in order to return mentally ill people to "productive" roles in their families, communities, and the economy. This chapter investigates the medical meanings of lobotomy in the early years of its use in the United States and shows how the argument of emotional impairment that served as lobotomy's scientific justification was mirrored in constraints on medical discourse. This connection is especially apparent in accusations of emotionality against lobotomy's critics, one of whom was chastised for "thinking with his thalamus" when he voiced his passionate objections to the procedure (Freeman 1970, 14–10).

"Passion" and "pathology" share a common etymological root in *pathos*, which is also the term for the most maligned of rhetorical appeals. Aristotle, for example, describes *pathos* as "those feelings that so change men as to affect their judgment" (1991, 1378a, 20–21), thus figuring emotion as an impairment to reason, a force that "warps" the "carpenter's rule" (1354a). To acknowledge emotion is to acknowledge one's embodiment, partiality, and attachment.[3] To acknowledge one's emotion in scientific or medical discourse is thus a risky endeavor, for calling attention to embodiment, partiality, and attachment challenges medicine's identity as an applied science, which draws its authority from norms of universalism and disinterestedness (Merton 1973).

In this chapter, we see how medical rhetors are more than mere discursive agents, that is to say, more than just users of language. Medical rhetors are also *"agenc[ies]* for a language that is already in circulation" (Segal 2005, 14, original emphasis). In this case, they are the agencies for the language of science and its attendant grammars. If discourses are more than mere words, but also "practices that systematically form the objects of which they speak" (Foucault 1972, 49), then it should come as no surprise that a discourse that dismisses strong emotion as evidence of impaired judgment would find strong emotion to be evidence of an impaired brain.

Cutting the Gordian Knot

Before Walter Freeman's work with psychosurgery began, he was employed as the senior medical officer in charge of the medical laboratories of St. Elizabeth's Hospital, a position he held from 1924 until 1935. Sprawling across nearly three hundred acres of land on the bluffs overlooking Washington, DC, St. Elizabeth's was the nation's first federal psychiatric facility and one of its largest psychiatric hospitals. At peak operation, St. Elizabeth's employed nearly four thousand hospital staff, and its wards housed seven thousand patients, including presidential assassin Charles Guiteau, would-be presidential assassin John Hinckley, and poet Ezra Pound (Holley 2007).[4] In his memoir, Freeman recalls that his role did not include engaging with St. Elizabeth's patients on "a personal level" and describes his initial reaction upon meeting them as "a rather weird mixture of fear, disgust, and shame. The slouching figures, the vacant stare or averted eyes, the shabby clothing and footwear, the general untidiness—all aroused rejection rather than sympathy or interest" (1970, 14–2).

Fear of mad bodies is built into the very architecture of the psychiatric institution and reflected in many of its technologies of control. Fear "works to align bodily and social space" by restricting movement in the space of preservation to already-authorized bodies (Ahmed 2004, 69). Locked doors, common areas, unauthorized areas, restraints: each restricts the movements of some bodies (patients) while facilitating the movement of others (doctors, nurses, and hospital staff). Moving throughout this fearfully designed space, Freeman remembered he also experienced "disgust" in response to the "shabby" and "untidy" bodies that approached him. If fear is an emotion that seeks to preserve boundaries, disgust is provoked by the violation of those boundaries, a reaction to the threatened dissolution of the limits between the disgusted body and something, or someone, else. As one body is disgusted by another, "it pulls away with an intense movement" (Ahmed 2004, 85). Instead of sympathy for these patients—a pulling closer—Freeman experienced rejection—a pulling away. Yet the motion of disgust is "deeply ambivalent," a double movement also "involving desire for, or an attraction towards, the very objects that are felt to be repellent" (84).

In the case of Walter Freeman and the St. Elizabeth's patients, this double movement is revealed by his deep desire for knowledge about them. Afraid of and disgusted by the living patients, Freeman allowed himself physical contact with their bodies in the safe, sterile space of the pathology laboratory, where he set out to learn "all [he] could about the brain of the psychotic" (1970, 14–2). When he examined the brains of St. Elizabeth's patients after their deaths, however, Freeman was "challenged" by his observation that people who appeared so abnormal on the outside were indistinguishable from "normal" people on the inside. Freeman's inability to find structural abnormality in the brains of deceased patients led to intense frustration that he "had done nothing important in either explaining mental disorder nor treating it" during his time at St. Elizabeth's (14–2). His work with lobotomy would serve both purposes, while also allaying his frustration.

Freeman often referred to mental illness as a "Gordian knot," in reference to a myth about Alexander the Great often used as a metaphor for an unsolvable problem. In the myth, Alexander travels to Gordium in Phyrigia, where he finds an ox cart bound to a stake with a number of complicated knots. According to legend, whoever successfully freed the cart would become the next king. Instead of untying the knot, however, Alexander abruptly unsheathed his sword and cut it—a bold action that was said to have delighted Zeus. Psychiatrists had likewise been trying in "their own compulsive fashion" to unravel the Gordian knot of mental illness for years, Freeman believed, and perhaps the time had come for the Alexandrian solution (1970, 14–10).

While still working at St. Elizabeth's, Freeman began teaching at George Washington University (GWU), and in 1928 he accepted a position as professor and chair of the university's Department of Neurology. With neurosurgeon James Watts, one of his GWU colleagues, Freeman developed what was known as the "precision method" of prefrontal lobotomy, which they adapted from Portuguese neurologist Egas Moniz.

Freeman first met Moniz at the 1935 International Neurological Congress in London, where both men attended a full-day session on the physiology of the frontal lobes. As part of this session, Yale physiologists John Fulton and Carlyle Jacobsen offered a presentation in which they described experiments with bilateral frontal lobe ablation in two chimpanzees. Fulton and Jacobsen reported that while the chimpanzees did not appear to suffer any intellectual deficits as a result of the operation, their "experimental anxiety" markedly decreased.[5] During the discussion period following Jacobsen and Fulton's paper, Moniz is reported to have asked whether their findings could be replicated in humans.[6] Fulton's "startled" and negative response did not sway Moniz, who returned to Portugal and began to operate on patients with neurosurgeon

Almeida Lima (J. Pressman 1999, 47).[7] Just one year later, Freeman and Watts shaved off Alice Hammatt's curly hair.

In a prefrontal lobotomy, surgeons drilled two holes through the skull, inserted a specialized instrument called a leucotome through the burr holes into the brain, and swept it back and forth to sever fibers between the frontal lobes, located immediately behind the forehead, and the thalamus, situated in the middle of the brain (for a detailed description, see Freeman and Watts 1950, 33–50). In 1946, Walter Freeman began performing the transorbital version of the operation for which he is now best known. Transorbital lobotomy was initially developed by Italian neurosurgeon Amarro Fiamberti in 1937. Despite performing over one hundred of these operations on his patients, Fiamberti never analyzed his results, and it appeared to Freeman that "Fiamberti and his colleagues were more concerned with defending the safety and simplicity of the transorbital approach than they were with demonstrating its effectiveness." Because Fiamberti's reports did not inspire much confidence in Freeman, it wasn't until 1946 that he "summon[ed] up courage to attack the brain through the orbital plate" (Freeman 1950, 51–53).

In Freeman's version of the transorbital operation, the patient was first rendered unconscious using an electroconvulsive therapy machine, an effect that lasted for only a few short minutes but that obviated the expensive services of an anesthesiologist. Instead of going through the top of the head, the technique of the prefrontal lobotomy, Freeman was able to reach the same area of the brain by hammering an instrument through the orbital plate and swinging it back and forth. Although he would later have an instrument specially made for the operation, Freeman performed his first transorbital lobotomy on Sallie Ellen Ionesco with an ice pick from his kitchen drawer.

The transorbital lobotomy, which took only a few minutes to perform and did not require the services of a surgical team, was touted by Freeman as a "minor" operation that was "simple," "safe," and cheap—an ideal solution for institutions high in patient populations and low in financial resources (1948, 261). Patients recovered rapidly and were able to return home the next day with only bruising around the eyes to indicate that anything had taken place. Some of these black eyes, Freeman commented, "are beauties, and I usually ask the family to provide the patient with sun glasses rather than explanations" (1950, 57). Freeman contended that with the right training, any medical professional could perform transorbital lobotomy—even those who, like him, were not trained neurosurgeons. This proposal eventually led to Freeman's professional split with James Watts, who firmly believed that any ablation of brain tissue required the services of a properly credentialed surgeon. Watts felt so strongly about this point that he included a separately authored comment elaborating his position in the 1950 edition of *Psychosurgery* (59–61). It is important to note that the dispute between Freeman and Watts did not necessarily concern the scientific merits or therapeutic value of transorbital lobotomy. It was primarily a territorial dispute over whose hand was authorized to hold the leucotome.[8]

The Emotional Nucleus

In his first publication on psychosurgery, in 1936, Egas Moniz admitted that his idea to treat mental illness with surgery was "audacious" ([1936] 1964, 1111). In part, Moniz's first surgeries were audacious because they relied on an idiosyncratic theory of psychopathology that identified the frontal lobes as the origin of mental illness. In his first publication on the procedure, Moniz identified the frontal lobes as an area where "psychic activity" occurred and then suggested that thoughts and ideas "are somehow stored in the nerve-fiber connections between brain cells" (1113). Certain mental illnesses emerged when ideas became "fixed" in the patient's brain, he posited, and these ideas "not only [dominate] their psychic life but also [direct] their actions and can lead them to suicide or crime" (1113).[9] After an idea became fixed within the brain's connecting fibers, Moniz concluded, it was necessary to sever these connections, and he believed "the principal ones among them are those that are linked within the frontal lobes" (1113). Moniz explained that he and partner Almeida Lima undertook the psychosurgery "experiment" solely "by reasons of theory." After two-thirds of their patients achieved "clinical recovery" or "ameliorations," Moniz declared the positive outcomes as evidence that both his theory of mental illness and his surgical remedy were sound (1111). According to Elliot Valenstein (1986), Moniz's theory of psychopathology "was so vague as to constitute no theory at all," but it "was repeated so often that it like the emperor's new clothes, in Hans Christian Andersen's famous story—acquired a veneer of truth and was accepted (or at least repeated) by many other people" (99).

Two of these people were Walter Freeman and James Watts. Although Moniz's rationale for the operation and his surgical technique had inspired the pair, they expanded his theory of psychopathology to emphasize the role of emotion. Freeman and Watts believed that the thalamus, which plays a role in processing sensation, was "the organ by which these sensations are endowed with emotional feeling tone" and that ultimately led to the fixed ideas of psychopathology (1942, 27; 1950, 306). In this theory, psychopathology was located neither in the frontal lobes nor in the thalamus—in fact, it wasn't necessarily *located* anywhere at all. Freeman and Watts's theory of psychopathology was "neither fully present nor absent, neither freely mobile nor totally static," but "poised undecidably between force and space, between dynamism and location," to borrow language from Elizabeth Wilson (1998, 186).

Emotion is part of the typical economy of the brain. Indeed, lack of emotion is considered a symptom ("flat affect") of conditions like schizophrenia. To frequently experience strong emotions, however, and especially negative emotions like sadness, fear, and shame, was to risk fixing ideas (Freeman and Watts 1950, 360). When ideas with a strong emotional charge were recalled repeatedly, Freeman and Watts suggested, they etched a sort of pathway in the brain that increased both the frequency of these ideas and their emotional intensity. If this "circuit" was not acted upon by severing the connections between the frontal lobes and the thalamus, "the emotional flow increases to the point where all cortical activities are submerged in the psychotic deluge. At first this is reversible, but as the process continues, the closed circuits, however extensive they are, continue with the reverberation but with more automaticity and less need for power input from the thalamus" (1950, 563).[10] It was this process—ideation powered and fixed by emotional excess—Freeman and Watts surmised, that eventually led to depression and anxiety, as well as mental illnesses "along the lines of somatic preoccupations (hypochondriasis), intellectual preoccupations (obsessive states), social preoccupations (paranoid reactions), or similar conditions" (1950, 307).

Remember that Freeman, who began his career as a pathologist, was motivated not just by the idea of treating mental illness but also by discovering its origins in the brain. Lobotomy thus promised both a treatment for patients and a "tool for the investigation of mental disorders" for researchers, and it ultimately promised "insight into the intellectual-emotional mechanisms that are such a potent factor in human behavior" (Freeman and Watts 1950, xxii–xxiii). Within this universal theory of psychopathology, mental illness came into view not as an abnormal idea or emotion, but as a disordered neural economy in which the supply of emotion exceeded the demand. The point of lobotomy, then, was to "reduce the affective charge" coming from the thalamus by cutting the fibers that led to the frontal lobes (75).

What did this "blunted" affect look like? As one man described it, before lobotomy his "conscience hurt"; after the operation, he explained, "I don't know where it is. It was down by my heart, but I can't feel it at all" (Freeman and Watts 1950, 130). One woman claimed that after her surgery, she blushed "without getting embarrassed. I'm just conscious of blushing now" (124). Perhaps the most vivid description of the emotional change in patients after lobotomy, however, is found in the transcript of a conversation between Freeman and a patient who remained, like many who received prefrontal lobotomies, awake throughout the procedure.[11] Freeman and Watts used the conversation to illustrate the "abrupt change from panicky apprehension to calm indifference" (1950, 129).

DOCTOR: Are you scared?
PATIENT: Yeh.
DOCTOR: What of?
PATIENT: I don't know, Doctor.
DOCTOR: What do you want?
PATIENT: Not a lot. I just want friends. That's all. How long's this going on?
DOCTOR: Two hours.
PATIENT: Two hours? I can't last that long. (Squeezes hand).
DOCTOR: How do you feel?
PATIENT: I don't feel anything but they're cutting me now.
DOCTOR: You wanted it?
PATIENT: Yes, but I didn't think you'd do it awake. O Gee whiz, I'm dying. O
   doctor. Please stop. O, God. I'm goin again. Oh, oh, oh. Ow. (Chisel.) Oh,
   this is awful. Ow (He grabs my hand and sinks his nails into it). O, God,
   I'm goin, please stop . . .
DOCTOR: How do you feel?
DOCTOR: You're grabbing me awful tight.
PATIENT: Am I? I can't help it. How long does this go on?
   (Right lower cuts)
DOCTOR: Glad you're being operated?
PATIENT: Yes, it makes me feel better . . .
DOCTOR: What will you do when you're well?
PATIENT: O, go back to work. Oh, I can't stand it.
DOCTOR: What job?
PATIENT: O, it's a good job, brakeman with a railroad.
DOCTOR: Scared?

PATIENT: Yeh.
DOCTOR: Sing God Bless America.
PATIENT: (He starts rather high and does a couple of lines) . . .
DOCTOR: What are you doing here?
PATIENT: Being operated on.
DOCTOR: What for?
PATIENT: There's something wrong with the brain.
DOCTOR: Is it all right now?
PATIENT: Where's the door?
DOCTOR: Afraid?
PATIENT: No.
DOCTOR: What's happened to your fear?
PATIENT: Gone.
DOCTOR: Why were you afraid?
PATIENT: I don't know.
DOCTOR: Feel okay?
PATIENT: Yes, I feel pretty good right now. (1950, 129–130)

Proponents of lobotomy operated with the conviction *that* it worked, and then, after observing the operation's effects on people like the railroad brakeman above, they reasoned back to *why* it worked. It might seem shocking that Moniz, Freeman, and Watts would perform surgery before they fully understood the neurological basis of its effects on behavior—or the physiology of the frontal lobes, for that matter, an area of the brain often called the "silent lobe" because neurologists understood so little about its function (J. Pressman 1999, 51). However, biological psychiatry still speaks in hypotheses with regard to the neural action of psychopharmacology and electroconvulsive therapy, the two most common somatic treatments for mental illness. Although new treatments now undergo randomized controlled trials and are subject to scrutiny by the Food and Drug Administration, neuroscientists have not yet come to a consensus about how, exactly, they work in the brain. Contemporary psychiatric treatments, chemical treatments in particular, are used for research as well as treatment, and they even play a role in developing diagnostic criteria. By observing behavioral and emotional changes in patients who respond to antidepressants, for example, researchers have carved out a negative definition of depression as the collection of symptoms that change in response to antidepressants (Healy 1999, 62).

We see this same logic at work in arguments for lobotomy, albeit on a much grander scale. By observing changes in patients after the operation, Freeman and Watts had evidence with which to construct a universal theory of psychopathology that rhetorically positioned emotion as the primary impairment of mental illness, a theory that corresponded exactly with treatment they had developed. Freeman and Watts were not interested in erecting discrete etiological boundaries around conditions like depression, schizophrenia, or obsessive-compulsive disorder. They sought to explain mental illness in general, which expanded the diagnostic categories for lobotomy, increased its potential pool of patients, and thus offered a compelling case for its widespread application (J. Pressman 1999, 144). Walter Freeman explained that his singular goal with transorbital lobotomy was to "apply a simple operation to as many patients as possible in order to get them out of the hospital."[12] Freeman often bragged that lobotomy "got them home," and at a time when state hospitals were packed with patients who were supported with state funds, increasing the number of patients able to be treated with lobotomy and removed from state budgets made the operation socially and even politically valuable.[13]

In 1952, for example, the West Virginia Board of Control commissioned Walter Freeman for a project in the mass application of transorbital lobotomy in its state hospitals, an event I will discuss in greater detail in chapter 6. In the West Virginia project, the metric used to judge lobotomy's success had very little to do with a patient's clinical outcome—what mattered was the patient's ability to live outside the hospital. In a 1954 article about the West Virginia project published in the *Journal of the American Medical Association*, Freeman reported that of the 228 people selected for the operation, only 4 had died, and 85 were released to their families in the year following surgery. He weighed this outcome against a "control group" of people who refused surgery. Of the 200 patients in the control group, only 5 had been released, and 2 had died. Using this metric, for Freeman and the state of West Virginia the project was an overwhelming success, particularly since, as Freeman explained in the article, the total cost of the 1952 project was only $2,300. Compared with the cost of a patient's daily care in a state hospital, Freeman estimated, the operation had saved West Virginia $48,000 over the course of a single year. In addition, as Freeman noted in the last line of the article, the income generated by discharged patients able to enter the workforce added up to more than the cost of the entire project (Freeman et al. 1954, 942).

Emotional impairment played a crucial role in these economic arguments for lobotomy's social value, which is exemplified by the rationale for operating on persons with schizophrenia. These patients initially were considered to be poor candidates for lobotomy due to a number of unfavorable outcomes. In a 1945 article in the *American Journal of Psychiatry*, Freeman and Watts proposed that the problem was not with the operation, but with the person selected for it. A person who had been living with schizophrenia for many years was thought to suffer from "emotional deterioration" (1945, 742). Many of these people, often the permanent residents of the back wards, were past even lobotomy's last resort. "Excitement, resistiveness, stupor, destructiveness, combativeness— these are favorable indications [for lobotomy], while docility, vagueness and true apathy are definite contraindications," the doctors explained; prefrontal lobotomy was only an option when a person was "still fighting his disease" (740).

Although lobotomy had the power to blunt the emotions, it did little to change the delusions and hallucinations characteristic of schizophrenia (Freeman and Watts 1950, 504). Yet it was not the delusions and hallucinations that were keeping people with schizophrena from social integration and economic value, they argued, but the disordered economy of emotion that "fixed" those ideas in the brain. "We are not particulary concerned if a patient retains his hallucinations and delusions," Freeman and Watts commented. "If a patient can take care of himself after operation we are satisfied with the results" (739). Self-sufficiency was deemed so therapeutically valuable that it superceded the loss of other cognitive functions, like creativity, which was often impaired after the operation. After lobotomy, if a patient

> is no longer able to paint pictures, write poetry or compose music, *he is, on the other hand, no longer ashamed* to fetch and carry, to wait on table [*sic*] or make beds or empty cans. If he has suffered some reduction in his personal dignity and vanity, he has gained in social adaptability and has at least a chance of earning his living. (748, my emphasis)

After surgery, it was rare for patients in the professions to return to their former careers, but lobotomy allowed the patient to to work *somewhere*, usually in the service sector, free of the feeling of shame that the doctors felt this type of labor might have normally induced (204). Lobotomy did not offer a cure for schizophrenia. What it offered was an emotionally dampened personality thought to be more amenable to "occupational adjustment" (1950, 203–225; see also Raz 2010).

Freeman and Watts often remarked that they would not operate on patients unless they were "threatened with disability or suicide" (1950, 203), and it is clear that in this discourse, disability—here positioned equally with death—meant disabled from the workforce. "Patients who come to prefrontal lobotomy represent failures in occupational adjustment," explained Freeman and Watts, and "usually they are bad failures, with no reasonable hope of restitution. Sometimes they have started out as failures, right from the time of high school or even grammar school, and have never been employable" (1950, 203). Although about a quarter of Freeman and Watts's patients were determined to be adjusting to life outside the hospital at the level of "household pet . . . [or] drone," (198–199), they reported with pride that after the operation, the majority of their patients returned to productive positions within the home or the workforce.

In the previous section, I began by describing Freeman's initial response to the St. Elizabeth's patients as one of disinterest. In his memoir, Freeman commented that this disinterest later shifted to interest when he began to look around at "the hundreds of patients and thought what a waste of manpower and womanpower" (1970, 14–1). There was a double economic argument for removing patients from state hospital beds: not only would these people contribute to their households and the US capitalist economy, but they would also no longer require public support. Lobotomy had the power to make "taxpayers" out of "taxeaters," Freeman believed, "and in these days," he casually remarked, "we need more taxpayers and will continue to do so for a long time to come" (Freeman 1950, 203). As Sharon Snyder and David Mitchell (2006) have argued, to be classified as economically dependent in the United States is seen by many as a moral failing in addition to an economic one, which adds an additional layer of meaning to Freeman's claims of success. "Getting them home" was more than just a medical and financial matter: it was a moral responsibility to the nation.

It is impossible to generalize about the experience of the tens of thousands of people who received lobotomies. As Freeman and Watts noted, their "standards change with different patients," and an outcome that might warrant classification as a "fair" result in one patient might be used to judge a "good" result in another (1950, 495). Yet it appears that very few people who received this operation ever achieved positions as titans of industry (like one of Freeman's patients frequently trotted out as an example of his success), and very few looked like the catatonic Randle McMurphy at the end of *One Flew Over the Cuckoo's Nest*. The reality for most lobotomy patients was somewhere in the wide gulf between these poles. A number of patients died from surgical complications on the operating table; one returned to his career as a doctor; one killed his father during a hunting trip; some patients returned home to raise families; some patients were angry at their doctors; and some, it must be noted, were grateful to them. And some patients, like John F. Kennedy's sister Rosemary, suffered severe brain damage and lived out the rest of their lives in institutions.

Rosemary Kennedy, born in 1918, was the third child of Joseph and Rose Kennedy. There is considerable controversy as to the exact nature of Rosemary's condition before the surgery and the reasons that led Joseph—against the expressed wishes of his wife—to request the operation, which in 1942 was still in an experimental stage. Some biographers of the Kennedy family, such as Laurence Leamer (1994), have suggested that Rosemary had a mild developmental disability and was sometimes physically aggressive (see also O'Brien 2004). Leamer's retroactive diagnosis follows statements by members of the Kennedy family who have since, when they have talked about Rosemary at all, described her as "partly epileptic as well as retarded" (quoted in Leamer 1994, 227). Other historians and biographers have seen the Kennedy family's public diagnosis as a public relations move for the image-conscious family, arguing that a diagnosis of developmental disability was preferred because it carried less stigma and that Rosemary was really depressed (Kessler 1996) or dyslexic (Gibson and Schwartz 1995).[14] While the nature of Rosemary's condition before her lobotomy may never be known, there is no question about her condition afterward. At some point during her surgery, Freeman and Watts made a mistake. Afterward, Rosemary could speak only a few words and was no longer able to care for herself. In 1949, she was placed in the St. Coletta School for Exceptional Children in Jefferson, Wisconsin, where she lived until her death in 2005.

In large part, the reason it is difficult to generalize about lobotomy patients is that the operation did not simply remove emotional impairment. Even in cases where the operation went as planned, the surgery traded one perceived impairment for another set of iatrogenically induced impairments that varied from patient to patient, what Pressman calls lobotomy's "therapeutic calculus" (1999, 206). As even Freeman and Watts admitted, "lobotomy has by no means always been entirely for the good; it seems quite certain that an individual wishing to be relieved of certain distressing symptoms has to pay a certain price" (1950, 377). Although the outcomes varied from patient to patient, in every case, the price of freedom—whether that freedom was envisioned as freedom from anxiety or freedom from the back wards of a state hospital—was paid for by sacrificing some element of a patient's emotional life. For some doctors, like Walter Freeman, getting patients home was worth it. For others, the costs were simply too great.

Lobotomizing the American Medical Association

Although lobotomy was well within the medical mainstream, it was not without its detractors, particularly since its peak in American psychiatry coincided with the peak of psychoanalysis. Although the paradigms of biological psychiatry and psychoanalysis were not necessarily incommensurable during this time (Metzl 2003; Sadowsky 2006; Raz 2008), many psychoanalysts resisted the proposal that mental illness ought to be treated by surgery. Freeman, for his part, despised his psychoanalytic colleagues and their methods.[15] Despite their private reservations about the operation, however, lobotomy's opponents were reluctant to criticize their colleagues in public, at least during the early years of its use (Diefenbach et al. 1999). A roundtable panel on psychosurgery arranged during a 1941 meeting of the American Medical Association, however, featured a rare example of semipublic criticism of lobotomy during its early years. In this heated exchange, and also in the publication of the exchange that followed in the *Journal of the American Medical Association* (*JAMA*), we can see how the argument of emotional impairment central to lobotomy's scientific rationale was also used to suppress ethical deliberation about the procedure.

Participants on the panel included James Lyerly, Edward Strecker, and Walter Freeman, all practicing psychosurgeons, and M. A. Tarumianz, director of the Delaware State Hospital, who provided detailed figures regarding how much a robust lobotomy program would save his institution over the course of the year (American Medical Association 1941a, 44).[16] The moderator of the discussion, neurosurgeon Paul Bucy, admitted it might "appear that this group in the main has been stacked in favor of the procedure" but insisted that it was not the organizers' fault, since so few of their colleagues were willing to voice their concerns (174).

The panel's voice of opposition was Roy R. Grinker Sr., a Chicago psychoanalyst who had been analyzed by Freud himself.[17] Grinker admitted he had no "personal" experience with lobotomy and had prepared for the meeting by talking with those in the field and reading all the "medical literature that has been available, including the Saturday Evening Post" (American Medical Association 1941a, 177). Referencing the magazine article was likely an intentional jab at Walter Freeman, since, as I will explain in the next chapter, the *Post* story, "Turning the Mind Inside Out," had engendered significant professional controversy (not because doctors were concerned about lobotomy, but because they were concerned that Freeman and Watts were advertising for their services).

Grinker began his critique by first pointing out that "emotional bias" motivated lobotomy's advocates as well as its critics. Advocates for the procedure had based their opinion on the "feeling that the psychoses have a definite organic basis," and critics of lobotomy were driven by an "emotional attitude toward an operation that destroys brain tissue [that is] as emotional as the attitude of the church toward abortions or contraception" (178). Grinker immediately threw the scientific basis for lobotomy up for debate, arguing that the organic basis of mental illness was a matter of feeling rather than fact, a comment that surely did not sit well with the devoutly organicist panel. Grinker noted the uncritical haste with which the psychiatric profession had adopted lobotomy, complained that other therapeutic modalities (like psychoanalysis) had not been given enough time to work, and expressed his strong disapproval of the use of an irreversible operation on children. The primary thrust of his comments, however, concerned the slippery concept of emotional impairment used as lobotomy's scientific rationale.

Since one of the primary symptoms ameliorated by lobotomy was anxiety, and since anxiety was not limited to one particular disorder, Grinker charged that it was "obvious" that lobotomy was being "devised for almost the whole field of psychiatry" (American Medical Association 1941a, 180). Moreover, since everyone exhibits some anxiety in their daily affairs, lobotomy was dealing in matters of degree rather than kind and matters of value rather than fact. Grinker challenged that it was "extremely dangerous" to assume that medicine had the power to determine "exactly what dose of anxiety is normal and what is pathological" to the point where the destruction of brain tissue could be warranted (187). Medicine was limited by the subjective nature of emotion, Grinker admitted: "I do not know how a schizophrenic patient feels, and my desire to know how much anxiety a depressed patient has is often fraught with a great deal of difficulty" (180).[18] Although Grinker granted that anxiety could breach "a certain pathological threshold," he also maintained that even strong anxiety could prove beneficial by motivating individuals to persevere in the face of difficulty (186). Although Grinker didn't critique the medicalization of emotion per se, he focused his opposition to lobotomy on the contingent nature of emotional impairment that served as its scientific foundation.

Walter Freeman regarded Roy Grinker and his arguments with thinly veiled contempt. Freeman did not object to Grinker's arguments *about* emotion; rather, he objected that Grinker was arguing *from* emotion. After telling the audience that he "always" took issue with the psychoanalyst from Chicago, Freeman stated, "I just want to say that throughout his discussion instead of saying, 'I think' or 'I know' or 'I believe,' he said, 'I feel'" (202–203). As if to later reinforce this point, in Freeman's personal copy of the roundtable transcript, the word "feel" is underlined each time it appears in Grinker's comments. In his memoir, Freeman remembers Grinker's argument as follows: "I feel these patients were not studied adequately; I feel they were given too short a time for other treatments; I feel they were rushed into operation; I feel, I feel, I feel . . . etc." (1970, 14–10). Freeman did not elaborate on this point, as his challenge to Grinker spoke for itself. The surgeons on the panel presented arguments that focused on anatomy and physiology, statistics, dollar signs, and case histories. Roy Grinker presented an argument that focused on emotions and values, and Freeman therefore believed it was not to be taken seriously, a point he emphasized by quipping during his closing remarks that Grinker had been "thinking with his thalamus" during the discussion (1970, 14–10).

The AMA psychosurgery roundtable was published in *JAMA* in 1941 under legendary editor Morris Fishbein, a hero in the medical profession for his efforts to combat quacks and frauds (see, e.g., Fishbein 1925). Fishbein's editorial standards were as strict as his standards for medicine—and indeed, he even described them in similar terms. In a 1928 address commemorating the one hundredth anniversary of the *Boston Medical and Surgical Journal*, for instance, Fishbein outlined his editorial philosophy in detail. After lambasting some lesser medical periodicals for appealing to "the baser emotions to which doctors as well as other men occasionally succumb," he presented a set of guiding principles for medical journal editors. In addition to impartiality and high scientific and medical standards, Fishbein declared that an editor should "be guided by good English style and diction but . . . avoid fancy writing and rhetorical bouquets" and advised potential contributors to "be as careful in literary publication as in surgical operation" (1928, 445). Given Fishbein's predilection for unaffected prose, it is not surprising that *JAMA's* version of the psychosurgery roundtable was lobotomized of the emotional intensity that characterized the original exchange.

Although Fishbein believed that his colleagues ought to take a cautious stance on lobotomy until more scientific evidence was available, he warned his readers that "an *emotional attitude of violent unreasoning opposition* to this form of treatment would be inexcusable" (1941, 535, my emphasis). In Fishbein's surgically edited version of the AMA psychosurgery roundtable, Freeman's critique of Grinker's use of the word "feel" is absent, as is his joke that his colleague had been "thinking with his thalamus." And perhaps most unfortunately, also missing is Grinker's impassioned rejoinder to Freeman during the panel's concluding remarks:

> Dr. Freeman mentions the fact that I have expressed myself here today in terms of feeling. I have not said " know" or "I am sure" or "I believe" because I do not know but I feel and perhaps some of you think, perhaps Dr. Freeman thinks that a prefrontal lobotomy may get rid of my anxiety, but truly I am anxious about it, I am extremely anxious about it, and I feel the anxiety which is projected into the future, the anxiety which has to do with the future care of . . . the general group of people floating around this country with psychoses and psychoneuroses who will, if we are not very careful, be mutilated by this operation. (American Medical Association 1941a, 209)

For Fishbein and for Freeman, an emotional attitude did not just signify an absence of reason, but a threat to reason, a *violent unreason*, an emotional impairment to the dispassionate judgment of medical science.

For Freeman and Watts, ethical objections to lobotomy were further polluted by popular attitudes that viewed the brain as sacrosanct and inviolable. "There is still a tendency to consider the brain as the 'temple of the mind,' the 'seat of the soul,' and the 'greatest gift of God,'" they protested, "and to decry any suggestion that such a holy structure is being tampered with. The shackles of medieval thought are difficult to strike off" (1944b, 535). To claim that there was something special about the brain and its functions was considered by Freeman and Watts not just to be evidence of a poor argument but, considering their use of the word "medieval," also suggested a time before the dawn of scientific reason.

Although Walter Freeman was likely seen by those in attendance to have "won" the roundtable debate about lobotomy in 1941, Roy Grinker's passionate ethical objections to lobotomy would eventually become dominant medical opinion. Grinker may have been the outlier of the 1941 AMA panel, but by the late 1950s, Freeman's firm conviction regarding lobotomy's value made him a pariah. In 1958, he extended his critique of Roy Grinker to all of his critics: "Psychosurgery in general has been condemned by many psychiatrists upon ethical and moral grounds since the idea of mutilating the brain is abhorrent to them. This represents an emotional status that is not to be influenced by argument or demonstration" (1958b, 430). Although Freeman continued championing lobotomy until his death in 1972, by the late 1950s his arguments failed to persuade his colleagues not because they were too emotional but because they were no longer paying attention to him.

Emotional Histories

Perhaps one of the greatest ironies of Walter Freeman's objection to emotional discourse about lobotomy, then, is that his personal attachment to lobotomy and his professional investment in its reputation led him to continue performing the operation for more than a decade after nearly all of his colleagues had abandoned it.[19] This emotional attachment is exemplified by a 1961 talk he gave at California's Langley Porter clinic regarding his use of transorbital lobotomy on children. To demonstrate the effectiveness of the procedure, he brought with him three adolescents who had recently been subjected to the surgery. In his memoir, Freeman recalls that the talk was met with a "barrage of hostile criticism":

> Even when I pointed out that these youngsters were adjusting reasonably well at home and some of them attending school, the specter of damaged brains prevailed. I had with me a box of Christmas greetings, over 500 of them, and dumped them on the table. I had lost my temper, and I challenged my chief antagonist: "How many Christmas cards did you get from YOUR patients?" (1970, 21–11)

Rather than interpret the crowd's response as evidence of his own failing or as representative of lobotomy's tarnished reputation, Freeman attributed the crowd's vocal resistance to their being "steeped in the Freudian tradition" (21–11). The crowd became particularly angry, however, when they learned that one of the boys on stage was only twelve. The boy's name was Howard Dully.

In "Adolescents in Distress" (1961), an article published in the *Journal of*

Nervous and Mental Diseases, Walter Freeman presents Howard Dully's case history. It reads:

> *Case 6: H.D.* was lobotomized at the age of 12 on December 16, 1960, hence is still (January 1961) in the early stage of social convalescence. His mother died of cancer when he was five years old. Shortly before her death she gave birth to a third son. Howard attacked the baby in its crib, fracturing its skull and crushing its chest so that this child is a cripple and mentally defective, now in a foster home. . . . Howard has always been a misfit. Among the stepmother's bill of particulars are lying, stealing, cheating, snooping, scaring, handling and smearing feces, urinating on the rug, teasing, bullying the younger boys, responding neither to affection nor punishment, showing neither anger nor pleasure (557).

Nowhere in the case history does Freeman suggest what, if any, complaints Howard might have had or how he felt that he was "in distress." The chief complaint came from Howard's father, Rodney, and his stepmother, Lou, who provided what Freeman called the "articles of indictment" against the boy (Dully and Fleming 2007, 77).

During research for the documentary "My Lobotomy," Howard Dully visited the Freeman and Watts archives at George Washington University, where he read his case file for the first time. When Howard read about the incident with his brother described in Freeman's article above, however, he stopped short. It had never happened. Howard Dully had gone to the archives in order to answer a question he had been asking his entire life: Had he done something to deserve the lobotomy? In the case file he found the answer, "and the answer was no. This was a lie. It was the biggest lie I ever heard. I never attacked Bruce. I *knew* that" (Dully and Fleming 2007, 231). Although the information in previous case-file entries was taken from interviews Freeman had conducted with his father and stepmother, the information about the attack was from a meeting his father had not attended. Rodney Dully later confirmed that his wife's charge had been fabricated (247). During an interview, Howard and producer David Isay encouraged Rodney to explain why he had given his consent for the operation. Yet he would say only that Lou, who had never liked Howard, had insisted it be done. "I got manipulated," Rodney explained, "pure and simple" (237).

Rodney's refusal to take responsibility for his son's lobotomy extended to his reluctance to emotionally engage with his decision to authorize the surgery.

During the interview, he chides Howard for "dwell[ing] on negative ideas," explaining that he tried to remain positive about the past (Dully and Fleming 2007, 237). Undaunted, Howard pushes his father to feel something by telling him about the tremendous impact the surgery had made on his life. Also trying to provoke some emotion in Rodney, a producer hands him a picture of his twelve-year-old son on the day of the operation. In the photograph—the same photograph used in *Asylum*—Howard is unconscious, and Walter Freeman's leucotome protrudes from his eye socket. It is a shocking, gruesome image. The few times I have shown it to others, many can't look, or if they do, they quickly look away. Rodney, however, claims to be unmoved. "It's just a picture," he tells the producer (237). In a second interview, Howard is more direct and asks his father if he is owed an apology. Rodney is adamant: "No. Because it serves absolutely no purpose. There is absolutely nothing to be gained by holding a grudge" (246). For Rodney, to feel what had happened was not just to remember the past, but to return there, to dwell there, and perhaps to take responsibility for what had happened. For Rodney, the past, his affective reaction to that past, and the lessons of that past seem to be intimately intertwined, and it is perhaps for this reason that he insists that he and his son remain in the present, figured as a nonaffective space of nonreflection. "I've got to live today," Rodney tells Howard, "and you have to live today" (244). For Rodney, the only permissible view of the past is one unencumbered by emotion. In this case, it is clear that emotion does not impair judgment but facilitates judgment, which may be precisely why Rodney avoids it.

It is tempting to return here to lobotomy as trope, perhaps by pointing to Freeman and Watts's description of their patients as living in a similarly emotionless present, with neither worries for the future nor rumination on past troubles. Yet this analogy fails. In the interaction above, it is Howard, not Rodney, who exhibits an exquisite depth of feeling. It is Howard who is fully engaged in the past as well as the present, with an eye toward his future. When confronting his father, Howard frequently chokes up when recounting the pain the operation has caused him. In the most moving part of the documentary, Howard tells his father that despite his anger over what happened, he still loves him. His father does not reciprocate the sentiment. When asked directly if he loves his son, Rodney evades the question. As the last interview concludes, Howard tells his father again how much he loves him. Rodney says that he "appreciates" it and adds: "I hope you're reassured about how you ended up—not about the problems you went through, but my perception of how you are *now*"

(Dully and Fleming 2007, 248, original emphasis). Although Rodney steadfastly remains in the emotionally unengaged present, for Howard, finding the truth about his past serves to weave that past together with his present, a cathartic clarity that not only produces but is also the product of strong emotion.

The lobotomy trope fails when measured against a real person's life, a failure that immediately suggests another: no matter how much context historians may provide in order to flesh out the case histories of biomedical discourse, this endeavor fails in one crucial respect, for "the medical case is not the patient's story—nor is it meant to be" (K. Hunter 1992, 164). Representing patients in medical history *only* through the mediation of the medical case history severs all nonmedically "relevant" information about the patient's biography and family; erases diagnostic controversy or uncertainty (or, in Howard Dully's case, outright lies); omits information about the treating physician, surgeon, or hospital; and elides the complex epistemological, ideological, economic, and, yes, *affective* forces that shape the clinical encounter.[20] By relying only on the medical case history to inform our understanding of lobotomy's patients, we exclude at least half of the history of psychosurgery and risk reproducing some of the same assumptions that served as evidence for permanently damaging their brains.

The professional strictures on emotional discourse in this chapter persist in the present. In a recent letter to *JAMA*, for example, physician Robert Brook explains that as rhetors, doctors have been taught "to present their science in what is called a 'flat manner': let the facts speak for themselves. Get rid of adverbs and adjectives, pictures, first person, and just let the science sing. However, science rarely sings" (2010, 2528). While Brook firmly believes that "medicine needs to be scientifically based," he also argues that doctors need to "be engaged through their passions and emotions" (2529). Brook wonders what harm could come from allowing researchers to include a brief statement in published articles about their feelings toward the subject matter. Rather than introduce bias, he writes in a later letter, acknowledging a researcher's affective investment might increase transparency,

> and it would let me, as a critical reader, understand something about how the writer views the world. Any change is risky. I think this risk is worth taking. It might even increase the amount of science that is actually read and at the same time, by making the author consciously aware of his emotions, increase the science's validity. (2011, 1096)

As Brook notes, in addition to serving a rhetorical function (attracting readership), acknowledging one's affective investments may also promote critical reflection, more honest deliberation, and, ultimately, better science.

Western cultural narratives about objectivity promote a cartoonish image of science in which disembodied scientists see everything from nowhere— what Haraway (1988) calls the "god trick." While few practicing scientists would be "caught dead" believing in this narrative (576), it is clear that the myth of disembodied scientific objectivity continues to animate the conventions of scientific and biomedical discourse (e.g., Lewis 2006, 10). What Brook wishes for is precisely what Haraway recommends: a vision of objectivity that embraces its embodied, and thus limited, view. This rhetorical position of "partial perspective" is more than just a textual posture—by allowing us to "become answerable for what we learn to see" (582–583), an embodied ethos also has ethical and political effects.

As Brook and Haraway suggest, giving voice to emotion in scientific and medical discourse may enhance, not diminish, the process of deliberation and ultimately may increase the quality of our judgments (see also Waddell 1990 and Price 2011). Yet overcoming the longstanding bias against emotion does not mean that we ought to simply flip the terms and privilege emotion over judgment, which only reinforces the false dichotomy already drawn between the two. A better approach might be to simply acknowledge the role that emotion is already playing in scientific and medical thinking, practice, and decision making: maybe as a premise in need of a conclusion, maybe as a feeling in need of acknowledgment and elaboration, maybe as a question in search of an answer, but most certainly as an invitation to further discourse.

CHAPTER 2

Domesticated Women and Docile Boys

Lobotomy and Gender in the Popular Press, 1936–1955

> That which an age considers evil is usually an unseasonable echo of what was
> formerly considered good—the atavism of an old ideal.
>
> —FRIEDRICH NIETZSCHE, *BEYOND GOOD AND EVIL* (1886)

For nearly fifteen years after lobotomy's introduction to American medicine in 1936, the American press proclaimed the operation to be the long-awaited miracle cure for mental illness. Walter Freeman believed that press accounts of lobotomy were such a significant factor in its history that he devoted an entire chapter of his memoir to the topic, going so far as to claim that "without the enthusiasm and occasionally embarrassing efforts of interpreting our work to the reading public there would have been a much slower tendency for lobotomy to develop along the lines that it has" (1970, 4–1). The positive press Freeman describes did not last. By the late 1940s bold claims of cure were tempered by qualifiers, and by the early 1950s they were replaced by skepticism and criticism. This shift is marked by discontinuities: there were a few negative stories about lobotomy in the 1930s and 1940s and a few positive stories about lobotomy in the mid-1950s. The general trend in the stories' tone, however, exhibits a significant change from positive to negative during lobotomy's lifespan in American medicine.

Using a mix of quantitative and qualitative analysis, Diefenbach et al. (1999) argue that early reports about lobotomy in American newspapers and magazines rarely presented known risks of the operation and frequently exaggerated its positive effects, leading the authors to conclude that "biased" press coverage of lobotomy was a significant factor facilitating its development in the United States. According to the authors, fierce competition in the midcentury American media marketplace led newspapers and magazines to publish dramatic stories of cure that inaccurately represented medical opinion regarding lobotomy's therapeutic value:

> This is a situation where human emotion undermines the foundation of the scientific process leading to a rush to press without justification, and stimulating public interest, without adequate information. It is true that with time the *full story of lobotomy was known*, but by then it was already too late for untold thousands of people who had undergone this irreversible procedure. (60, my emphasis)

Yet what was the "full story" of lobotomy that the authors suggest these early stories suppressed in their "emotional" rush to publication? By suggesting that early reports provided only a partial story, the authors appear to rely on a contemporary perspective that condemns lobotomy as poor science and bad medicine. In this way, the "full story" of lobotomy may *only* be told by the later negative stories. In this chapter, I argue that there is a more nuanced story to be told about representations of lobotomy in the popular press, and it reveals much about the social value attached to the operation—in particular, its power to enforce gender norms.

In 1946, for example, a young woman from Michigan became the subject of headlines across the country. The press described the "attractive" and "nice-looking" woman as what Italian criminologist Cesare Lombroso (1911) might have called a "born" criminal. She began stealing at the age of four "for no reason" and spent her early life in and out of reform schools, was arrested for shoplifting and arson, had been thrown out of bordellos for "injuring patrons," and "boasted" two murders, although they were never confirmed ("Kill or Cure" 1946). After Detroit police arrested the woman on an unspecified charge, they sent her to the Wayne County General Hospital for psychiatric observation and evaluation. While incarcerated there, she was said to have lied to her nurses and doctors, and the hospital staff described her as generally uncooperative. According to the press, Dr. Aage Nielssen performed the country's one thousandth prefrontal lobotomy on the woman, who became known in the press simply as "Case 1000." Case 1000 sang during the operation, the *American Weekly* reported, and she "lost her sense of tone only when actual brain cutting occurred" (Lal 1947, 24).

Remarkably, press stories about Case 1000 did not describe her as mentally ill. Instead, she was depicted as a violator of laws and social norms, and the latter certainly seems to have been of greater concern to the press. Many stories led into a discussion of her case by highlighting the fact that she enjoyed smoking cigars, and headlines routinely presented the case as a moral issue rather than a medical one:

> "Surgeons Hope Brain Operation Will Make Woman Criminal 'Good'" (1946)
> "Reformed by Brain Surgery" (Lal 1947)
> "Brain Surgery Invoked to Curb Evil Impulses: Outlook Changed, Says Woman Criminal" (1946)
> "Operate on Brain to Reform Woman" (Ruch 1946)
> "Surgery Is Tried in Morals Case: Part of Degenerate's Brain Cut to Aid Her Character" (1946)

The Case 1000 stories all close with a variation on the same ending: just a month after surgery, the woman had received a "new outlook on life," and she appeared "more relaxed, more composed emotionally, and friendly and sociable" (Ruch 1946). Lobotomy was said to produce a result that judges and prison wardens could only dream of: not only had Case 1000's "urge" to commit criminal acts disappeared, but she also expressed "genuine embarrassment about her past conduct" (Lal 1947, 24). As the example of Case 1000 illustrates, press stories about lobotomy did much more than correctly or incorrectly reflect medical opinion: they also offered arguments for its value supported with interpretations of the operation's effects.

In these stories, lobotomy was accorded social value as well as therapeutic value, and indeed, the operation's therapeutic value was often measured in social terms. Intriguingly, when arguments about the lobotomy's therapeutic value shifted from positive to negative, the gender of patients used as evidence also shifted. Positive stories about the surgery most often featured examples of women to support their claims of cure, and suggested that lobotomy restored proper gender behavior in women like Case 1000. Negative stories about lobotomy, in contrast, frequently drew on examples of damaged men and diminished masculinity, which rhetorically positioned the operation as a social threat.

In the first section of this chapter, I expand on Walter Freeman's claim that "no account of lobotomy would be complete without a discussion of the effect that newspapers and magazines had upon the development of the procedure"

(1970, 4–1) by focusing on Freeman and Watts's ambivalent relationship with the popular press, which drew welcome public attention to the surgery and unwelcome professional attention to the doctors themselves. I then turn to the role gender played in medical discourse about lobotomy, exploring how gender performance was used as an indication for psychosurgery and also deployed as evidence of its success. In the final sections of the chapter, I examine press stories about lobotomy, first positive and then negative, with attention to their rhetorical use of gendered case histories. I conclude by showing how the narrative of these early press stories was reproduced—with a very different conclusion—in accounts of actress Frances Farmer's supposed lobotomy in *Shadowland* and *Frances*.

The Fourth Estate

The chapter of Walter Freeman's autobiography dedicated to the popular press is entitled "The Fourth Estate," a term that describes a nonpolitical force or institution that strongly influences political action. Although traditionally applied to the media's effect on politics, the term also aptly describes the media's powerful influence on medicine. In 1946, *Time* reported that the "chief U.S. lobotomy centers" were "swamped by demands for lobotomy by alcoholics, criminals, frustrated businessmen, unhappy housewives and people who are just nervous" ("Medicine: Losing Nerves" 1947), and there is no question that praise for lobotomy in venues like *Time* led many potential patients and their families to doctors like Walter Freeman. Reporters followed Freeman's travels across the country, and he and Watts received a "sizable sheaf" of newspaper and magazine clippings from "people who were earnestly hopeful that something could be done for their Johnny's who had been in hospitals for years with deteriorating dementia praecox, or whose Willie's had been subject to epileptic fits for ever so long" (6–7). Press interest in lobotomy was not simply a matter of reporters chasing a good story, however.

In the decade before his work with lobotomy began, Walter Freeman realized that reporters "played a very definite part in the development of a scientific subject by virtue of their ability to catch the imagination and enlist the sympathy of the public, to disseminate information in such a way that members of the profession are almost obliged to subscribe to the newspapers and periodicals to keep abreast of recent developments" (1970, 4–2).[1] Considering Freeman's belief in the power of the press, it is therefore not surprising that he and Watts introduced the procedure to journalists *before* they introduced it to their medical colleagues. In 1936, after the doctors had operated on Alice Hammatt and two other patients and had achieved some measure of success, they realized the announcement of their work would generate headlines (1970, 4–7). Concerned that reporters might distort or exaggerate their research, Freeman preemptively contacted Thomas Henry, the science writer for the *Washington Evening Star*:

> "Tom," [I asked.] "Would you like to see some history made?"
> His ears pricked up. I continued:
> "We've done a few brain operations on crazy people with interesting results.
> Would you like to see one?" (4–8)

Henry agreed and visited Freeman and Watts's clinic in Washington, DC, where he met patients before and after surgery and observed a prefrontal lobotomy in its entirety. After finishing a draft of his article, Henry sent it to Freeman and Watts for their feedback. In a vivid illustration of the power of the fourth estate, the doctors were so impressed with the quality of Henry's story that they used some of his language in their presentation to the 1936 meeting of the Southern Medical Association (SMA), the venue where they announced the results of their first surgeries to their colleagues (4–8).

During the discussion that followed Freeman and Watts's SMA paper, renowned psychiatrist Adolf Meyer complimented the team, commenting that while he had some reservations about the procedure, he nonetheless found lobotomy to be "very interesting." However, Meyer concluded by cautioning those in attendance about the dangers of publicizing the operation, stating, "it is important that the public should not be drawn into any unwarranted expectations" (quoted in Freeman and Watts 1937, 22). A number of Meyer's colleagues echoed his concern. In the editorial in *JAMA* accompanying the AMA roundtable I discussed in the previous chapter, for example, Morris Fishbein (1941) wrote that "there is no excuse for dissemination of discussions or of any statements laudatory of this procedure to the general public" (535). Three years later, one psychiatrist complained it was a "pity" that lobotomy was being discussed in the popular press. He went on to say, "We can only deprecate very strongly the action of medical men who have encouraged this" (Fleming 1944, 486). Without a doubt, the "medical men" in question were Freeman and Watts, who by the early 1940s had become familiar faces in the United States, much to the detriment of their professional reputations.

At the 1941 meeting of the American Neurological Association, there was informal discussion about expelling Freeman and Watts from the organization after one member "walked down the aisle brandishing a copy of the *Saturday Evening Post* and demanded an investigation with possible punitive action" (Freeman 1970, 4–12). The *Post* story that caused such a stir was "Turning the Mind Inside Out," a multipage feature by Waldemar Kaempffert, the longtime science and engineering editor for the *New York Times*. Like Thomas Henry, Kaempffert had visited Freeman and Watts in Washington, DC, on a number of occasions, watched a prefrontal lobotomy, and interviewed patients. And like Henry, Kaempffert had submitted a draft of the article to Freeman and Watts for their input. After obtaining Freeman and Watts's approval, Kaempffert went even further: he requested that the Medical Society of the District of Columbia vet the article for medical accuracy, and he also submitted it to John Fulton, whose experiments with the frontal lobes of chimpanzees had inspired Egas Moniz's initial foray into psychosurgery.

John Fulton did not mince words in his condemnation of the story, according to Walter Freeman. Fulton was incensed by Kaempffert's decision to publish the story with the *Saturday Evening Post*, which he derided (without explanation) as an "un-American institution" and a "Nazi rag" (quoted in Freeman 1970, 4–14). After Kaempffert submitted the first draft of his article to the *Post*, Freeman recalls, the editors refused to publish it unless it contained "liberal" references to the doctors discussed in the story. The "editorial demand for personalization" was exacerbated by prominent photographs illustrating the doctors in action. According to John Fulton, the decision to include photographs was "regrettable and both Watts and Freeman should have known better than to release them" (quoted in Freeman 1970, 4–14).

Fulton's concern, echoed by the ANA, was that publicity was tantamount to advertisement, which had been forbidden by the American Medical Association's first statement on ethics in 1847. This prohibition was loosened somewhat in 1976, after physicians challenged the ban on the basis of the First Amendment, but in 1941 it would have been enforced by the AMA at national and state levels, and the antipublicity sentiment would have extended into specialty organizations like the ANA as well (Canby and Gellhorn 1978). Walter Freeman was well aware of the professional interdiction against advertising, and both he and Watts "realized that we were courting censure by the various medical societies to which we belonged if the article went beyond the scientific presentation and dealt too much with personalities" (1970, 4–7). Largely because of the photographs, however, this is precisely how Freeman and Watts's colleagues received the *Post* story. While Freeman and Watts may not have intended to advertise for their services, press stories about lobotomy clearly were very persuasive to potential patients and their families. Freeman describes one of their patients, for example, as having been "lured by the publicity of our first paper."[2]

In that paper, Freeman and Watts (1937) emphasized that although they had obtained positive results in their first six cases, they made "no claims whatsoever to having a cure for any mental diseases" (21). Thomas Henry's story repeated and emphasized this claim in his story for the *Washington Star* and included an additional note from the pair:

> We wish to emphasize also that indiscriminate use of the procedure could result in vast harm. Pre-frontal lobotomy should at present be reserved for a small group of specially selected cases in which conservative methods of treatment have not yielded satisfactory results. It is extremely doubtful whether chronic deteriorated patients would be benefited. Moreover, every patient probably loses something by this operation, some spontaneity, some sparkle, some flavor of the personality, if it may be so described. (1)

As news of the surgery began to spread, however, headlines began to tell another story, freely claiming that lobotomy offered a "cure" for mental illness. In his memoir, Freeman comments that "some of these articles were well written but most of them conveyed the idea that there was a brand new method, infallible, that could be applied in all sorts of nervous and mental disorders without danger and with good prospects of restoration of the suffer[er] to normality" (1970, 4–16).

When scientific and medical discourse is translated into journalism, a process exemplified by these early accounts of lobotomy, the prose undergoes a number of rhetorical transformations. Jeanne Fahnestock (1998) argues that when scientific discourse is directed toward a scientific audience in the form of a research article or conference presentation, it exhibits the characteristics of forensic rhetoric, which seeks to establish the validity, nature, or cause of the matter under consideration (333). Scientists addressing other scientists are held to professional discursive norms that demand careful qualification of claims, narrowness of scope, consistent attention to refutation, and, as I discuss in chapter 1, a dispassionate tone. Conventions of scientific argument foreclose bold claims of significance, and since a discovery's meaning and value are "largely understood" by a scientific audience, they rarely warrant comment. When the audience for scientific discourse changes from an audience of scientists to an audience composed primarily of nonscientists, however, the argument's rhetorical character shifts from forensic to epideictic, a genre of discourse that celebrates (or condemns) its subject matter (333). Forensic rhetoric is primarily discourse about fact. Epideictic rhetoric, in contrast, is discourse about value.

In addition to shifting genre from forensic to epideictic, science journalism also frequently undergoes a change in argumentative intensity. In the small space given to journalists,

> there is no room for the qualifications a more knowledgeable audience would demand, qualifications that show the author's awareness of the criticism and refutation that an expert audience could raise against his inferences. To protect himself from such refutation, the scientist-author has naturally hedged his account. But because he fears no such challenge, the accommodator is far more certain of what is going on. (Fahnestock 1998, 338)

When scientific and medical discourse is translated into popular venues, in other words, its claims solidify and strengthen, a process well illustrated by these early reports about lobotomy. In these stories, the qualifications Freeman and Watts offered to an audience of their colleagues (qualifications that also appeared when the doctors had some measure of control over the writing, as with Thomas Henry's story) were removed as science writers emphasized and exaggerated lobotomy's potential, and the treatment of last resort became the miracle cure.

While many of lobotomy's cure stories may have been uncritical, they were not irrational. Journalists built a case for the operation, citing numbers of patients released from the hospital, providing basic physiological explanations for how and why the operation worked on the brain, and noting its utility in shrinking the populations of state hospitals. Most persuasively, however, many also presented examples of patients who had benefited from the surgery. Although some descriptions of patient outcomes were drawn from interviews with individual patients and their families, most appear to have been taken from interviews with doctors and surgeons or adapted from case histories presented at association meetings or published in professional journals. Before analyzing the representation of gender in press stories about lobotomy, then, it is worth pausing in order to consider how gender was represented in the primary source material.

Fixing Bad Girls

Although men constituted the majority of patients in American psychiatric institutions in the mid-twentieth century, a 1951 study of the nation's hospitals found that nearly 60 percent of patients subjected to lobotomy were women (Kramer 1954). In a study of California's Stockton State Hospital, Joel Braslow (1997) confirms that men outnumbered women during the time lobotomy was performed there. With regard to psychosurgery, however, Braslow discovered a significant difference with regard to gender: 85 percent of the 241 lobotomies performed at Stockton were performed on women. Of the fourteen patients who received multiple lobotomies, all but one were female (154). Braslow concludes that physicians' preference for surgical intervention in women reflected a gendered "therapeutic rationale" in which the body, feminine gender performance, and psychopathology were bound together (152).

The epistemological tendrils of this rationale are long. They reach back into ancient Greek theories of hysteria as the wandering womb; they extend into Silas Weir Mitchell's prescription of bed rest for the exhausted nerves of neurasthenic women; and they even curl forward, as some feminist scholars have claimed, into contemporary hormonal and neurobiological explanations for the etiology of depression (Ussher 2011). As Phyllis Chesler (1972) writes in the landmark book *Women and Madness*, since the body itself is pathologized in these theories of psychic distress, a diagnosis of mental illness often functions as a "penalt[y] for *being* female" (16, original emphasis). Elaine Showalter (1985) argues that the cultural association between women and mental illness extends even into our systems of representation, which have "typically situated [women] on the side of irrationality, silence, nature, and body, while men are situated on the side of reason, discourse, culture, and mind" (4). Within this gendered Cartesian framework, mental illness has become the quintessential "female malady" reflected both in representations of madness as feminine as well as in women's disproportional rates of psychiatric diagnosis.

Situated in a patriarchal heteronormative society, psychiatry reproduces a "notion of gender that normalizes married women, men doctors, and other requisite components of a heterosexual symbolic order while pathologizing the lesbian, the ambitious woman, the homosexual man, and other threats as diseases in need of a cure" (Metzl 2003, 21). In this way, if *being* a woman makes women vulnerable to psychiatric diagnosis, so too does "daring or desiring not to be" (Chesler 1972, 16).[3] Vividly illustrating this idea, Braslow found that Stockton's female patients often were called "bad girls" (no matter their age), and it is clear that in this clinical context, "bad girl" meant "bad *at being a girl*" (Braslow 1997, 158). Gender violations such as the use of "foul" language, consumption of alcohol, aggression, and the neglect of house and family were all interpreted as signs of pathology in Stockton's female patients. In one case, doctors criticized a woman who worked outside the home for not properly caring for her children, a "strange behavior" that was translated as a symptom of illness (rather than evidence of ambition or a result of financial need) and contributed to her diagnosis of dementia praecox (159).

Violations of sexual norms, such as homosexuality, masturbation, and "excessive" sexual behavior, were also employed by Stockton's physicians as symptoms of disorder and used to justify surgical intervention into women's genitals as well as their brains. Braslow discovered that five women at Stockton had received clitoridectomies to remedy their supposedly abnormal sexual behavior; four of these women also received lobotomies. Similar sexual behaviors in men, when deemed clinically significant enough to merit mention in their files, did not prompt a similar prescription. Not a single male patient was castrated or had his penis removed, Braslow adds, for violating sexual norms (1997, 165).

In *Psychosurgery in the Treatment of Mental Disorders and Intractable Pain* (1950), a six-hundred-page tome that contains the most detailed patient case histories in the lobotomy literature, Freeman and Watts also employed gender-specific metrics of sexual behavior to evaluate patients' conditions before and after surgery. In contrast to the logic that led Stockton's physicians to prescribe lobotomy in order to reduce women's sexual desire and pleasure, the doctors observed that lobotomy *increased* sexual desire in women as well as men. Notably, two symptoms that lobotomy was said to relieve were "frigidity or impotence," which were included in the same classification (1950, 502). For men, any increase in sexual desire was spoken of as a positive development, even if the man was not married.[4] One man, for example, was prescribed psychosurgery in part because he was "hysterical" and "afraid of women." After his operation, "he was introduced to a rather good-looking young girl and showed no evidence of embarrassment" (1950, 76). Another unmarried man, who had "religious obsessions" before surgery and who had "denied himself intercourse for more than twenty years," commented on the "renewed pleasure he experienced [afterward], complaining only that the girls cost him more money than he could afford" (1950, 178).

Unlike the behavior of the newly virile bachelors described above, women's extramarital sexual activity was evidence that the operation had produced "dubious results" (Freeman 1958a, 344). When Freeman and Watts evaluated women's sexual desire as positively changed, it was always within the confines of marriage. One woman, for example, who had "experienced no sexual pleasure with her husband" before surgery, began "kissing her husband passionately" afterward, and the husband of another reported to her doctors that his wife's affections were "just as deep, only possibly somewhat calmer" after her lobotomy (Freeman and Watts 1950, 178).

Despite a number of positive outcomes in patients' sex lives, Freeman and Watts admitted that "exaggerated" sexuality was sometimes a problem for men, a situation they described with some measure of amusement. One patient, for example, "a very dignified, reserved middle-aged gentleman, would emit a low whistle every time the nurse stooped over to pick something up from the floor," and for another, "it seemed the natural thing to do to slap the nurse on the rump every time she turned around and gave him the chance" (1950, 152–153). The "increase in sexual appetite and performance" exhibited by some men sometimes developed into a "ticklish situation" for their partners, a description that seems to be a euphemism for sexual assault:

> A woman who has been the target of her husband's criticism all day long may well be excused for avoiding his embraces when bedtime comes, particularly since the sexual act is carried out only for his own gratification. Refusal, however, has led to one savage beating that we know of (Case 43), and to several separations. Physical self-defense is probably the best tactic for the woman. Her husband may have regressed to the cave-man level, and she owes it to him to be responsive at the cave-woman level. *It may not be agreeable at first, but she will soon find it exhilarating if unconventional.* (1950, 195, my emphasis)

Unlike the descriptions of sexuality above, this passage is not included under the heading "Sex" but in the chapter "The Patient Comes Home," which focuses on the family's responsibility during convalescence. Although sexual assault is not presented as a benefit of lobotomy, neither is it used as evidence of its failure. Instead, the "exaggerated" sexuality of lobotomized men and the "ticklish situations" it occasioned are described as side effects that women must manage and even enjoy.

Psychosurgery's portrayal of lobotomy as a gender adjustment is enhanced by photographs that depict patients' physical appearance before and after surgery. Freeman (1950) believed changes in facial expression offered reliable evidence of a patient's mental state because they often "betray suffering better than the patient's words" (19), and consequently, many of his papers and presentations featured dramatic photographs of patients before and after surgery. In the "after" photographs, most postlobotomy patients are smiling, and many previously disheveled patients are neatly dressed; men are usually shaved, and women are coiffed and carefully made up. One "before" photograph of a bespectacled young man in *Psychosurgery* describes him as "perplexed, unable to solve the simplest problem." In the second photograph, the young man has lost his hair (due to surgical preparations) and his glasses, but he has gained a cigar. Only ten days after surgery, the young man was no longer troubled, Freeman and Watts reported, and he "seemed rather pleased with himself" (1950, 248).

Although photographs supported positive claims of personality changes in both men and women, Freeman and Watts gave the appearance of women special attention. Although the doctors claimed not to be "sufficiently acquainted with the mysteries of the boudoir to know just what happens following operation in regard to cosmetics, creams, lotions, rouge, lipstick, perfume and the rest," they noted that a number of their women patients were more apt to use cosmetics after surgery: "Even during the stage of primary inertia some young women will show interest when given their makeup kit and will apply lipstick with skill" (Freeman and Watts 1950, 172). An illustration provided as evidence shows a woman before the procedure, a few days after, and seven months after the operation. In the first photograph, the woman looks directly at the camera with a pained expression. In the second, her head is bandaged, and lipstick is garishly smeared across her lips. The caption indicates that she has "applied lipstick unskillfully but with pleasant effect." In the third photograph, she is shown impeccably dressed, with earrings, a hairdo, and lipstick precisely applied, framing the slight smile she gives the camera (172). Another woman, in a description that could have been taken from an advertisement for an antiaging cream, looked "so different from the photographs taken before operation that we hardly recognized her. She appeared years younger and her features had toned up; her eyes were bright and she was modishly dressed" (Freeman and Watts 1950, 78). In contrast to these descriptions of women, many lobotomized men were said to exhibit "indifference to personal appearance," although they were noted to "shave with precision" and did not cut themselves, even when shaving for hours at a time (172). This last point received no further comment.

The use of women's appearance as evidence for surgical outcome was not limited to Freeman and Watts. In one 1949 article from the *American Journal of Psychiatry* that described the results of a lobotomy program at Connecticut's Fairfield State Hospital, doctors justified their disproportional use of lobotomy on women (78 percent) by claiming that women were more violent and aggressive and offered "greater problems from the standpoint of general management in a state hospital" (Oltman et al. 1949, 743). When reporting the results of lobotomy, an "encouraging therapeutic weapon for a very malignant disease," the doctors commented that it was "truly gratifying to observe a patient who was previously a tremendous problem in management . . . [take] pride in her personal appearance" after surgery (750).

As I discuss in chapter 1, the criteria used to evaluate lobotomy's success had little to do with curing whatever the underlying psychiatric condition was said to be. The best evidence of surgical outcome was the extent to which patients "socially adjusted" at home and in their communities, and it is clear that social adjustment was directly tied to the proper performance of a traditional gender role. "[What mattered] was that the woman was restored to the abstract category 'woman,' irrespective of her psychological state," Braslow explains. "If she could cook, clean, care for the children, and provide sex, her recovery was considered complete" (1997, 162). For women at Stockton State Hospital, this often meant returning to the home and domestic duties. One patient, for example, was discharged after her doctors determined her husband was more "satisfied" (162).

For Freeman and Watts, although returning women to their roles within the household was sufficient as evidence for a successful surgical outcome, it was not necessary evidence. The doctors warned their readers not to expect too much from lobotomized women with regard to domestic performance. "In comparison with running a typewriter or a taxicab or a spot welder," they explained, "keeping house is an infinitely complex task that demands a great deal more of the person" (1950, 215). After surgery, women might half-cook the family's food or reduce a steak to "leather," and the family might sometimes be deprived of its right to dessert (1950, 215–216). In fact, lack of attention to household duties was sometimes framed as a *positive* result: Freeman (1953) claimed that a "beneficent effect" of lobotomy could be observed in the "greater freedom from tension in the household—the full ash trays, the book on the floor, the nylons in the bathroom—things that would have made the finicky housekeeper uncomfortable before the advent of mental trouble" (272).

Although the complexity of keeping house made this an unfair measure of a woman's surgical outcome, bearing and caring for children provided Freeman and Watts with some of their "best examples" of women's social adjustment after surgery (1950, 216). In one case, after giving birth to an "imbecile" child who later died, one of Freeman and Watts's patients fell into a "brief psychosis," and her husband subsequently left her (1950, 217). After lobotomy, the woman was "rewarded" with children after her remarriage to a farmer, an event the doctors pointed to "with considerable pride." Freeman and Watts noted that she was able to maintain a "home of this type with its multifarious activities of canning, preserving, gardening, and what not," and that, although a "bit indolent and somewhat of a gossip, [she was nonetheless] well liked in her community" (217). A studio photograph of her smiling family is featured in the 1950 edition of *Psychosurgery*.

For Freeman, the act of childbirth was not only possible for lobotomized women but also desirable.[5] Childbirth is cited as a "stabilizing influence" in many women's postoperative lives—even for women who gave their children up for adoption (1958a, 344).[6] "The pregnancy and delivery have seemed to give an additional push to a patient who was making a marginal adjustment," Freeman commented on one case, "with the result that the woman was able to secure employment and maintain her independence" (344). Freeman did not expand on this claim, nor did he offer physiological or psychological reasons why pregnancy and childbirth might have positively contributed to the woman's mental health or her financial independence. One is left to assume that by achieving the telos of biological womanhood (Leavitt 1986), the female body provided lobotomized women with "the additional push" toward gender normativity and successful convalescence.

Psychiatric patients have dual citizenship "in the world of meanings as well as the world of matter" (Berkenkotter 2008, 5). As I argue in chapter 1, it is impossible to generalize about what men and women were really like before or after lobotomy. Nearly all of the information we have about lobotomized people is found in their doctors', nurses', and families' representations of their lives. As psychiatrist Jay Hoffman (1949) wrote with regret in the *New England Journal of Medicine*, although the "opinions of the relatives and of the doctors and the nursing staff concerning this procedure are known . . . the opinion of the patient himself is not known," a silence he believed compromised any thorough evaluation of surgical outcome (234).[7] As the individual is interpellated as patient, her language is interpreted as sign and symptom within the psychiatrist's "interpretative framework" (Berkenkotter and Ravotas 2008,

146), distilled into a case history, and sometimes employed as an exemplar. This interpretative framework depends on a number of paraphrases and translations: language is translated as action; actions are translated into behaviors; behaviors are interpreted as symptoms; and symptoms are known according to a normal/pathological binary given meaning, in part, by gender ideology.

Domesticated Women

In its first story on psychosurgery, the *New York Times* claimed lobotomy could "transform wild animals into gentle creatures in the course of a few hours" (Laurence 1937, 1). While the *Times* did not describe any patients specifically, subsequent positive stories often featured stories about patients cured by the surgery, and the "wild animals" domesticated in these stories were overwhelmingly female. In 1947, for example, the *Seattle Post-Intelligencer* reported that doctors at Western Washington State Hospital "are watching the unfolding of what gives promise as a medical miracle," after lobotomy was performed on eight women and five men there. Although all patients were "cured" enough to be sent home to their families, the story focuses its attention on the personality changes in the women and mentions none of the men specifically. Three women are said to have been carried into the operating room bound in straitjackets, and one "was given to clawing and scratching at hospital attendants." After lobotomy, when the clawing woman was asked if she wanted to leave the hospital, she "pertly" replied, "that's up to the staff and I never debate with the staff." The article explains that "her suspicion had changed to trust; her anti-social behavior to cooperation." Another woman was said to have "brightly" declared after her operation, "Oh, doctor, I want to do anything you ask" (L. Cohen 1947).

Other cure stories added an additional layer to the domestication narrative: lobotomy had the power to clothe naked women. One 1953 story in *Newsday*, for example, supports a positive evaluation of lobotomy by referencing the case of the "the meanest woman in the building," whom doctors had dismissed as a "hopeless case" before her operation. Like the women in the *Post-Intelligencer* story, this woman is described in abject terms: "she kicked, shouted and spat at her attendants, stripped off her clothes in the dining room, and required forced feeding by three husky attendants." After surgery, the woman became a "mild, well-liked woman, completely competent for her limited job" (Burton 1953). In a similar 1940 story in the Washington, DC, *Times-Herald*, the woman whose case history supports the claim that lobotomy produces "amazing results" is described as "violent," someone who "frequently flew into rages" before surgery and often ripped off her clothes. After surgery, she "consented to keep her clothing on" ("Brain Surgery by D.C. Doctors" 1940).

Although not described in these animalistic terms, before surgery Case 1000 was nonetheless suggested to be living outside the boundaries of "decent" society (Lal 1947, 24). Gender figures prominently in descriptions of her case, beginning with the headlines, which frequently refer to her as a "woman criminal."[8] *Time*'s account of Case 1000, entitled "Kill or Cure," positions its description of her postoperative condition in a section called "The New Woman." Yet unlike the "new woman" of the 1920s who challenged conventional gender norms, the new woman of lobotomy upholds them: after surgery, Case 1000 became "neat," "polite," "friendly," "cooperative," and "demure."[9] This brief article raises a number of questions, beginning with its title, "Kill or Cure." Who is in danger of being killed? The article's positive tone, and its omission of any data about surgical complications, suggest that the "or" linking these two terms does not refer to the two possible outcomes of the surgery. Instead, audiences were faced with a choice between the "cure" of lobotomy and letting the woman fully realize her homicidal potential. Yet lobotomy is said to have had another effect on Case 1000's antisocial behavior: not only had her physical aggression abated, but her "aggressive sexuality" and "abnormal desires" had also "apparently vanished" (67). The *New York Times* account of the case hints that lobotomy's power to decrease "abnormal desires" may have a juridical application as "a new avenue of attack on sex crimes," even though Case 1000's only "sex crime" appears to be a history of prostitution (Ruch 1946).

Lobotomy's moralizing power is also vividly illustrated by the *Jet* article "Can Surgery Cure Evil Women?" (Wright 1953). While few press stories about psychosurgery mentioned patients' race specifically, the *Jet* article focuses on case histories of African American women. The article, which answers its title question in the strong affirmative, presents four examples of "evil or wicked" women whose mental "disorders" were sexual and/or domestic in nature. One woman's marriage was "doomed to failure because she could not get along with her husband or her children," a situation complicated by an "uncontrollable sexual drive which her husband could not satisfy." Lobotomy "freed" the woman from her "mental disturbances," and she was able to "return to her husband and children and live a happier life" (25).

A second case history focuses on a "young Chicago girl" said to suffer from a "compulsive sexual drive" that embarrassed her family. After a gynecological exam revealed an "over-sized clitoris," a "few deft turns of the scalpel . . . changed her into a normal young woman, [which] enabled her to marry and find perfect connubial life." The article does not mention whether the operation performed on the girl was a lobotomy or, as it sounds, a clitoridectomy. The use of surgery to cure oversexed women extended to women who sought sexual pleasure outside of the marital bed, such as a minister's wife with a reputation for "meanness," who one day quit her church, left her husband, and began dating another man. After a "short, painless prefrontal lobotomy," the woman became a "happy, respected helpmate for her husband" (26). And in the final case *Jet* presents, a woman was sent for surgery because she was "irritable" and "habitually drove her husband out of the home by throwing things at him." After surgery, she became a "normal, happy wife," "free" of the problems that "threatened to wreck her marriage" (26). By restoring "connubial" heterosexual relations and decreasing women's sexual desire, surgery "cured" these unhappy marriages and fixed their broken homes. While Jet claimed lobotomy helped women to fulfill proper adult gender roles, other press accounts suggest it had the opposite effect: transforming women into little girls.

Lobotomy, Freeman and Watts (1943) explained, might best be described as "a surgically induced childhood" (803). This result was apparently so common that the doctors warned patients' families that although "more mature reactions develop in due course" (1950, 188), they ought to expect loved ones to return as "enfant terrible[s]" (1944a, 299). It was common for patients to lose tact and other social graces, eat whatever they pleased, make "poor" jokes, and exhibit "childish exuberance" at the world around them (1950, 186–187).[10] Postoperative "childishness" was enhanced by the doctors' recommendation that families *treat* their loved ones in recovery as though they were "overgrown child[ren]" (1943, 803). Families were told to bring dolls, teddy bears, picture books, and crayons to the hospital to keep patients occupied. In the hospital, tickling by doctors and nurses appears to have been a common practice (Freeman and Watts 1950, 163) and even recommended as a means of punishment, as illustrated by advice the doctors gave to one frustrated mother:

> It would not hurt at all if you treat [her] as a child and tell her she is crazy, to shut up, to stop telling fibs, and so on. . . . Pull her around and push her around

and if she is disobedient tickle her in the ribs or slap her on the behind, make fun of her. You will find that she has lost a certain reserve or dignity which will make her a pleasanter companion to get along with. She will get a little petulant at times, but this should not disturb you. Rose is growing up all over again. (Freeman and Watts 1950, 428)

Rose was thirty-nine years old. Her mother later committed suicide, the doctors reported with surprising candor, because she "couldn't take" life with her lobotomized daughter, and the woman's death was described as a "tragic by-product" of her daughter's lobotomy (429–30).

While childishness was occasionally mentioned in positive stories about lobotomy, it was rarely used as evidence that the operation had failed. Instead, such behavior was subsumed into the dominant cure narrative or presented without further comment. In *Time*'s "Kill or Cure" story, for instance, Case 1000 reported that she felt "dopey" immediately after surgery and "cried, sucked her thumb, and splashed in her bath like a two-year-old." In the *Newsday* story above, the "meanest woman in the building" was "made almost childlike by her operation" but nonetheless was "full of friendliness and docility." In these stories, childlike behavior is either presented as a temporary state or presented without comment as unproblematic, perhaps owing to a long history in which women, and disabled women in particular, have been infantilized (E. Barton 2001).

Though women outnumbered men in cure stories, case histories of men sometimes surfaced in support of positive claims about lobotomy. Like the examples of women above, the few positive stories in which men are used as evidence also tended to portray lobotomy as a force for gender normalization. The headline of one 1953 story from the *Los Angeles Times*, "Brain Surgery Seen as Aid for Christine," makes reference to Christine Jorgensen, the first public face of sex reassignment surgery. I reference the case not because Christine was "really" a man but because of the assumptions about lobotomy's effect on masculinity within the story. When a reporter asks Walter Freeman if lobotomy might have "helped" Christine Jorgensen, he replies that he isn't sure, "but 1500 operations performed under my direction indicates the operation has a good chance to cure people of abnormal behavior. It should be of value in restraining men from their drive to dress in women's clothes" (W. Barton 1953). The article then provides a brief case history of one of Freeman's male patients:

a business executive who, because of trouble with his wife, fired six shots into his head. He survived and the operation was performed. At first this patient was very disagreeable. But he divorced his wife. After that he received several promotions, the last of the presidency of an oil company.

The man's attempted suicide is attributed to marital discord, not to any underlying psychopathology. In this story, the breakup of the man's marriage is interpreted as a positive effect. The patient's choice to divorce his wife (presented as a unilateral decision) contributed to the man's professional success, almost more so than the lobotomy, which at first made him "very disagreeable." At no point does the story mention anything about mental illness. Instead, lobotomy is praised for its potential not just to restore masculinity but to enhance it—which translated into financial success.

"Miracles in Brain Surgery," which ran in the weekly newspaper supplement *American Weekly* in 1946, also features a man (Potter 1946, 11). Like the unhappily married man from the previous story, the man of this story is not described as mentally ill. Instead, the story characterizes him as a "shy, mousy little bookkeeper, the kind that is the butt of all office pranksters." Also like the man in the previous example, lobotomy enabled career advancement. After surgery the mousy bookkeeper transformed into "a gregarious hail-fellow-well-met type, who could sell anything to anybody" and was later promoted to president of his company. The pathology represented in the "Miracles" narrative is not the abject insanity represented in many cure stories about women; rather, the man's only infirmity appears to be a chronic case of shyness and an emasculated position at the office. Lobotomy has the power to restore the bookkeeper's masculinity, and the erect cigar in his hand in the "after" illustration accompanying the story suggests that it has been restored indeed. The illustration also reveals a second miracle. In the "before" illustration, we see the office's prankster secretary, who has pinned a "kick me" sign to the mousy bookkeeper's back. After lobotomy, this same secretary sits demurely, legs crossed, taking dictation from the newly "gregarious" company president. The real miracle of lobotomy in "Miracles of Brain Surgery" is that it has the power to render an aggressive woman docile, *even though the operation was performed on someone else*. As if to solidify this point, the illustration provides a diagram of a brain inside the head of a woman who looks very much like the prankster secretary.

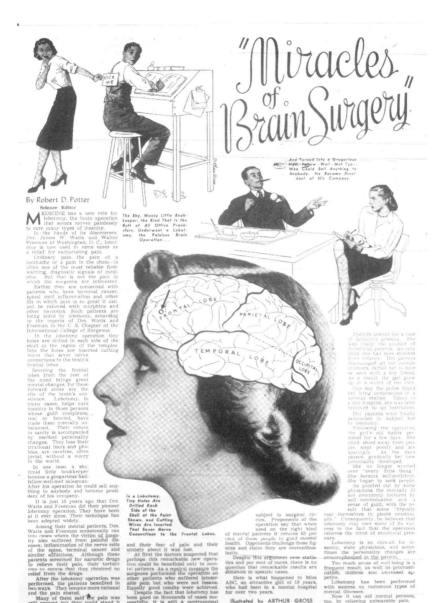

Fig. 2. "Miracles in Brain Surgery," 1946. (Courtesy of Hearst Newspapers, LLC/ American Weekly.)

Docile Boys

When the press's position on lobotomy began to shift from praise to blame, so did its rhetorical use of gender. A 1950 article in *Scientific American* entitled "Prefrontal Lobotomy: Analysis and Warning," for instance, expressed strong reservations about the operation, cautioning that it produces a "defect" that may be "more disastrous to the patient than the disease it is intended to relieve" (Goldstein 1950, 47). The article illustrates this warning using four examples of patients changed for the worse. All four are men. After surgery, one patient is said to exist in "a kind of vacuum"; "no friendship is possible; one can neither like nor dislike him." Another man, previously a "skilled craftsman," seemed to "have resigned himself to being a routine worker." The final case, an unemployed minister, was able to work. However, the minister's problem was his motivation, for he appeared "not in the least concerned that he is out of work. He is passive, shows poor initiative, [and] depends on his wife to decide everything" (47). The "warning" of the article's title suggests that even though lobotomy may have returned these men to their homes, their lives fell far short of the domestic ideal promoted by the cure stories. In the final example, lobotomy is blamed for *reversing* traditional gender roles. Not only is the unemployed clergyman unwilling to support his family, but he has become "passive," and his wife has taken over as head of the household.

Negative stories about lobotomy were fewer in number and featured fewer patient examples than the cure stories, which is not surprising: even today we are much more likely to read about scientific discoveries and medical breakthroughs than mistakes and retractions. In instances when examples of patients were used to portray lobotomy as unsuccessful or even as an unmitigated disaster, however, they were overwhelmingly case histories of men. These failure stories sometimes read as mirror images of the cure stories—in some, lobotomy is said to produce aggression rather than diminish it; however, like the cure stories, they also employ gender norms as a yardstick with which to measure patient outcomes. And so while violence and aggression indicate an unsuccessful outcome in these stories, so does docility, which is presented as evidence that the operation had *failed*. And childishness, presented as an unproblematic trait in most cure stories featuring women, is marshaled as evidence that, for men, the "miracle cure" was no cure at all.

The 1953 *Newsday* story I discuss in the previous section begins with the case of the "meanest woman in the building," who emerged from lobotomy "childlike," "full of friendliness and docility," and competent for her "limited" job. In the next paragraph, however, the story takes a turn: "That is a pleasant story, conjuring up visions of a medical miracle, but the results are not always so pleasant." The article's title, "How to Prevent a Murder (Sometimes)," refers to the case of Theodore A. Trent-Lyon, a lobotomy patient who shot and killed his former psychiatrist. In contrast to the wild women and emasculated men of the cure stories, the story describes Trent-Lyon as a "brilliant student" at the Harvard Divinity School, who was elected president of the student body before becoming mentally ill. Lobotomy was performed in order "to remove his aggressive drives—which is what the operation is supposed to do. It didn't" (Burton 1953, 65).[11] The story blames lobotomy for not curing, and for perhaps exacerbating, Trent-Lyon's violent behavior. Although the operation made him "silly," the brilliant divinity student was still rational enough to have made a list of people to kill, with his doctor's name at the very top.

After lobotomy, the article explains, the best a patient can hope for is to emerge from the operation "much like a child," which, in the case of the "meanest woman in the building," is cause to consider the operation a "medical miracle" *in the same story*. In a strange turn, the story concludes with the example of a man whose aggressive and violent tendencies were abated by lobotomy, but whose case is nonetheless described as a failure:

> Violent before the operation, [the patient] became an amiable idiot afterward. . . . He is as happy as a clam, and can't say too many nice things about the pre-frontal lobotomy. The family is now wondering if there isn't some way to sew his brain back together and make him into the same old violent Pa they used to visit at the State Hospital. (66)

"Literally," the story explains, strengthening the claim from Freeman and Watts's *Psychosurgery*, "lobotomy is a surgically-induced childhood." In a letter to his surgeon, violent Pa's son writes, "frankly, I know no way to cause *the deterioration of a whole family* more effectively than through a pre-frontal lobotomy" (66, my emphasis). In this article, lobotomy not only threatens public safety, illustrated by the homicidal Trent-Lyon, but, in the case of "violent Pa," it also threatens the patriarchal family, for a father (even an unhappy, violent, institutionalized father) is preferable to a happy child.

The production of a childlike personality is also denounced in "The Operation of Last Resort" (Wallace 1951), a double-length feature published in the *Saturday Evening Post*. In 1941, the *Post* had published Waldemar Kaempffert's "Turning the Mind Inside Out," an uncritical report about lobotomy's promise as a treatment for mental illness. Ten years later, "The Operation of Last Resort" takes a strongly negative view of lobotomy and the new personality it created. The article is richly detailed, and, pointing to author Irving Wallace's later career as a successful screenwriter and novelist, it also builds narrative tension and character identification not found in other press stories about lobotomy, positive or negative. Wallace first appears to approach the surgery evenhandedly, quoting Freeman and Watts's claim that "life is particularly agreeable to [lobotomy patients] and they enjoy it to the fullest." In the next sentence, however, Wallace points to another "school of thought" that believes lobotomy

> converts patients into *docile, inert, often useless drones*, stripping them of their old powers, giving them convulsive seizures, making them indifferent to social amenities, filling them with aggressive misbehavior and impairing their foresight and insight. There are those who feel the operation tampers with the God substance, who feel that if it cuts out a man's cares, it also cuts out his soul and his conscience. (24, my emphasis)

There is no question which school of thought Wallace finds more persuasive, demonstrated by the story's primary focus: the case history of a man Wallace calls "Larry Kennedy."

Unlike the cure stories, which provide little biographical information about patients outside of their clinical identity, with much more space at his command, Wallace paints a detailed portrait of Larry's life before and after surgery. Before lobotomy, Larry is described much like Theodore Trent-Lyon: a man of privilege and Ivy League education who spiraled into suicidal depression after entering Princeton (a depression attributed, by one family member, to Larry's discovery of Schopenhauer). Creative and "brilliant," with an IQ over 150, Larry was in the "near genius category," finishing in the top ten of his class and working as a writer until drafted into the army as "officer material" in 1942 (Wallace 1951, 79). Wallace spends half of the article detailing Larry's slow descent into depression. Unlike the brief case histories of the women above, many of whom were described as abject to a point where the audience could not possibly have identified with them, Wallace fashions Larry into a sympathetic, multidimensional character, a rhetorical move that amplifies the tragedy of his drastic personality change.

Lobotomy "unquestionably" made Larry happier, but Larry's happiness, like that of Violent Pa's, came at a price. Like many lobotomy patients, he gained weight: "his face is round, young, cherubic, and he's getting plump around the middle." While Wallace reports that Larry retained most of his cognitive capacity, his now-"dulled" brilliance was "erratically mixed with terrible streaks of childishness," an effect presumably enhanced by his now-cherubic face. After surgery, Larry's depression subsided, replaced by a "carefree" and "happy-go-lucky" attitude. Lobotomy "badly scrambled" Larry's memory, but he still remembered all of his friends and relatives, "though without much depth of feeling toward them one way or another." "People who meet him for the first time," Wallace writes, "always accept him as a perfectly normal citizen. They regard him as intelligent, jovial, though somewhat egotistical and impatient." However, "after they meet him a second or third time, they begin to suspect something is wrong with him" (94).

The article also builds sympathy for the Kennedy family, particularly Larry's brother Jack, who authorized the operation. The decision to lobotomize the wild women of the cure stories seems to be no decision at all. We do not hear from the women's families, only from doctors and hospital staff. In contrast, the audience agonizes with Jack over the choice to lobotomize his brilliant brother. As Larry is wheeled into the operating room, we hear Jack's inner conflict about his decision: *I will never see him again as I've known and loved him all my life. He will soon be returned from that room, the same name, the same face, the same body, but a different human being forever, for the rest of his life and ours* (90, original emphasis). To secure our identification, Wallace invites his audience to put themselves in Jack's place:

> About this time on Saturday nights, Jack is always tired, and he reaches up to turn off the lamp. He walks through the darkened house to his room, with Larry's heavy breathing following him. Were they right or wrong about Larry? Jack will never know. Anyway, it's a helluva thing to answer at two o'clock in the morning. After all, Jack asks, "What would you have done?" (95)

Filled with literary flourish, "The Operation of Last Resort" reads much like the pulp novels and sentimental films Larry prefers to Schopenhauer after his surgery, and the last line calls out for sympathetic reflection with Jack and the gut-wrenching decision that has changed his brother into someone else.

By looking closely at accounts of lobotomy in the popular press, we see how claims about the operation did not merely correctly or incorrectly reflect medical attitudes about the operation's therapeutic value. Press stories argued for lobotomy's therapeutic value supported by interpretations of its social value—specifically, its power to uphold or subvert traditional gender roles for men and women. The image of the docile lobotomy patient in these press stories has had remarkable staying power in American popular culture, an image most vividly illustrated in *Frances* and *One Flew over the Cuckoo's Nest*. These two texts are often positioned together as an illustration of lobotomy's power to enforce conformity and subdue dissent; however, when read against the gendered backdrop of this chapter, we can see that they come to slightly different conclusions about the meaning of docility.

In November 1942, American actress Frances Farmer was arrested for driving drunk in a wartime dim-out zone. When taken into custody, Farmer reportedly told the arresting officer, "You bore me." As a condition of her release, Farmer was ordered to abstain from alcohol. In January 1943, after she reportedly attacked a hairdresser on set, police arrived at Hollywood's Knickerbocker hotel to arrest her again for violating parole. When officers entered her hotel room, they discovered Farmer in the nude and "forcibly attired" her ("Actress Frances Farmer" 1943; "Frances Farmer, Actress, Jailed" 1943). The image of Farmer resisting arrest (fig. 3) was widely reproduced in the media, sometimes positioned next to one of Farmer's glamorous headshots in a dramatic before and after, as the papers tried to make sense of what had happened to the accomplished actress. During Farmer's court appearance, when the judge reminded her that she had been told what would happen if she "took one drink of liquor or failed to be a law-abiding citizen," she brusquely interrupted him: "What do you expect me to do? I get liquor in my orange juice—in my coffee. Must I starve to death to obey your laws?" ("Frances Farmer to Serve Six Months" 1943). Instead of serving the sentence, Farmer was released to her mother, Lillian, who sent Frances to a convalescent home in California. On March 23, 1944, Lillian Farmer committed Frances to the Western Washington State Hospital in Fort Steilacoom, Washington, where she would spend much of the next six years.

The details of Farmer's hospitalization have been the subject of intense scrutiny and controversy. According to *Shadowland*, William Arnold's 1978

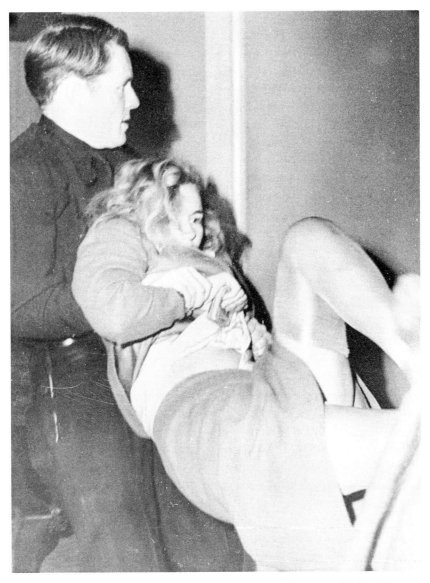

Fig. 3. Frances Farmer resisting arrest, 1943. (Courtesy of Bettmann/Corbis/AP Images.)

biography, Walter Freeman performed a transorbital lobotomy on Frances Farmer in 1948. Arnold came to this conclusion after a journalist phoned him with information that "the final step for Frances at Steilacoom had to do with something or somebody named Freeman" ([1978] 1982, 157). Arnold claims that like many psychiatrists, Walter Freeman was "fascinated" by Farmer's case, and he operated on her during one of his cross-country tours demonstrating transorbital lobotomy for hospital superintendents (161). After her lobotomy, Arnold writes, the ebullient actress was "meek and submissive and she generally did exactly what she was told" (162).

Arnold's account of Frances Farmer's lobotomy was repeated in the 1982 biopic *Frances*, in which the story of Farmer's life is presented as a tragic tale of nonconformity. Throughout the film, Frances repeatedly challenges the powers that be—authoring an essay entitled "God Dies" while a high school student, espousing leftist political beliefs and her support for organized labor, resisting the image of the Hollywood starlet, and challenging her diagnosis and subsequent maltreatment by psychiatrists. The film also includes a violent scene of sexual assault, dramatizing a claim from *Shadowland* that Farmer was raped "hundreds of times" by orderlies, their friends, and a "drunken gang of soldiers" (Arnold [1978] 1982, 141). *Frances* suggests that lobotomy finally freed Farmer from Steilacoom, cutting from the Freeman character explaining that "lobotomy gets them home" to Farmer's 1958 appearance on *This Is Your Life*. In the film's recreation of her television appearance, Frances slowly answers the host's questions, pauses frequently, and attributes her recovery to her belief in God. Watching this appearance is Frances's longtime love interest, Harry, a political radical who is clearly unsettled by her performance and her newfound faith. Harry seeks Frances out, and when they reunite, she smiles and haltingly asks him—twice—how she looks. The film ends with the platonic pair walking slowly away from the camera.

In 1983, William Arnold sued the makers of *Frances*, claiming that the film violated copyright by repeating large portions of *Shadowland* without his permission. There is no question that the film follows Arnold's biography closely. However, since one cannot copyright historical facts, a similarity between them did not necessarily violate the law. Remarkably, then, Arnold's case against *Frances* depended on the assertion that he had fictionalized a number of incidents in *Shadowland*, including Farmer's lobotomy at Western Washington State Hospital.[12]

According to an itinerary included in his memoir, Walter Freeman appears to have performed lobotomies at Fort Steilacoom during the time Frances Farmer was institutionalized there (1970, 18–3). However, it is doubtful that Walter Freeman lobotomized Frances Farmer during one of these visits. Independent reporter Jeffrey Kauffman (2004) has vigorously contested the lobotomy claims in *Shadowland* and *Frances*, citing the 1983 court case as well as interviews with Farmer's family members and information from the archives of Western State Hospital. Freeman biographer Jack El-Hai agrees with Kauffman's assessment, adding that if Walter Freeman had lobotomized Frances Farmer, he likely would have touted her as one of his success stories (2005, 242). I must point out that the summary of the 1983 lawsuit mentions that the defendants "established a factual basis" for the incidents Arnold claims he fictionalized. However, the overwhelming evidence to the contrary leads me to agree with Kauffman's and El-Hai's assessment that Frances Farmer was never lobotomized.

Yet one does not need lobotomy to create a tragic arc for Frances Farmer's life. During Farmer's real appearance on *This Is Your Life*, she remembers her time in Fort Steilacoom as traumatic and painful, commenting that she and other women had received "shots," hydrotherapy, and electric shock to "relax us and keep us quiet, which it did." The conversational pauses *Frances* attributes to Farmer's lobotomy appear to be provoked by these uncomfortable memories as well as her clear annoyance at host Ralph Edwards, who persists in asking her deeply personal questions in a patronizing tone. When Edwards describes her as "uncooperative," "violent," and "mentally ill," Farmer frequently cocks an indignant eyebrow at him. "I didn't think then, and I still don't, that I was actually sick," she tells him, "but if you're treated like a patient you're apt to act like one." These incisive words are reproduced in *Frances*. However, in line with the film's narrative, Frances says them *before* her supposed lobotomy, not afterward.

As told by *Shadowland* and *Frances,* Farmer's life is a tale of transformation that vividly mirrors the cure stories in this chapter, in which a rebellious, drinking, smoking, fighting, desiring, and even nude woman is thoroughly domesticated. The early cure stories recounted in this chapter celebrate this personality change as evidence of lobotomy's success. In contrast, *Shadowland* and *Frances* paint Farmer's domestication, like the failure stories in this chapter, as a tragic loss. Scripted in the late 1970s, this image of Frances Farmer was made possible in part by decades of feminist efforts to change what it means to be a woman, efforts that included a strident critique of psychiatry. Although one can hardly describe *Shadowland* and *Frances* as feminist texts (e.g., Johnston

1993, 24), they nonetheless have molded Frances Farmer into a representative character for women's oppression by psychiatry and a patriarchal culture in which women's docility is praised. In the intervening years, Frances Farmer has become something of a feminist martyr. However, in the fictional world of *Shadowland* and *Frances*, Farmer's sentence is not death but a docile life, a life so unremarkable that it warrants little commentary. Even though the real Frances Farmer went on to have something of a comeback in the late 1950s and 1960s, acting in a number of plays and television dramas and even hosting a successful television show from 1958 to 1964, *Shadowland* and *Frances* effectively end her narratable life with her lobotomy.

Like *Shadowland* and *Frances*, lobotomy is used to punish nonconformity in Ken Kesey's 1962 novel *One Flew over the Cuckoo's Nest*, which, combined with the 1975 Academy Award–winning film, offers the most well-known depiction of lobotomy in American culture. Set in a large state mental hospital, *Cuckoo's Nest* follows the protagonist Randle McMurphy, who fakes mental illness in order to avoid being incarcerated for statutory rape. Throughout the story, McMurphy rallies his fellow patients to challenge the system represented by hospital matriarch Nurse Ratched, who manages the details of the men's lives down to the number of cigarettes each is allowed. McMurphy describes the Big Nurse as a "bitch and a buzzard and a ballcutter" (Kesey [1962] 1999, 58) who emasculates the men of the ward, "getting you where it hurts the worst" (57). After years of suffering through the dominance of Nurse Ratched and her attendants, who periodically subject the men to gang rape, the men have become docile, passive, and reluctant to question the authority constraining their lives. McMurphy, in contrast, enters the hospital as the picture of virile masculinity, described by his friend "Chief" Bromden as having a "voice like papa":

> He's got on work-farm pants and shirt, sunned out til they're the color of watered milk. His face and neck and arms are the color of oxblood leather from working long in the fields. He's got a primer-black motorcycle cap stuck in his hair and a leather jacket over one arm, and he's got on boots gray and dusty and heavy enough to kick a man in two. (17)

After the final confrontation with Nurse Ratched, during which McMurphy almost kills her, McMurphy receives a transorbital lobotomy. Wondering what McMurphy would have thought of this development (and assuming that the body in front of him has been evacuated of subjectivity), the Chief explains, "I was only sure of one thing: he wouldn't have left something like that sit there in the day room with his name tacked on it for twenty or thirty years so the Big Nurse could use it as an example of what can happen if you buck the system" (308). Rather than leave McMurphy to suffer the indignity of lobotomized life, the Chief smothers "the big, hard body" with a pillow (309) in what we are to understand as McMurphy's final act of resistance. In the masculine world of Cuckoo's Nest, even death is preferable to docility.

One Flew Over the Cuckoo's Nest's gender anxiety reflects a larger postwar climate in which masculinity was thought to be in crisis, a crisis with significant political implications. In a Cold War cultural and political environment "that put a new premium on hard masculine toughness," male docility was imagined to be a "potential threat to the security of the nation" (Cuordileone 2000, 516). During this period, lamentations for the nation's "lost" masculinity "crystallized into a recognizable refrain: American males had become the victims of a smothering, overpowering, suspiciously collectivist mass society—a society that had smashed the once-autonomous male self, elevated women to a position of power in the home, and doomed men to a slavish conformity not wholly unlike that experienced by men living under Communist rule" (522–523). Within the cultural and political climate of the Cold War, lobotomy, and the conformity and docility it supposedly produced, thus came to be seen as more than a threat to the individual or family—it became a threat to the nation. In the next chapter, I explore that threat in detail.

CHAPTER 3

Someone Else

The Cold War Politics of Personality Change

> When you talk about being a member of the Communist party,
> I'm not so much concerned about whether they have a card in their pocket
> saying, "I am a member of the party." I'm concerned about those men
> who are doing the job that the Communists want them to do.
>
> —SEN. JOSEPH MCCARTHY, *MEET THE PRESS*, MARCH 19, 1950

Nearly every history of lobotomy ends with the same explanation for its demise: the ascendance of psychopharmacology in the mid-1950s (e.g., Smith and Kiloh 1974; Valenstein 1986; Shorter 1997; J. Pressman 1999). This narrative is so common in medicine that it has been described as a "dogma" (Sterling 1978, 135). And indeed, the mid-1950s saw the invention of antipsychotics like Thorazine (1954), anxiolytics like Miltown (1955), and antidepressants like Tofranil (1955) and their rapid dissemination in private psychiatrist's offices and state hospitals alike. The new drugs promised many of lobotomy's emotional "blunting" effects discussed in chapter 1, but with fewer risks and, most important, without the permanence of surgery. Indeed, many of these drugs were favorably referred to as "chemical lobotomies" when they emerged on the psychiatric scene, which suggests that many of the operation's effects were still desirable (cf. Freyhan 1955; Lehmann 1955; Lehmann 1989) even if the surgical vehicle was not.

Like lobotomy, psychopharmacology received lavish praise in the American press as psychiatry's newest miracle cure, which led many members of the reading public to ask their doctors for the pills by name. By the mid-1950s, many of Walter Freeman's patients and their families began to inquire about the newest treatment they saw in the press, as evidenced by many requests for Thorazine and Serpasil in Freeman's correspondence. By 1958, America's "dean of lobotomy" lamented that the procedure he had defended and promoted for nearly two decades was now in "eclipse, overshadowed by the tranquilizers and euphoriants" that had captivated public and psychiatric attention alike (1958b, 429). By the late 1950s, there is no doubt that psychopharmacology had become the dominant somatic treatment for mental illness, and the lobotomy era was over.

However, the "dogma" that drugs simply replaced lobotomy is flawed. According to neuroscientist Peter Sterling (1978), lobotomy peaked in 1949 and rapidly declined thereafter—almost five years *before* drugs came to dominate somatic psychiatry. Sterling argues that lobotomy "died" in the United States not because of the advent of drugs, but "under its own weight" (135). By this, Sterling means that lobotomy was not providing the results its practitioners had hoped for. Although they come to different conclusions, Sterling's explanation for lobotomy's decline and the historians' explanation are anchored in the same fundamental premise: changes in medical practice are caused by the evolution and refinement of scientific knowledge about the human body.

As Thomas Kuhn (1970) famously argued about changes in scientific thinking, however, shifts in paradigm do not simply reflect new discoveries or better visions of nature (94). Changes in scientific thinking follow the assent of a scientific community in response to persuasion, and it is reasonable to extend this proposition to biomedicine as well. While it is wrong to view the movement between psychiatric treatments as an abrupt shift in paradigm, as many historians have argued, there is no doubt that the number of lobotomies in America began to decline at roughly the same moment when psychopharmacology began to ascend.[1] Yet, however tempting it may be to write the history of lobotomy as a teleological narrative of biomedical progress—that is to say, the replacement of a less effective treatment with a more effective one—it is more accurate to say that psychiatrists, presented with a number of treatment options in the mid-1950s, were persuaded away from surgical treatments for mental illness and toward something else.

To account for shifts in biomedical knowledge and clinical practice without succumbing to the temptations of teleology, Judy Segal (2005) suggests that rhetorically minded historians might follow the principle of *kairos* rather than the principle of *chronos* that organizes most medical histories. Kairos is a rhetorical term from the ancient Greek sophists that refers to "right" time. Chronos—from which we get the word "chronological"—signifies a quantitative, measurable sense of time, while kairos speaks to a "a *qualitative* character of time, to the special position an event or action occupies in a series, to a season when something appropriately happens that cannot happen just at 'any time,' but only at *that* time, to a time that marks an opportunity which may not recur" (Smith 1986, 4, original emphasis). According to Carolyn Miller (1992), *kairos* "calls attention to the nature of discourse as event rather than object, shows us how discourse is related to a historical moment," and enables an understanding of history not only as a diachronic procession through time but also as a synchronic collection of discursive events at a particular moment (310).[2]

Approaching medical history from the perspective of *kairos* rather than chronos widens our view beyond medicine to the culture in which it is situated, Segal argues, and we begin to see how "popular and medical interests converge on certain themes" at particular times (2005, 36). Following this line of thought, the question that guides this chapter is not *why did psychopharmacology replace psychosurgery?* Rather, I ask, *under what conditions were psychiatrists persuaded to choose between psychosurgery and other treatment modalities for mental illness?* As such, my objective is not to construct a causal argument or a chronological narrative of lobotomy's decline, but to sketch the contours of the rhetorical environment in which the shift away from lobotomy took place.

One way to reconstruct this kairotic moment is to examine what lobotomy came to mean in the American imagination in the 1950s, a meaning I argue was shaped by fears of personality change in the early years of the Cold War. In this chapter, I trace the origins and impact of this meaning in a disparate group of texts yoked together by what Timothy Melley (2000) calls "agency panic"— the fear that the individual has lost autonomy and uniqueness in the face of pervasive social control. In the United States, agency panic operates in a liberal political register, in that it attempts to rescue and reinforce the individual as a sovereign subject, "a rational, motivated agent with a protected interior core of beliefs, desires, and memories" (14). Yet the panic we see in the texts discussed in this chapter exceeds mere anxiety over individual agency: they reveal a pervasive fear that a person can become a *different person*. This fear cuts to the core of foundational concepts of personhood. For instance, in John Locke's ([1694] 1975) classic definition, the person is "a thinking intelligent being, that has reason and reflection, and can consider itself as itself, *the same* thinking thing, in different times and places" (335, my emphasis).[3] For Locke, a defining element of the person is its immutability: if the person has, as Melley puts it, an "interior core" that must be "protected," then what it must be protected against is change.

The fear that you or someone you love could become someone else appears again and again in the 1950s: in fiction like *Invasion of the Body Snatchers*; in media and film accounts of "brainwashed" prisoners of communism; and, most vividly, in far right claims that mental health professionals were conspiring to alter the American personality—invading the country by literally changing the minds of its citizens. These texts reference each other to such a dramatic extent that "intertextuality" does not do the phenomenon justice. A better term is "echo," and I use the verb frequently in this chapter. To be sure, the direct indictment of lobotomy in many of these texts did not necessarily cause a wholesale shift from surgery to psychopharmacology; however, it certainly contributed to the rhetorical environment in which the choices that characterize the shift were made.

Invasion of the Mind Snatchers

"No emotion." I said it aloud, but wonderingly, speaking to myself.

—MILES BENNELL, IN JACK FINNEY'S *INVASION OF THE BODY SNATCHERS* (1954)

Nowhere is the Cold War fear of personality change better illustrated than in Jack Finney's *Invasion of the Body Snatchers*, first published as a serial in *Collier's* magazine in 1954, expanded into the novel in 1955, produced into Don Siegel's unforgettable film in 1956, and remade into successive films that surface at least once a generation. *Body Snatchers* has become widely known as a Cold War parable in spite of the protestations of those involved. Jack Finney, for his part, was insistent that his novel should not be interpreted as "a cold war novel or a metaphor for anything" (cited in Corrigan 2011), and Don Siegel frequently denied that his film was a commentary on either communism or anticommunism, which, in typical Cold War irony, are the two themes most frequently attributed to the film. Ignoring Finney's and Siegel's claims, scholars have proffered a number of sociopolitical interpretations of *Body Snatchers*, such as its representation of Cold War anxieties (Samuels 1979); race and immigration (Mann 2004); and gender and sexuality (Steffen-Fluhr 1989; Byers 1989; Hendershot 2001). One overlooked aspect of *Invasion of the Body Snatchers*, however, is its trenchant critique of the psychiatric profession. The novel features a number of medical references, beginning with its title, which points to the age in which doctors, not alien pods, snatched the bodies of the recently deceased for the purposes of dissection. But as we will see, it is psychiatry that is *Body Snatchers'* primary target. Although *Invasion of the Body Snatchers* is not necessarily a text *about* lobotomy, the deep anxiety *Body Snatchers* expresses about personality change and its strong suspicion of psychiatry are an excellent introduction to the rhetorical environment this chapter maps.

At the beginning of the novel, protagonist Dr. Miles Bennell is visited by Becky, his high school sweetheart, who is deathly worried about her cousin Wilma. Wilma has become convinced that her uncle Ira is an imposter. Although the man looks like her uncle, he simply doesn't *feel* like her uncle. In fact, Wilma explains that her uncle doesn't feel at all: "There *is* no emotion," Wilma explains to Miles, "only the pretense of it. The words, the gestures, the tones of voice, everything else—but not the feeling" (Finney 1954, 21). Flummoxed but convinced that the trouble is with Wilma, not Ira, Miles refers her to his friend Mannie Kaufman, the local psychiatrist.

Mannie first appears in a meeting in which he, Miles, and two other doctors discuss the unusual cases that are appearing with greater and greater frequency in their offices. During the meeting, the psychiatrists' profession is treated with levity by both Miles and Mannie, who quips that if patients like Wilma continue to accumulate without treatment, "it'll kill our racket." Miles continues the joke, telling his colleagues that psychiatry, still in its "infancy," is "the backward stepchild of medicine" (26). Later, when Miles calls Mannie in the middle of the night, he is treated to a flurry of curses. "Why doctor," Miles teases, "where in the world did you learn such language? From your patients' foul and slimy subconscious, I suppose. How I wish I were a head-doctor, charging seventy-five bucks a throw just to sit and listen and improve my vocabulary" (54). Despite the digs at his friend's profession, Miles clearly has a great deal of respect for Mannie, whom the novel repeatedly refers to as a man of considerable intelligence.

Soon, however, Miles is confronted by the truth of what is happening to the citizens of Mill Valley. They are being replaced with identical replicas of themselves, bodies grown in alien pods that have floated to Earth from outer space. After Miles discovers a pod template for Becky, he panics and turns to Mannie for help. Instead of rushing to his aid, however, Mannie dismisses Miles's fright as yet another case of the mass hysteria he believes is sweeping over Mill Valley. Miles grudgingly agrees with Mannie's diagnosis. But then, with horror, he realizes that something is wrong with his friend:

> *Mannie, Mannie, Mannie,* I thought to myself suddenly. . . . He'd explained our delusion last night, and now this morning every patient I talked to seemed to

mention his name ecstatically and gratefully; he'd solved everything in no time, and single-handed. For a moment I thought of the Mannie Kaufman I'd always known, and it seemed to me he'd always been more cautious, slow to form final opinions. Then the notion roared up in my mind full-blown; this *wasn't* the Mannie I'd always known. (92, original emphasis)

Mannie, Miles suspects, has become a pod person. Moreover, the trust the new Mannie seems to inspire in the pod townspeople has made him one of their leaders. In one of the final scenes of the novel, Mannie and his pod colleague L. Bernard Budlong, a professor of biology, discover Miles and Becky hiding in a doctor's office. After staring hard at Mannie's face, Miles explains to the reader, "I knew. It's hard to say how I knew—possibly the eyes lacked a little luster; maybe the muscles of the face had lost just a hint of their usual tension and alertness; and maybe not—but I knew" (170).

Even though the pod body—down to its fingerprints—can be replicated, the one difference between the pod people and their originals is emotion. Melissa Littlefield (2011) argues that the novel's discussion of emotion should be understood as the tension between emotion, defined by Eric Shouse (2005) as "the projection/display of a feeling," which can be feigned, and affect, the "non-conscious experience of intensity" (114–115), which cannot. Although the pod people can display emotion externally, they cannot feel it internally. Affect may be interior, but it lends the exterior performance authenticity, since some measure of performed affect is used to judge the credibility of an emotional display. There are tears, and there are crocodile tears: after all, Wilma knew that "Uncle Ira's" emotions were not real feeling, only "pretense."

Disgusted by the prospect of a life without feeling, Miles declares to Mannie and Budlong: "You live in the same kind of grayness as the filthy stuff that formed you" (182). Reminding Mannie of the book he used to work on "every spare minute," Miles tells the pod psychiatrist that although he might still be able to read books, without feeling and creativity he won't be able to write them anymore (183). Mannie is predictably nonplussed by Miles's outburst and assures his friend that despite its gruesome appearance, the process of body snatching is painless. In addition, pod life—that is, life without feelings—has its advantages. In words that could easily have come from Walter Freeman, Mannie tells Miles, "'Ambition, excitement—what's so good about them?' he said, and I could tell that he meant it. 'And do you mean to say that you'll miss the strain and worry that goes along with them? It's not bad, Miles, and I mean that. It's peaceful, it's quiet'" (183).

Three years before American audiences were thrilled by *Body Snatchers*, magazine readers were treated to a similar terrifying scenario of forced personality change in the *Saturday Evening Post*. However, the *Post* story was not a work of science fiction. It was Irving Wallace's double-length feature "The Operation of Last Resort" (1951), a story I also discussed in the previous chapter. The article briefly mentions the case of one woman who accused her husband's doctor of giving her "a new husband. He isn't the same man." Another woman, in a comment that easily could have been uttered by a concerned relative in *Body Snatchers*, observed that after lobotomy her daughter "is my daughter, but yet a different person. She is with me in body, but her soul is in some way lost. Those deep feelings, the tenderness are gone" (95).

As I discuss in the previous chapter, most of the *Post* story focuses on the personality changes in "Larry Kennedy" after his lobotomy. As Larry is wheeled into the operating room, his brother Jack muses, "he soon will be returned from that room, the same name, the same face, the same body, but a different human being forever, for the rest of his life and ours" (Wallace 1951, 90). Wallace's story carefully details the personality change in post-op Larry, who has transformed from an intelligent man with depression into someone else, and the similarities between Wallace's description of Larry and Finney's description of Mannie are striking. Larry before lobotomy was measured in his judgments, "never expressing an opinion until he'd read all sides of a subject, and even then he'd always say he wasn't sure" (79). In this way, pre-op Larry mirrors pre-pod Mannie, whom Miles remembers as "cautious, slow to form final opinions." Much like Miles's observations of post-pod Mannie, after lobotomy Larry rushed to judgment and formed "flash opinions" (92). Although Larry was still able to read after the operation, the article explains that, like post-pod Mannie, "he would never be able to do creative work, like writing, again" (84). Lobotomy may have offered a more peaceful and quiet life for Larry, but "it had also removed his old personality" (89).

Toward the end of "The Operation of Last Resort," Wallace quotes the eminent psychoanalyst D. W. Winnicott, who worried that lobotomy might be exploited for political purposes: "What guarantees have we that a [John] Bunyan in prison will be allowed to keep his brain intact and his imagination free?" Like Winnicott, *Invasion of the Body Snatchers* expresses deep unease about the power of the psychiatric profession to pathologize dissent. When the residents of Mill Valley, including Miles, voice concern about the changes in their loved ones and seek to act against the pod powers-that-be, Mannie Kaufman diagnoses the situation as a mass delusion. In the 1956 film, after Miles Bennell escapes the pod people, he stands alone on the side of a dark California highway, screaming to the rush of passing cars about what has happened to his hometown. When Miles is rescued by the police and tells them his story, however, they do not take him back to the station. They take him to a psychiatric hospital.

Reflecting on the popular culture of his 1950s childhood, Martin Scorsese remembers that his imagination was "filled with images from *Invasion of the Body Snatchers*, practices like lobotomies, and fears that the Communists could steal our souls" (quoted in Brody 2010). For Scorsese and for many others of the time, *Invasion of the Body Snatchers* was merely one element of a larger discourse of personality change in which the lines between fact and fiction, psychiatrists and communists, lobotomized people and pod people, began to blur. In what follows, I seek to bring those lines into focus.

Brainwashing America

The Cold War is often described as a war of words: an ideological conflict fought on a mental battleground with rhetorical weapons in order to claim territories of opinion, attitudes, and loyalties. In this context, the development of effective communication strategies and propaganda programs became as strategically important to the United States as the buildup of its nuclear arsenal. These communication programs sought to understand (and thereby increase the efficacy of) techniques of persuasion (Parry-Giles 1994), but they also endeavored to strengthen American resistance to the seductive communist message, a project often characterized as a matter of health. US diplomat George Kennan (1946) wrote in his famous "long telegram" to the Treasury Department, for example, that resistance to communism began at home by promoting the "health and vigor of our own society," which would presumably act as a bulwark against outside influence. J. Edgar Hoover (1947) echoed Kennan's metaphor in a speech before the House Un-American Activities Committee (HUAC) in which he compared communism to a "disease that spreads like an epidemic; and like an epidemic, a quarantine is necessary to keep it from infecting the nation." The metaphors of health and illness that dominated early Cold War discourse strongly urged the United States to train its body politic to resist outside influence in order to safeguard the nation's identity. Shortly after Hoover's speech to the HUAC, two events appeared to validate his paranoia about the power of communist influence: the confession of Hungarian cardinal József Mindszenty and the "brainwashing" of US prisoners of the Korean War.

In 1949, the newly formed People's Republic of Hungary tried Cardinal József Mindszenty and sentenced him to life in prison after he confessed to a number of crimes against the state. During the Second World War, Mindszenty had become a national icon when he opposed and was subsequently imprisoned by the occupying Nazi forces. When Hungary was occupied by the Soviet Union after the war ended, Mindszenty once again became an oppositional figure. Once the Hungarian Communist Party assumed power in 1948, it quickly moved to diminish the role of religion in Hungarian life, dismantling religious education, stripping theological programs from state universities, forbidding religious orders, and confiscating property from religious communities (Schanda 2011, 17). Mindszenty vocally opposed these developments, and on December 26, 1948, he and a number of other clergy members were arrested and charged with treason and espionage.

The trial that followed quickly became an international cause célèbre. In the United States, Catholics were the first to rally to Mindszenty's defense in response to calls from church authorities like New York's Cardinal Spellman, and concern for Mindszenty's plight soon spread across the country. "No recent move by the Communists seems to have stirred up so fierce a reaction as the Mindszenty trial," mused one *New York Times* editorial, which noted that the case was "discussed with unusual attention" even in the largely Protestant South ("Upper South" 1949, cited in Carruthers 2009, 137). American citizens sent letters to President Truman urging him to intervene in the Mindszenty case, and massive parades and rallies were held across the country to demonstrate American sympathy and support for the embattled Cardinal ("Mindszenty Upheld" 1949).

At the start of his trial, the stalwart anticommunist who had resisted German soldiers confessed he had planned to steal the crown jewels and was conspiring to start another world war so that he might seize political power in Hungary for himself (Streatfeild 2007,3). Although Mindszenty's confession disturbed many people, it came as no surprise. Before the trial, Mindszenty had released a letter warning that any confession he might make would come as the result of duress and should be discounted. Just as he had predicted, in his testimony before the court Mindszenty recanted the letter and announced to the packed courtroom: "I did not see certain things as I see them now" ("Their Tongues" 1949, 28). Although Mindszenty appeared thin and exhausted, no bruises or lacerations were visible on his body, and many correspondents present at the trial believed Mindszenty was "perfectly normal in every respect" ("Eyewitness" 1949; G. Pressman 1949).

A photograph of the cardinal that circulated widely after the trial, however, appeared to suggest that *something* had happened to Mindszenty during his time in captivity (fig. 4). According to one British newspaper, "in contrast to all earlier photographs, the photographs of the Cardinal . . . which appeared in the London newspapers last Saturday showed, as was widely noticed, a man clearly under great strain, with brows tautly knit and eyes staring, in contrast to all earlier photographs" ("Cardinal's Trial" 1949, 118). In the image, Mindszenty perches on the side of the bench, his gaunt face tightly drawn. His darkly circled eyes, which seem almost to bulge out of his head, stare intently at something out of the frame.

Mindszenty's odd gaze was only one aspect of his strange performance in court that day. According to observers at the trial, the cardinal also appeared bewildered and tottered unsteadily on his feet. He suffered from frequent lapses in memory. Normally eloquent, with a fiery voice, the cardinal initially spoke in a "low, almost inaudible voice" when he addressed the court, and he often made grammatical mistakes. Later in the day, however, when Mindszenty offered his final statement, he spoke in a "much clearer, more decisive manner" and "gave some evidence of being an orator," which discounted any theories that the cardinal may have been merely tired. People continued to speculate about the cause of Mindszenty's unusual behavior even after he was convicted and sentenced to prison. Although the trial was over, wondered one eyewitness, "the question remains: what made the Cardinal act as he did?" (G. Pressman 1949).

One answer was that Cardinal Mindszenty had undergone a total change of personality. During the trial, Mindszenty's family members and friends reported that the man sitting in the courtroom was "not the man we knew" and that his words and behavior appeared "wholly unlike what we know of the real Cardinal's personality." Even Mindszenty's handwriting—long held to be the trace of the unique personality—was noted to have changed during his imprisonment, which led graphologists who examined Mindszenty's signature to declare that "the mind which compelled the pen in the first instance was not the mind which impelled the pen in the second instance" (quoted in Streatfeild 2007, 3–4). Nearly all observers agreed that "a different Joseph Mindszenty" sat in court that day ("Their Tongues" 1949, 32). Yet *how* his captors had managed this "miracle of evil," *Time* mused, "nobody knows. Somehow they broke Joseph

Fig. 4. Cardinal József Mindszenty at his trial, 1949. (Courtesy of AP.)

Mindszenty, man of burning courage. Somehow they made him say things he had denied with the utmost vehemence, and with full knowledge of the consequences, until his arrest 40 days before" ("Their Tongues" 1949, 28).

In 1950, US-based Freedom Productions, Inc., offered an explanation for Mindszenty's personality change in *Guilty of Treason*, a film that critic Leonard Maltin aptly describes as a "preachy Red Scare time capsule" (2012).[4] After Mindszenty's arrest, the film's audience is treated to a closed-door meeting between Hungarian officials, the Soviet commissar, and a psychiatrist, who deliberate over how to wrest a confession from the recalcitrant cardinal. Since the confession is to be used as propaganda, it is crucial that it appear genuine. The psychiatrist runs through a list of possible techniques and technologies (including drugs like the "truth serum" scopolamine) before settling on hypnosis for its power to "radically" alter the patient's personality. "Very well then, doctor," declares the commissar. "If we can change the personality of the defendant Mindszenty, let us change it by all means." The group readily agrees to the proposition, Mindszenty is hypnotized, and he confesses. Mindszenty later speculated in his memoirs that he may have been drugged, although he could not say for sure (1974, 104).[5] However, there is no evidence that he was either hypnotized or tortured to induce his confession (Rév 2002, 63).

Although many Americans were deeply disturbed by what had happened to Cardinal Mindszenty, what became known as the "Mindszenty treatment" endangered only those on the other side of the Iron Curtain.[6] However, when the United States entered Korea in 1950, the Mindszenty treatment, now known by a terrifying new word—*brainwashing*, became a dreaded threat to captured US soldiers.

When the Korean War is remembered by Americans—if it is remembered at all—the focus is on the thousands of Americans captured by North Korean and Chinese forces. Shortly after the war ended, stories began to swirl in the press about the conduct of many American POWs in the camps. According to Eugene Kinkead's controversial and widely read book *In Every War but One* (1959), nearly one in three American POWs collaborated with their captors, and one in seven "seriously" collaborated to the point of making false confessions and petitioning politicians in the United States to end military intervention in Korea (16).[7] In a highly publicized case, Colonel Frank Schwable confessed that the United States had used bacteriological warfare in Korea, a charge he later denied, claiming he had made it under psychological duress. Like Schwable, most soldiers who "collaborated" with their captors renounced their actions when they returned to the United States, attributing their behavior to physical and psychological maltreatment. To the nation's dismay, however, twenty-three American POWs not only refused to retract their statements against the United States but also refused to come home.

Instead of repatriating with the thousands of other POWs released during Operation Big Switch, the men expressed a desire to move to China in order to study Marxist and Maoist philosophy and work in Chinese factories and farms. In late September 1953, the soldiers were transferred to a neutral prison camp in the demilitarized zone between North and South Korea, where attempts were made to "explain" to them why they should return to the United States.[8] The men steadfastly refused to listen to the appeals, which included impassioned pleas from their own family members. In early 1954, the soldiers traveled to China, where they lived for a number of years before returning one by one in the late 1950s and 1960s. Two of the men, James Veneris (who later took the name "Lao Wen") and Howard Gayle Adams, remained in China for the rest of their lives ("Ex-Army Private" 1981).

Unlike other POWs who had worked with their Chinese and North Korean captors, the twenty-three soldiers did not appear to have been tortured or otherwise coerced into their decision. According to one foreign correspondent present when the men were delivered to the neutral camp,

> many [observers] gave the group the benefit of every doubt and took into consideration that the men might be rundown physically and mentally and should not be condemned for their actions. But with the appearance of two truckloads of bronzed young men, obviously well fed and seemingly in the best physical condition, at the prison camp, opinions changed. . . . When the twenty-three arrived they were singing the "Internationale," the song of international communism, and shouting that the Soviet Union would free the world. As they sang and shouted they raised their fists in unison and alternated between waving greetings to near-by Communists and scowling at United Nations officers and Allied correspondents. Their attitude did not seem to be that of bewildered young men. (MacGregor 1953, 4)

The men did not appear to be opportunists eager for better rations or privileges, but "true believers," to use a term popular at the time (Hoffer [1951] 2003).

As with the Mindszenty trial, American attention immediately focused on the question of *how* and *why* these particular soldiers had turned toward the enemy, in large part because their guilt or innocence depended on the answer.[9] If the soldiers had willingly gone Red, they were guilty turncoats worthy of the nation's scorn. However if, like Mindszenty, they had undergone some irresistible "miracle of evil," they were innocent victims worthy of the nation's sympathy. In interviews with the Associated Press, the men's families all expressed surprise and disbelief at their sons' and brothers' odd behavior ("Families Shocked" 1953). The POWs were not just acting strangely, their families claimed. They were not acting like themselves. One man's mother stated firmly that "this boy is not really her boy, not really the Billy who marched off from Dalton so proudly in 1949" (Pasley 1955, 49). Speculation about the soldiers began to percolate in the national media, and the explanation that came to dominate all others was that the men were not acting like themselves because *they were not themselves.* They had been brainwashed.

Brainwashing, wrote a *New York Times* columnist in 1956, "the word and the technique, burst like a bombshell upon the American consciousness" during the Korean War (Leviero 1956). The word "brainwashing," a translation of the Mandarin phrase *xi-nao* ("brain wash"), was coined by journalist Edward Hunter in 1950.[10] *Xi-nao* is an idiomatic version of the formal Chinese name for programs of ideological realignment and political education, known as *si-xiang gai-zao,* which means "thought reform."[11] In *Thought Reform and the Psychology of Totalism*, his 1961 study of brainwashing, psychiatrist Robert Jay Lifton ([1961] 1989) wrote that although the idea of brainwashing and thought reform may have horrified many Americans, who saw programs of political education and indoctrination as coercive, it was "important" to realize that many "Chinese Communists view [the practice] as a morally uplifting, harmonizing, and scientifically therapeutic experience" (15). Lifton's emphasis on perspective was echoed by other academics of the early 1960s, like sociologist Albert Biderman (1963), who defined brainwashing as

> a word that has become embedded in our language to refer to the attempts of Communist functionaries to coerce, instruct, persuade, trick, train, delude, debilitate, frustrate, bribe, threaten, promise, flatter, degrade, torture, isolate. . . . By extension, the term "brainwashing" is used in our language to refer to the attempt to persuade people to act [in ways] of which the user of the term disapproves. (141)

For Biderman, to call a method of influence "brainwashing" revealed more about the person using the term, and that person's attitude toward the outcome, than it did about the method used to obtain it. Brainwashing was not a practice, but a signal of one's ideological position.

Kenneth Burke (1966) took a similarly measured look at brainwashing in *Language as Symbolic Action,* writing:

> We hear of "brainwashing," of schemes whereby an "ideology" is imposed upon people. But should we stop at that? Should we not also see the situation the other way around? For was not the "brainwasher" also similarly motivated? Do we simply use words, or do they not also use us? An "ideology" is like a god coming down to earth where it will inhabit a place pervaded by its presence. An "ideology" is like a spirit taking up its abode in a body: it makes that body hop around in certain ways; and that same body would have hopped around in different ways had a different ideology happened to inhabit it. (6)

Anticipating later theories on language, ideology, and human agency, Burke writes that one is *acted on by* ideology and moved by it as an irrational force, like a body possessed by a spirit, a movement that Burke identifies as characteristic of *all* ideologies, not just communist ideology. Following these calls for perspective, it is necessary to point out that while American prisoners of war were said to be undergoing "brainwashing" in Chinese and North Korean prison camps, Chinese and North Korean POWs were also undergoing "civilian information and education" in some of the United Nations and US prison camps, which sought to teach "Western values" to prisoners in order "correct their distorted ideas about Western democracy" and also incorporated Christian elements into the curriculum (Haga 2012, 100).

Although academics later dismissed brainwashing as the reification of an image in popular culture rather than a reflection of what had really happened in China and Korea, in the paranoid years of the early Cold War, brainwashing was perceived to be a very real threat that extended far beyond "our boys" in Korea. Vivid pictures of brainwashing were painted in books like Edward Hunter's *Brain-Washing in Red China* (1951) and *Brainwashing: The Story of Men Who Defied It* (1956), which warned Americans that brainwashing "must be stopped and counteracted, and the mentally maimed must be cured if we ourselves are to be safe ourselves from 'brain-washing' and 'brain-changing'—and 'liquidation' and 'evaporation'" (1951, 302), drawing a direct comparison between the threat of brainwashing and nuclear holocaust.[12]

For Hunter, brainwashing was a "sinister" practice in which the brainwashee's beliefs and ideological commitments were replaced by the thoughts, beliefs, and desires of the brainwasher. Anticipating Biderman's later critique, Hunter insisted that brainwashing could not be described "by some familiar expression such as *education, public relations, persuasion . . . mind reform and re-education.* None of these could define it because it was much, much more than any one of them alone" (1956, 3, original emphasis). There was something "diabolical," almost supernatural, to the process (1951, 70). The result was equally mysterious. Describing one Chinese victim, Hunter writes that

> he appeared to be under a weird, unnatural compulsion to go on with a whole train of thought, from beginning to end, even when it had been rendered silly. . . . He was no longer capable of using free will or adapting himself to a situation for which he had been uninstructed; he had to go on as if manipulated by instincts alone. This was Party discipline extended to the mind; a trance element was in it. It gave me a creepy feeling. (1956, 14–15)

A number of Hunter's words bear mention here. First are his own feelings ("weird," "creepy") when observing the brainwashed man. According to Freud ([1919] 2003), when applied to a living person, feelings of uncanniness arise when we ascribe "evil motives" to a person that have their origin outside the ego, such as from the realm of the spirit or even the body itself. Persons possessed and persons in the grips of an epileptic seizure elicited similar feelings of uncanniness, Freud surmised, because although they moved, they did not act of their own will (cf. Burke 1966, 53). I will return to this idea shortly.

Hunter's vivid descriptions of brainwashing captivated the American public, particularly when fictionalized in stories like Sidney Herschel Small's "The Brainwashed Pilot," published in the *Saturday Evening Post* in 1955. In the story, nurse Anne Holmes seeks to reunite with her husband, Johnny, who has been shot down in North Korea and subsequently imprisoned in China. Anne bides her time in Hong Kong, where she assists at a local hospital. After one of the hospital's machines breaks, one of Anne's patients tells her of a "white man" in his village who is skilled at repair, "although his head was of little use to him" (62). The man is revealed to be her husband, of course, and Anne is overjoyed at their eventual reunion. As Anne talks with him, however, it becomes clear that Captain Holmes is not the man he used to be. Not only does he not recognize his wife, but he also does not recognize himself. He does not respond to his name, telling Anne: "they call me Yan Hai" (66). Like Hunter's description of the brainwashed Chinese prisoner, Johnny Holmes cuts an uncanny figure in the story, which describes him as a "shell" with "large, unwinking eyes" (62) that appear "unfathomably strange" (66). This description is enhanced by a large illustration, which bears a striking resemblance to the photograph of Mindszenty that circulated only a few years prior. In the image, the strong-jawed Holmes does not look at his wife, who strokes his face; instead, he stares wide-eyed into the distance, gaze fixed on something—some person, some memory—we cannot see.

When joined with media reports of Cardinal Mindszenty and the Korean War POWs, stories like "The Brainwashed Pilot," not to mention the later *The Manchurian Candidate* (novel 1959, film 1964), created an image of brainwashing that was so persuasive that it began to be treated as fact rather than speculation, in part because it was energized by two powerful ideological forces: fear of communism and racist attitudes toward the "mysterious" East. According to Albert Biderman, "for most Americans" of the early 1950s, "the Oriental was a strange fellow" (1962, 552), and reports of a mysterious practice in which a person could be changed into another merely fulfilled those expectations. While scholars like himself slowly gathered evidence about what had happened to American soldiers in Korea and China, Biderman writes, "popular writings established an image of 'brainwashing' as, in the words of Lifton, 'an all-powerful, irresistible, unfathomable, and magical method of achieving total control over the human mind' (p. 4)" (549). Academic studies of brainwashing lagged behind their cultural counterparts, and as a result, "brainwashing" became a diffuse, imprecise term of little use and was burdened with "almost ineradicable connotations" (549). Even worse for Biderman was that many scholars had hastily taken their cues from the image, such as claims by his colleagues in the social sciences that brainwashing "was 'really' conditioning á la Pavlov's dogs or was accomplished by using drugs, hypnotism, or the sensory deprivation effect" (1962, 552). Taking note of Biderman's final comment, we might add a third element to his list of why brainwashing became such an attractive idea to the American public in the early 1950s: a creeping suspicion of psychiatry, which was linked to brainwashing in a number of ways.

In *Brain-Washing in Red China*, for example, Hunter draws explicit parallels between Chinese brainwashing techniques and American psychiatry. As his informant "Mr. Chi" described the practices used on political dissidents in China, Hunter recalls, he began to have a feeling of déjà vu. He remembered an incident a few years earlier when one of his friends had been hospitalized after a nervous breakdown. One day while visiting, Hunter spoke to one of the hospital's psychiatrists, who boasted that "he had just won a glorious victory—the fight for a man's mind" (1951, 6). The feelings that came over Hunter in that "most modernized institution," he realized,

> were the same as those I felt as I listened to Chi's story: the same disquieting sense of probing into dangerous fields. Chi's experiences in North China had been similar to that of the patients in the American institution. It was as if the most advanced mental hospital with a staff of psychiatrists had stopped treating the insane and had begun treating only the sane, without changing the treatment. (6–7)

Hunter's connection of brainwashing with psychiatry is reiterated a few pages later, when he argues that learning about the mind has led to controlling the brain. Hunter illustrates his claim with a bizarrely expansive list of examples, which include Maoist self-criticism meetings, hypnotism, public relations, movie posters, and—buried in the middle—psychosurgery:

> Man has learned not only some of the theoretical processes that go on in a man's head but also how to direct his thoughts, and to do this in a "democratic group discussion," in a "self-criticism meeting," *on the operating table*, or in the hypnotist's chamber. The whole field of psychology has been brought to embrace everything that influences thought and attitude, from the first crude publicity put out for a movie actress to Ivy Lee and psychological warfare, and the whole wide range of activities that lies within—in effect, our entire field of modern communications media, from public opinion surveys to aptitude testing. It is used by individuals in private and public life, by small firms and big corporations, by political parties and governments. (12, my emphasis)

For Hunter, psychologists and psychiatrists, like Chinese brainwashers, had violated a taboo against "tampering" with the "divine creation" of the brain. Violating the sacred human brain was akin to violating nature by splitting the atom: "such discoveries can be utilized, like primitive fire, for good or for evil" (11). If the atomic bomb threatened the United States from outside its borders, brain control—which for Hunter was embodied in both brainwashing and mental health—threatened the nation from within the heads of its citizens, a *pharmakon* that tilted toward poison, not cure.

In 1956, the tabloid magazine *Suppressed* took the connection between brainwashing and psychiatry a step further. It claimed that the brainwashing of Cardinal Mindszenty and the twenty-three Korean War POWs had been accomplished with transorbital lobotomy, which the article calls a "surgical brainwash." The article provides a remarkably accurate account of the procedure, correctly identifying both the anatomy and the surgical technique involved. While the article admits that the surgery may cure many "dangerous mental ills," it also warns that many patients "acquire personality traits which can be equally as troublesome as the disease they sought to alleviate." In an echo of the press stories of the previous chapter, the article soberly informs the reader that the personality trait lobotomy most commonly produces is "docility" (Lamb 1956, 36).

Although the *Suppressed* story is easy to write off as typical tabloid pabulum—in the same issue, readers are offered stories about Prince Rainier's pet chimpanzee collection, the FBI's catalog of Americans' fingerprints, "Europe's exclusive club for wayward women," cheesecake photos, reincarnation hoaxes, and ads for hypnotizing aids—the connection it makes between psychosurgery and brainwashing was neither new nor limited to fringe publications. Shortly after József Mindszenty was convicted, a 1950 article in the *New York Times* suggested that the cardinal might have been subjected to a transorbital lobotomy in order to induce his confession. Consulting biologist Charles Marc Pomerat, the *Times* told its readers that transorbital lobotomy

> is performed by cutting nerve fibers on either side of the brain, thus separating the rear part of the brain from the front. Dr. Pomerat said he thought the Communists may use a variation developed in Portugal which consists of removing an eyeball, severing two nerves in back of the eyeball and replacing it. He said this leaves no outward scar. ("Confessions to Reds" 1950)

Although the *Suppressed* story provides medically accurate information, the story from the *Times* couldn't have been further from the mark. In the transorbital lobotomy, no eyeballs were removed, no optical nerves were severed, and the procedure was developed in Italy or the United States, but not Portugal. While the facts may have been fuzzy, the fear was clear: just as one could be brainwashed without evidence visible to outsiders, or even to oneself, one could also be secretly lobotomized. In the scenario the *Times* paints, one of the benefits of transorbital lobotomy—that it leaves no visible scar tissue—is reframed as one of its most diabolical characteristics. This fear was not entirely ungrounded: Walter Freeman (1950) observed that many patients who received the transorbital procedure denied that they had received any operation at all, and some even denied visiting the hospital (57). Similar stories connecting brainwashing and lobotomy appeared in other newspapers as well, which speculated that communists may have used the operation to obtain false confessions from other political prisoners ("Surgical Brain-wash" 1955; "Scalpel Brain-Washing" 1955).

The connection between lobotomy and brainwashing was not limited to newspapers and magazines. For example, in his luridly titled book *The Rape of the Mind* (1956), Joost Meerloo, formerly the chief psychologist for the Dutch military and a member of the Columbia Medical School faculty, also speculated that psychosurgery could be used as a political weapon. Meerloo's preferred term for brainwashing was "menticide," which he had previously defined in the *American Journal of Psychiatry* (1951) as "psychic homicide." Like many accounts of brainwashing, *The Rape of the Mind* crafts a strong tie between brainwashing and psychiatry. Meerloo singles out psychosurgery as one of psychiatry's most dangerous tools, which, he warns, "could be misused by dictators to make zombies out of their competitors" (71). Those subjected to menticide were still alive, but in a liminal existence comparable to the state of zombiehood Meerloo describes as the effect of psychosurgery—a new personality that emerged from the death of the old. This new personality, which Meerloo argues was characteristic of citizens in totalitarian states, was hardly a personality worthy of the name. It was merely an empty vessel that thought the thoughts, spoke the words, and obeyed the orders of someone else. The imagined community of Totalitaria, Meerloo warned, was a "society of robots, not men" (111).

Communist Zombies and Mental Robots

Although zombies and robots are now familiar characters in science fiction literature and horror films, in the postwar years these terms were deployed as a trenchant political critique of lobotomy's power to alter the individual personality. The *Suppressed* story about Mindszenty and the Korean War POWs, for example, is entitled "A Surgical Brainwash That Makes Men Zombies." A story from New York's *Daily Independent* reported, "the Reds have developed a specialized brain surgery to reduce their captive victims to 'zombies'" (Arnot 1955). Another editorial intoned:

> Those who have seen post-lobotomy patients in the state mental hospitals or who have observed them after release from confinement, can testify to the striking effect the operation has on the mentality and personality of the patient. Although different patients react in slightly different ways to the radical surgical treatment, most seem to lose all capacity for original thought or philosophical speculation. While "zombie" is described here as an "extreme" and "dramatic" term for lobotomy patients, it is nonetheless "correctly" deployed as a trope for docility, dripping with agency panic. ("Scalpel Brain-Washing" 1955, my emphasis)

While "zombie" is described as an "extreme" and "dramatic" term to describe lobotomy patients in this example, it is nonetheless "correctly" deployed as a trope for docility, dripping with agency panic.

"Zombie" was readily available as a personification of the agency panic that powered stories of personality change in postwar America. The United States was introduced to the first zombie on film in Victor Halperin's 1932 colonial fantasy *White Zombie*, followed closely by *Revolt of the Zombies* (1936), *King of the Zombies* (1941), and *I Walked with a Zombie* (1943). Unlike later uses of the zombie as a trope for conformity and consumerism, like those found in George Romero's iconic film *Night of the Living Dead* (1968), these early films portray zombies not as flesh-eating aggressors, but as sympathetic slaves obliged to cater to their masters' every whim. Audiences are led to fear not the zombies, but those who created them. According to Joshua Gunn and Shaun Treat (2005), what these early zombie films share is "the notion of a hypnotic, totalizing, determining force that lobotomizes the subject into a mindless, laboring zombie . . . put into the service of a fascistic authority" (151). (Note how easily Gunn and Treat use the word 'lobotomize" here.) The zombies of the mid-twentieth century, in other words, were docile zombies.

Like "zombie," "robot" was also circulating in the midcentury as trope for docility. The first printed use of the term "robot" is found in Karel Capek's 1920 play "R.U.R. (Rossum's Universal Robots)," which features artificial humans who serve their human masters without complaint. Capek used the Czech word *robotnik* to describe the perfect mechanical slave, a term that means "forced laborer" or "serf."[13] It is this meaning of "robot" that far right activist Lewis Alesen employed in his book *Mental Robots* (1958), which took aim at a number of medical developments Alesen believed were in the process of changing the United States "from a land of opportunity and individual freedom into just another minor way station of the international Welfare-Police-Slave State" (9).

Alesen cites Capek's play directly near the beginning of the book, describing it as a "beautiful foretaste of what has been and is now happening to individuals all over the world" (1958, 52). Intriguingly, Alesen then references the Haitian "voodoo" practices (or, more accurately, colonial fantasies of Haitian *vodou*) upon which the early zombie films were based. There is only a short distance between purchasing a love potion or a hex, Alesen asserts, and "the modern and more sophisticated practice of participating in the consummation of a grand and master plan to make zombies of all but the chosen few who seek to be our masters and direct our destinies" (53). This plan was put into practice by the burgeoning art and science of "robotry," which, though loosely defined in Alesen's text, might be summed up as mind control. Of all the fields affiliated with robotry (Alesen names economics, sociology, and philosophy), the most potent robotrist practice is psychiatry:

> Under its skillful use the human can be, and has been in countless instances, so altered as completely to transform the concepts previously held and to prepare the individual so treated for a docile acceptance of all manner of authoritarian controls. *The psychiatrist boasts that he possesses the power to alter human personality*, and he has certainly made good his boast in many respects, at least to the extent of being able to force phony confessions out of men like Cardinal Mindszenty. (68, my emphasis)

Alesen does not provide examples of how psychiatrists were able to change Mindszenty's personality (or evidence that psychiatrists were involved in the Mindszenty case, for that matter); he merely presents this information as common knowledge, an assumption warranted by the many connections drawn between brainwashing and psychiatry in public culture at the time.

Lewis Alesen was not a conspiracy theorist handing out tracts on the street corner. He was a surgeon who served as chief of staff at the Los Angeles County General Hospital and was elected president of the California Medical Association in 1952. In his president's address to the association, Alesen urged his colleagues to take an active interest in politics in order to fight what he saw as a rising tide of collectivism in America's public institutions. Instead of remaining safely tucked away from public view in examination and operating rooms, Alesen exhorted his fellow physicians to embrace their roles as leaders in civic affairs (1952b) and join him in "the fight to uphold basic American principles above the muddy flood waters of socialism, communism and fascism that have engulfed so much of the world" (1952a, 367). *Mental Robots* thus seems to be Alesen taking his own advice.

Alesen's alert about the emergence of robotry was echoed by another physician, Reuben Swinburne Clymer, who declared in his 1958 book *The Age of Treason* that in psychiatry Americans were facing "the greatest danger ever known." *The Age of Treason* is a long, rambling screed, which begins with its full title: *The Age of Treason: The Carefully and Deliberately Planned Methods Developed by the Vicious Element of Humanity, for the Mental Deterioration, and Moral Debasement of the Mass as a Means to Their Enslavement Based on Their Own Writings, and the Means Already Confessedly Employed.* The book is a bricolage of quotes from ultraconservative tracts and mainstream magazines and newspapers, and it is peppered with Clymer's idiosyncratic argumentation and writing style, which often uses all-capital letters for emphasis.

Like Alesen, Clymer's intention is to sound an alarm about the robotization and zombification of his fellow citizens, which he connects to a loss of one's humanity/masculinity:

> Imagine yourself BECOMING CONSCIOUS you are gradually losing your manhood—that your mind is rapidly deteriorating so that you are no longer able to think clearly; unable to plan your future actions; that your resistance is becoming so weak you are no longer master of actions. In short, that you are rapidly developing into a moron, a robot, a zombie, readily subject to the dictates of others. (1958, 13)

In addition to repeating the common tropes of zombie and robot, Clymer takes aim at a number of familiar targets of the far right, such as polio and influenza vaccination programs and the fluoridation of the water supply. The real question is not whether these treatments are effective in eradicating disease, Clymer declares, but rather "when and how will serums and viruses be impregnated for the purpose of the *deterioration of men's minds, often resulting in insanity*?" (45, original emphasis). Ironically, the plot to destroy the nation's minds was being hatched from within the very profession that claimed to protect them.

Clymer spends a number of pages condemning the use of "happy pills," a recent development he felt was particularly scandalous, since the pills were "of purely American origin—and the victims are fellow American subjects" (150), but he reserves most of his vitriol for lobotomy, which he calls a "diabolical operation" (153).

Clymer begins his denunciation of lobotomy by quoting liberally from "Living Bodies without Souls," an article that first appeared in the ultraconservative newsletter *Task Forces* in 1957. Although Clymer agrees with the article's conclusions, he initially takes issue with the article's title, which suggests that the soul can be destroyed. Lobotomy's real danger was not its destruction of the soul, but its destruction of the mind, which would "hold the soul in *status quo* until death of the body relieved it. The method practiced more or less extensively in America, and now openly admitted, *destroys reason, and without reason man becomes less than an animal*" (1958, 168, original emphasis). After explaining that the operation "causes a particular nucleus of brain cells in the powerhouse of emotions, the thalamus, to *degenerate permanently*," Clymer contradicts his previous statement about the inviolability of the soul, which he locates in the thalamus: "If the Thalamus degenerates, or is made to degenerate, by any means, then according to one of the oldest beliefs of man, the Soul is destroyed. Man becomes less than animal. Another co-worker with God has been eliminated" (180, original emphasis).

Unlike Alesen and others on the far right, Clymer takes a rather sympathetic view of American lobotomists. Clymer declares that no "American born" physician would ever perform the operation "except possibly on the criminally insane, vicious Sadist[s], or those guilty of rape, or suffering from moral degeneracy," and Walter Freeman is said to "regretfully" discuss the lobotomies he performed. Physicians like Freeman, men of "the highest reputation," were not acting out of their own free will, Clymer maintained; rather, they had been "beguiled by the swan song of foreign surgeons" (1958, 179).

Clymer's characterization of American lobotomists as puppets of their foreign peers and his description of lobotomy as a foreign operation are supported by a number of historical "facts" about lobotomy he takes from an article entitled "Bodies without Souls." The article, written by Stephanie Williams, a conservative activist, claims that Adolf Hitler and Josef Stalin used lobotomy on German and Russian citizens. Williams repeated these figures in another article, "Lobotomy Is a Dangerous Weapon," published in the more mainstream conservative magazine *American Mercury*, in which she warns her readers about the operation that "can turn a man into a living corpse" (1957, 139). Lobotomy, Williams states, "is an essentially fascist technique" (141–142). According to Williams, not only did Hitler perform "mass lobotomies" on Germans, creating "approximately 10 million morons . . . so that they could be put to simple but useful tasks," but "medical men in Germany, France, and Italy have [also] added another 3 million to that deplorable number," and Stalin in particular is "supposed to have had over 10 million slaves turned into living zombies."[14]

Characterizations of lobotomy patients as zombies and robots also found their way into medical discourse. In 1949, for example, Nolan Lewis, director of New York's State Psychiatric Institute, told *colleagues at the American Psychiatric Association that he was* "disturb[ed]" by the "number of zombies that these operations turn out" ("Lobotomy Disappointment" 1949, 51). By the mid-1950s, zombie and robot critiques were so pervasive that Walter Freeman felt the need to rebut the terms directly. In his regular column on psychosurgery for the *American Journal of Psychiatry*, for example, Freeman provided a case study of the "average" lobotomy patient. After surgery, the patient "participated more in group interchange by giving suggestions, opinions and orientation and he was altogether more productive. . . . Zombies and human vegetables," Freeman directed (presumably at Nolan Lewis), "take note!" (1955, 518). In a 1961 article, Freeman wrote that his intention was to "enter another wedge of doubt, constructive doubt, into the opinions commonly expressed, that lobotomy kills the soul [and] converts the patient into a robot" (555).

However hyperbolic the warnings about zombification and robotization might seem today, these terms served as a powerful critique of psychiatry's perceived threat to agency at a point when American agency panic was arguably at its peak. In these texts, agency panic is not merely a fear that one cannot freely act. It extends into paranoia that one's agency has been replaced with another's. In conspiracy theory, the other is by definition envisioned as a powerful network (in this case, psychiatry), which is personified as a rational, conscious entity "with the will and the means to carry out complex plans" (Melley 2000, 13). Melley calls the attribution of intentionality to organizations and networks a kind of "postmodern transference" (13), but the transference in the claims of this chapter might also be understood in its modern, psychoanalytic form. In the nightmare of transference described above, however, the psychiatrist does not replace the patient's mother or father. Instead, the psychiatrist replaces the patient with himself.

Psychopolitics

In the wake of Joseph McCarthy's censure by the Senate in 1954, a number of grassroots political organizations concentrated in the southern California suburbs took up the senator's zealous mission against communism. Many of these "kitchen table activists" (McGirr 2002) were women, who organized study groups, wrote impassioned letters to the editor, ran for school boards, circulated petitions, and rallied their friends and neighbors to fight what they saw as the growing influence of communism in American society and policy. In addition to writing articles like "Living Bodies without Souls," Stephanie Williams founded the American Public Relations Forum, a women's political organization that sponsored a number of campaigns against state and federal mental health legislation.[15] Anticommunist groups were prolific. They published countless newsletters and tracts for their adherents, and many mainstream articles in which they claimed that the field of mental health was a "Trojan Horse" for a Russian plot to take over the United States (Nickerson 2004, 119). One piece of literature distributed by Stephanie Williams's American Public Relations Forum and a number of other far right groups was *Brain-Washing: A Synthesis of the Russian Textbook on Psychopolitics* (1955).

Brain-Washing claims to reproduce a speech from Lavrentiy Beria to American students at Lenin University in which Beria laid out the blueprint of a secret Soviet plan to infiltrate the American mental health system. The slim volume describes that plan, the art of "psychopolitics," as "capturing the minds of the nation through brainwashing and fake mental health—the subjecting of whole nations of people to the rule of the Kremlin" (i). Psychopolitics was brainwashing applied en masse: a personality change on a national scale.

The Russian brainwashing textbook is, without question, a fake. In an article for *Look* magazine in 1965, journalist Donald Robison consulted Benjamin Mandel, the research director of the Senate Internal Security Subcommittee, who asserted that he did not believe the book to be genuine. In his book *The Hoaxers*, Morris Kominsky (1970) cites a number of sources that confirm the fraudulent nature of the textbook, including a source from the CIA who pointed out that not only was Beria not in Moscow when the speech was allegedly given, but the term "psychopolitics" is also not found anywhere in the Russian language (540). He also contacted Edward Hunter, who told Kominsky that to his mind, the Russian textbook was a fictional and inferior version of his *Brain-Washing in Red China* (545). *Brain-Washing* was not a textbook on the Russian program of mind control. However, as a piece of homegrown political discourse, *Brain-Washing* offers an ideal rhetorical primer on the far right's campaign against psychiatry in the mid-twentieth century.

Many versions of the textbook circulated in the 1950s and have continued to circulate in the decades since. One can still find recent editions of the textbook available for sale as well as digital copies on the Internet, with different covers, prefaces, and conclusions. An Internet search also readily yields countless contemporary references to the textbook on far right and mainstream conservative websites, where it often is presented as a historical document (e.g., Makow 2004). The copy I will refer to was printed and distributed by Kenneth Goff, an ultraconservative activist and minister of the Christian Identity movement, a loose grouping of churches and individuals that preached white supremacy (Kaplan 2000). Although it's hard to know for sure, some critics (Kominsky 1970) have identified the Russian textbook as Goff's handiwork, while others (Corydon and DeWolf 1987; Introvigne 2005) assert that its use of the term "dianetics" and its focus on psychiatry indicate that the *Brain-Washing* was written by L. Ron Hubbard, founder of the Church of Scientology.[16] Although the true author of the textbook will likely never be known, one thing is certain: its author was not Levrentiy Beria, architect of Stalin's Great Purge.

In the editor's note, Kenneth Goff confesses that he once was a "card-carrying" Communist Party member who later testified against his former comrades in front of the HUAC in 1939. Goff attests that as a young man, he was trained at the Eugene Debs labor school in Milwaukee, where he was instructed in "all phases of warfare, both psychological and physical, for the destruction of the capitalistic society and Christian civilization," and where *Brain-Washing* was part of the curriculum. After his supposed political and religious conversion from young atheist communist to wizened Christian patriot, Goff became a prolific speaker and writer, publishing over twenty-eight books and tracts; the magazine *Pilgrim's Torch*; and bulletins on a host of pet issues of the far right: fluoridation programs, the "narcotizing" of America's youth, and the "one world order" represented by the United Nations (Kaplan 2000).

Goff explains that he decided to reveal the Russian textbook to the American people not in order to warn them of what *might* happen if communists began their psychopolitical plot to invade the United States, but to sound an alarm that it already was taking place. Psychopolitics, Goff declares, could be observed first in the brainwashing of our boys in Korea, and then in the well-financed drive of mental health propaganda by left-wing pressure groups, wherein many of our states have passed Bills which can well be used by the enemies of America to subject to torture and imprisonment those who preach the gospel of our Lord and Saviour Jesus Christ and to oppose the menace of communism. (*Brain-Washing* 1955, 1)

One of the bills Goff refers to is the 1956 Alaska Mental Health Bill, which proposed a grant of land and money to the Alaskan government so that the territory could provide hospitalization for its citizens, who had been forced to travel to Oregon in order to receive psychiatric care. Goff charged that the Alaska bill would establish a "mental Siberia" in Alaska, "which could be turned into a prison camp under the guise of mental health for everyone who raises their voice against Communism and the hidden government operating in our nation" (1). The "mental Siberia" line was not Goff's invention. It was a frequent slogan of the far right campaign to kill the Alaska bill. Some of the bill's most vocal opponents were anticommunist groups like the American Public Relations Forum and the Minute Women of the USA, whose Leigh F. Burkeland exposed the bill's "true" intent in a letter to the *Santa Ana Register* entitled "Now—Siberia, U.S.A." Both Williams and Burkeland testified against the bill in front of Congress in 1956; Burkeland's "Siberia" letter was later entered into the *Congressional Record* (US Congress 1956, 141–142).

According to the textbook, the creation of a "mental Siberia" was not the primary danger to the American public from psychopolitical operatives. The ultimate goal of psychopolitics was to replace mental health professionals in the United States with communist agents in order to achieve "psychopolitical rule" (6). To achieve full control over the minds of Americans, *Brain-Washing* instructs its students to produce "maximum chaos in the fields of mental healing" until "every teacher of psychology unknowingly or knowingly teaches only Communist doctrine" and "every doctor and psychiatrist is either a psychopolitician or an unwitting assistant to our aims" (3). In the terrifying world of psychopolitical control, in other words, even psychiatrists could be turned into robots and zombies.

Brain-Washing expends considerable effort to undermine the scientific claims of psychiatric diagnosis and the therapeutic claims of all forms of psychiatric treatment. Psychoanalysis, for instance, is described as a "spiritual

Alice-in-Wonderland voyage" that is "singularly lacking in success" (11). Electroshock therapy is said to be worthless (19). And psychosurgery, the text reports, "has no statistical data to recommend it *beyond its removal of the individual personality*" (20, my emphasis). Although somatic treatments are said to lack therapeutic efficacy, the textbook nonetheless praises them as effective methods of subduing patients and ensuring their obedience. Consequently, the psychopolitician is directed to promote somatic treatments in public venues by listing "large numbers of pretended cures" and having on hand "innumerable documents which assert enormously encouraging figures on the subject of recovery by reason of shock, brain surgery, drugs, and general treatment" (50). In the Russian textbook's nightmarish vision of the American mental health establishment, psychiatrists are characterized not only as ineffective doctors and communist collaborators but also as violent political terrorists whose "brutalities are committed in the name of science" and whose ultimate goal is control, not cure (31).

The textbook singles out electroshock therapy and psychosurgery as especially effective in this regard. The two treatments are said to be "Russian developments" (20)—a particularly odd attribution, since the USSR had instituted a ban on psychosurgery in 1953.[17] In a chapter entitled "Violent Remedies," the textbook admits that psychopolitical operatives would probably encounter public concern about the "brutality" of these treatments. However, since the public understands that a certain amount of psychiatric violence is "reasonable," by "starting from a relatively low level of violence, such as straight-jackets and other restraints, it is relatively easy to encroach upon the public diffidence for violence by adding more and more cruelty into the treatment of the insane" (54). The Russian textbook concludes its praise of violent treatments by returning to the familiar conservative trope of the zombie, explaining that by increasing the public's exposure to electroconvulsive therapy and psychosurgery and the personality changes they cause, "they will at last come to tolerate the creation of zombie conditions to such a degree that they will probably employ zombies, if given to them" (55).

Although *Brain-Washing* may have been a fake document, it was a powerful fake with a very real and remarkably large audience. The Russian textbook circulated widely among far right groups, and the text was widely printed, reprinted, and excerpted in a variety of more mainstream media (Kominsky 1970). Portions of the text also appear in Lewis Alesen's *Mental Robots*, discussed above, as evidence of the robotization of the US mental health system. In addition to its circulation in far right enclaves, the textbook also found its way into national political discourse.

On June 13, 1957, for example, Representative Usher Burdick (R-ND) entered an article entitled "Beware of Psychiatrists" into the *Congressional Record* in a text that acts as an echo chamber for many of far right critiques of psychosurgery discussed above. "The destruction of the mind is less obvious and not an open act of murder," Burdick writes in the strains of Joost Meerloo's *Rape of the Mind*, "but the millions who have had their minds destroyed . . . are as dead as they ever will be." After briefly describing the technique used in transorbital lobotomy, Burdick—likely having read Stephanie Williams's articles—attests that "Hitler used this method on millions of his subjects and Stalin had over 10 million slaves or prisoners operated upon and turned into mere beasts of burden." Then Burdick details the terrible result of the "five minute" operation. A person lobotomized "loses his animation as a living object and becomes a zombie," and afterward, "the subject does not know what has been done to him." And in the most damning comment of all, Burdick claims that lobotomy castrates the patient, whose "productive organs wither up" after surgery so "he is incapable of resistance" (Burdick 1956, 9060). Although Burdick provided no scientific evidence to back up his assertion, his meaning was clear: lobotomy was a national political crisis of phallic power.

In keeping with the title of the piece, Burdick also directs his audience's attention to the doctors performing the operation. Unlike R. Swinburne Clymer, who believed that American psychiatrists had been duped by their foreign colleagues, Burdick attests that "in the United States today a large percentage of the psychiatrists are foreigners, most of them educated in Russia. The percentage runs as high as 80." To support his argument, Burdick then quotes directly from the last line of the Russian textbook, which declares: "upon these people can be practiced shock and surgery so that never again will they draw a sane breath." "There you have the Communist assault on the minds of men," Burdick soberly concludes. "Is this the practice this country is going to follow in mental health cases?" (1957, 9061). Later that day, Burdick entered a second item into the *Congressional Record*. "Mr. Speaker," he declared, "to apprise the people of this country just what the Communist practice was and probably still is in regard to the treatment of so-called mentally sick persons, I have decided to reprint the entire speech made by Communist Beria to a class of American students at Lenin University" (1957, 9113).

Although there was no refutation of Burdick's arguments (not even a response from his colleagues in the House), the Representative's extensive citation of *Brain-Washing* shows that the ultraconservative attack on psychiatry was a force to be reckoned with. Psychiatrists, wrote Alfred Auerback in 1963, were little match for their "well organized," "well financed and vociferous" critics from the far right and their mainstream political allies, who so thoroughly dominated public discourse on the subject in the mid-1950s that "whenever mental health work is being attacked the phrases used are identical to those first appearing in the period of 1955–1958" (105–111). Even worse, Auerback complained, the citation of far right texts by members of Congress and the *Congressional Record* had given them credibility. Many conservatives pointed to statements by people like Usher Burdick, Stephanie Williams, and Leigh Burkeland in the *Congressional Record* as "implying governmental approval" of their arguments (1963, 111). According to Donald Robison's 1965 *Look* article, a number of psychiatrists had been threatened on a regular basis by persons suspicious of their political allegiances. These attacks also affected potential patients, many of whom were reluctant to seek help from mental health professionals. Jack B. Lomas, a clinical professor of psychiatry at the UCLA School of Medicine, told Robison he knew of a number of people who had chosen suicide instead of seeking treatment because of the fear stoked by the far right's campaign against psychiatry (Robison 1965, 30).

Not only were activists successful in derailing the federal Alaska bill, but they also successfully targeted state mental health policy. Pressure from the far right led lawmakers to abandon proposed mental health legislation in Wisconsin, and although activists were not successful in stopping a bill in Utah in support of community mental health clinics, they managed to add two powerful amendments. The first made it a felony to provide psychiatric treatment to anyone without written permission from their next of kin. The second amendment made it a felony to provide psychiatric treatment, including psychoanalysis, drugs, shock treatment, or lobotomy, with the "purpose of changing [the patient's] concept of, belief about, or faith in God" (Robison 1965, 31; Auerback 1963, 107). (In response, one psychiatrist Robison interviewed wondered, only half-joking, "What do I do if my patient thinks he *is* God?") In Southern California, activists targeted the opening of a free mental health clinic in Los Angeles. Although the City Council eventually endorsed the center, protests against the clinic were so fierce that donors became afraid to contribute to it, and it never opened (Robison 1965, 31). Auerback urged his colleagues to respond to far right critiques of the profession by writing "dispassionate" rebuttals to publications that published them and by sending "commendations" to publications that expressed their support for mental health. "The issues at stake," he concluded, "no longer permit psychiatrists to remain uninvolved" (1963, 111).

Psychiatrists were understandably concerned by these attacks on their profession and, as Auerback had urged, in some cases responded publicly to them. On November 16, 1961, Tom Sullivan, an employee of the "Free Enterprise Department" of the California's Coast Federal Savings and Loan Association, gave a speech to the Women's Auxiliary of District 6 of the Los Angeles County Medical Association in which he liberally quoted from the *Brain-Washing* textbook in order to show how a "considerable amount of the concern about our declining mental health has been engendered by Kremlin agents for the purpose of demoralizing the American people" (San Fernando [1961?], 13). Illustrating Auerback's concern that the insertion of the Russian textbook into the *Congressional Record* had implied governmental approval of its contents, Sullivan claimed that "documentation" of the textbook could be found as Senate Document 2646, noting that Congress had "use[d] it as a reference for their own material" (13).

In the speech, Sullivan took aim at a number of developments in state and national mental health policy: the Alaska bill; the development of a Mental Health Department of Los Angeles County; and the 1957 Community Mental Health Services Act, also known as the Short-Doyle Act, which allowed the state to reimburse local governments up to half the cost of their mental health services. He also criticized California's Welfare and Institutions Code, which made a provision for the use of emergency psychiatric treatment in a seventy-two-hour period, without court order, if a person was determined to be dangerous or at risk of harming himself. According to Sullivan, during this period, it was possible to undergo electroshock therapy, psychosurgery, or "anything else" psychiatrists recommended (San Fernando [1961?], 3). When Sullivan later received a public commendation from a local medical society, mental health professionals in the area were outraged (Auerback 1963, 107).

In response, the San Fernando Valley Doctors Committee on Mental Health (SFVDC) self-published a point-by-point refutation of Sullivan's speech entitled *The Doctors Speak Up: An Answer to Irresponsible Attacks on the Mental Health Program*, which they "prepared as a public service." They noted in the introduction that it was their "obligation" to present the information and the obligation of "an intelligent and informed citizen" to read it. In the response, the committee reproduced Sullivan's speech in its entirety, interspersed with refutations of his facts and supplemental commentary, including the statement that emphasized without qualification that "emergency psychiatric treatment never includes psychosurgery" (San Fernando [1961?], 4). In addition to charging Sullivan with "outright lies" (19), they also criticized his rhetorical strategies connecting their profession with the Kremlin as "smear tactics." For the San Fernando Valley doctors, the far right's campaign against psychiatry was doing more than just spreading "insidious rumors and unfounded charges." By standing in the way of mental health research and care, the far right's attack was also "hurting the mentally ill" (23). The document was signed by over eighty MDs, with a note that the tight deadline had prevented the listing of additional members.

Although the claims of the far right might seem outrageous and their rhetorical tactics unsavory, they were undeniably effective. Auerback estimated that "millions of Americans are being exposed to them over and over again. In addition to thousands of pamphlets and brochures repeating them there are many radio and television stations across the United States which routinely broadcast this philosophy" (1963, 108). Yet the problem for Auerback wasn't just that his fellow citizens were being exposed to these arguments. The problem was that many Americans were *listening*. And as we have seen in this chapter, they had been listening to many of these arguments, saturated with agency panic and powered by anticommunist anxieties, for well over a decade.

In his influential essay "'Personality' and the Making of Twentieth-Century Culture," Warren Susman (1984) argues that a culture's definition of the self offers a powerful lens on a particular people at a particular place and time. Building on Susman's thesis, Andrew Heinze (2003) shows how new discoveries of the "split" or "multiple" personality during the first decade of the twentieth century were projected onto public anxieties over its changing demographics. "Given the predilection to compare the psyche and the nation," Heinze argues, "ascendant views of the human personality as fragmented or maladjusted could easily conflate with rising public uneasiness about ethnic fragmentation and maladjustment" (235). Within this new vision of the personality, concerns over immigration and race relations became anxieties over the "health" of the nation's personality, in what Heinze calls "ethnotherapeutics" (234).

As we have seen in this chapter, the ethnotherapeutics Heinze describes as characteristic of the late nineteenth and early twentieth centuries was also in full force in the postwar years, illustrated by a flood of public discourse that worried that the individual personality and, by extension, the American personality were vulnerable to change. In the early years of the Cold War, as the nation worried about its borders' vulnerability to unseen nuclear missiles and submarine strikes, it closely guarded the psychological borders of its body politic and expressed deep concern over its vulnerability to influence. One of the best defenses against the looming Red menace was a mind that resisted persuasion and a personality, nourished by individualism and liberalism, that resisted change. Within this discursive context, psychiatry was seen by many as a suspicious line of work at best and, at worst, a threat to national security. In 1960, three psychiatrists reflected on the power of the rhetorical connection between communism and psychiatry in the *American Journal of Orthopsychiatry*. When "the social climate renders the risks especially great such as during the height of McCarthyism," they wrote, "some of those in the health professions retreat into less controversial areas of work" (Marmor, Bernard, and Ottenberg 1960, 343).

There is no question that psychiatry moved away from psychosurgery and toward psychopharmacology in the mid-1950s. Yet there is also no question that at the same kairotic moment, psychosurgery had become the most controversial technique within an already-controversial field. During the American cultural moment that produced HUAC hearings, Red hunts, and Hollywood blacklists; a moment in which the personality became a matter of national significance and national security; a moment in which psychiatry and lobotomy were characterized as politically suspect, it was risky to specialize in a surgery that permanently changed the human personality. It was this rhetorical environment in which the contemporary image of lobotomy as an authoritarian operation was forged and given power. And it is within this rhetorical environment that the decline of lobotomy in American medicine ought to be understood.

CHAPTER 4

The Rhetorical Return of Lobotomy

The Campaign against Psychosurgery, 1970–1973

> Words which formerly were simple terms become slogans; sentences which
> once were simple statements become calls to battle. They no longer influence
> the mind through their logical meaning—indeed, they often act against it—
> but rather they acquire magical power and exert a mental influence simply
> by being used.
>
> —LUDWIK FLECK, *GENESIS AND DEVELOPMENT OF A*
>   *SCIENTIFIC FACT* (1935)

In 1972, shortly before he died, Walter Freeman wrote a letter to the *American Journal of Psychiatry* in what seems to be an attempt to rewrite his legacy. Freeman claimed three major successes for the operation he championed for nearly four decades: he claimed that lobotomy diminished his patients' suffering, relieved their "wear and tear," and ultimately "got them home" (1315). He reported that the majority of his patients were "aging in comfort and decency." Some were married; some had children and grandchildren; and some were professional men and women who had returned to their careers. Despite these declarations of success, Freeman admitted that a number of surgeries had failed. He attributed these failures not to the operation itself, but to the "poor choice of patients" on the part of surgeons and "incisions into the frontal lobes that were too extensive and erratic." After patients subjected to failed lobotomies "continued to accumulate in the hospitals," Freeman explained, a pall descended on the procedure, and "a wave of pessimism set in." Yet even in 1972 Freeman stubbornly refused to admit that the lobotomy era had ended. Perhaps, he suggested, it was just in "limbo" (1315).

Although medicine had abandoned lobotomy by the time Freeman wrote this letter, in the mid-1960s, bolstered by developments in neurobiology, brain imaging technology, and surgical technique, research interest in psychosurgery began anew. Papers began to appear in medical journals investigating the use of thalamotomy (Andy 1966); amygdalotomy (Heimburger, Whitlock, and Kalsbeck 1966; Vaernet and Madsen 1970); and cingulotomy (Ballantine et al. 1967; Brown and Lighthill 1968); and in perhaps the most striking development, in 1970 the International Congress of Psychosurgery convened in Copenhagen—the first time the group had met since 1948. The group selected Walter Freeman and Alemeida Lima as their honorary presidents (Lipsman, Meyerson, and Lozano 2012, 349). Yet unlike lobotomy, which was publicly celebrated as a cure for mental illness for nearly fifteen years, the renewed interest in psychosurgery in the late 1960s was met almost immediately by public outrage. The vanguard of the fight against this "second wave" of psychosurgery was psychiatrist Peter Breggin, who spearheaded a campaign to eradicate the practice in the United States, an effort that led to state and federal investigations, Senate hearings, and a five-year comprehensive study of psychosurgery by the National Commission for the Protection of Human Subjects of Biomedical and Behavioral Research.

Despite his role as the public face of the campaign against psychosurgery in the early 1970s, Breggin is noticeably absent in histories of psychosurgery. I suspect Breggin's absence in these histories is not due to his insignificance; rather, I believe it reflects his reputation. Although he is a trained and practicing psychiatrist, Breggin has been a gadfly to his colleagues for nearly forty years, and he has taken somatic treatments like psychopharmacology, ECT, and psychosurgery as his primary targets. Recent book titles include *Toxic Psychiatry* (1991), *Talking Back to Prozac* (1994), *Brain-Disabling Treatments in Psychiatry* (1997), *The War against Children of Color: Psychiatry Targets Inner-City Children* (1998), and *Your Drug May Be Your Problem* (1999). Breggin's hostility to somatic psychiatry has led some prominent psychiatrists to label him an "outlaw," a "pariah," and a "flat-earther" (Gorman 1994). These charges are instructive: as pariah, Breggin is thrust outside the social boundaries of the profession; as outlaw, he is pushed outside its norms and conventions; and as flat-earther, perhaps the most damning epithet of all, he is positioned outside its paradigm. Breggin's reputation is not helped by the fact that he once had a connection to the Church of Scientology or the fact that he has presented his case to the public in forums like *The Oprah Winfrey Show*. Circulating between medicine and popular culture, between allopathic and alternative medicine, and between praise and blame, Breggin's reputation is highly contingent. To some, Breggin is a "know-nothing" (M. Hunt 1999), while to others he is an outspoken hero, a *parrhesiastes* who courageously speaks truth to power (e.g., Foucault 2001). Breggin's public opposition to somatic psychiatry might compromise his ethos as a scientist or physician in the eyes of many of his colleagues; however, there is no getting around the fact that he has been tremendously effective at getting people to listen to him.

In this chapter, I analyze how lobotomy functioned in Peter Breggin's campaign against psychosurgery in the early 1970s as a "condensation symbol" (Graber 1976) crafted by lobotomy's marvelous history. Condensation symbols are a form of rhetorical shorthand: terms that evoke emotions and "compress (or condense) images, attitudes, reactions, and evaluative judgments into a verbal form" (Jasinski 2001). I begin by describing the changes in surgical technique and technology that were the hallmarks of the psychosurgeries developed in the mid-1960s, as well as developments in neurobiology that shifted the target of psychosurgery from the frontal lobes to the limbic system. I then explore the relationship between these biomedical developments and a number of social and political concerns of the late 1960s and early 1970s. In the second section, I look closely at Breggin's frequent claim that lobotomy had returned to American medicine. I argue that Breggin's assertion that "lobotomy has returned" relied on a metonymic association between lobotomy and its behavioral effects that allowed Breggin to classify *all* psychosurgery as lobotomy. Ultimately, I contend in this chapter that the controversy over psychosurgery in the early 1970s was not just a struggle over a surgical practice, but a struggle over the *meaning* of that practice—a meaning that was electrified by lobotomy's marvelous history and the articulation of that history with the social and political tumult of the late 1960s and early 1970s.

New Technologies, New Controversies

As I explain in the previous chapter, by the mid-1950s, psychopharmacology had become the dominant treatment option for somatically oriented psychiatrists. Just a decade later, however, some psychiatrists, neurologists, and neurosurgeons began experimenting once again with psychosurgery, albeit on a much smaller scale. Supported by developments in neurophysiology and neurosurgery, including new instruments and technology, the new psychosurgeries differed from lobotomy in a number of ways.

First, new developments in surgical technique resulted in greater precision.

In both the prefrontal and the transorbital versions of lobotomy, surgeons inserted a leucotome through the brain without a way to see what they were doing, damaging much tissue en route to the connecting fibers between the thalamus and the frontal lobes. Lobotomists plotted their incisions according to the logic of anatomical norms, using areas of the skull as external landmarks that corresponded to the location of internal structures. Although most human brains are laid out in roughly the same way, they vary in shape and size. And so, in addition to its numerous other drawbacks, lobotomy relied on an imprecise surgical method with drastic effects of miscalculation—cerebral hemorrhage was one of the many risks of the operation. Most psychosurgeons of the 1960s, in contrast, used stereotaxy, which used a three-dimensional system of coordinates and internal, rather than external, landmarks. Developed in 1947 and refined in subsequent years, stereotactic procedures employed a large metal frame that wrapped around the skull and neuroanatomical "atlases" to plot individual brain structures in three-dimensional relation to internal points of reference (Gildenberg 1988). This technique also relied on the landmark logic of anatomical norms; however, ventriculography, electroencephelography (EEG), and computerized tomography (CT scans) eventually allowed surgeons to "see" the individual brain upon which they worked, improving their ability to locate and target a particular area.[1]

Innovations in surgical instrumentation also made the ablation of brain tissue less traumatic. While many neurosurgeons continued to use scalpels, new techniques (such as the localized injection of liquid nitrogen) and new tools (such as focused ultrasound, high-frequency sine wave generators, and radiosurgical techniques like the "gamma knife") quickly gained favor in neurosurgical practice (Gildenberg 1988, 5–6). In addition, some surgeons began to abandon targeted ablation altogether in favor of electrodes, which were used both to identify the location of neurological functions and to stimulate particular areas of the brain.

Perhaps the most important distinguishing feature of the new psychosurgeries, however, was the fact that they focused on different areas of the brain. Lobotomy, as I discuss in the first chapter, severed the fibers between the frontal lobes and the thalamus. Most of the newer psychosurgeries, in contrast, targeted areas of the limbic system directly. In line with Ernst Haeckel's theory that ontogeny recapitulates phylogeny, the limbic system is often referred to as the "oldest" part of the human brain and frequently (though reductively) as the "feeling" brain. This is the area of the brain that develops first in the fetus, and the patterns of development roughly follow evolution from "lower" to "higher" animal life forms (Gould 1977). As a concept, the limbic system emerged from the evolutionary perspective of Paul MacLean (1949), who argued that since only mammals were believed to have a neocortex, and since cognition and memory are well developed in mammals and particularly in humans and other primates, these brain functions were the product of the "higher" neocortex alone. Other cortical areas, MacLean believed, which were thought to regulate emotion, were "lower-order" parts of the brain; while clearly not vestigial, such areas of the brain were nonetheless neurobiological traces of our evolutionary past. MacLean's theory (now discredited by many) is where we get terms like "lizard brain" to refer to involuntary, emotional, and instinctual behavior in humans, and its hierarchy of location is very much in line with the privileging of cognition over emotion discussed in chapter 1.[2] In the late 1960s, some prominent neuroscientists drew on theories of limbic system function in order to argue that these areas of the brain housed violence as well as emotion—a claim with profound social and political implications.

Violence and the Brain

In the wake of a number of assassinations, social unrest, and a perceived rise in random criminal acts, American concern about violence was at a frenetic pitch in the late 1960s and early 1970s. In 1972, for instance, Senator Edward Kennedy identified violent crime as one of the biggest issues facing American society, calling "the threat of the criminal . . . [a threat] that all of us feel directly and daily. It is a threat that we all sense is growing. It is one that we all as individuals feel powerless to deal with, *a disease beyond our control, an infection which we cannot really protect ourselves against*" (23, my emphasis).[3] Kennedy was speaking metaphorically here, but only a few years earlier research into the etiology of violence had begun to flourish not only in social sciences like sociology, psychology, and criminology but also in the medical sciences. Of course, claims about the biological underpinnings of violence are not new. In the nineteenth century, for example, Cesare Lombroso (1911) developed an intricate taxonomy of anthropological criminality based largely on facial features and head shape. In the late 1960s, however, corporeal signs of violence and criminality were sought inside, rather than outside, the skull.[4]

One tragic event that appeared to illustrate the connection between brain pathology and violence was a mass shooting by Charles Whitman on the campus of the University of Texas in 1966.[5] On August 1, Whitman climbed the campus clock tower with a rifle and shot and killed fourteen people and wounded thirty-two others with a sniper's precision. Before the tower shootings, Whitman had also stabbed his wife and mother to death. Afterward, authorities found a suicide note in which the former marine complained that he had been experiencing persistent violent thoughts in the months leading up to the murders. "After my death," Whitman directed, "I wish that an autopsy would be performed on me to see if there is any visible physical disorder. I have had some tremendous headaches in the past and have consumed two large bottles of Excedrin in the past three months." Whitman also directed that any remaining life insurance funds be donated to a mental health foundation so that "research can prevent further tragedies of this type" ("Suicide Note" 2006). After the murders, Texas governor John Connally convened a massive team of psychiatrists and neurologists and charged them with explaining Whitman's actions. An autopsy revealed a tumor growing between his thalamus, hypothalamus, and amygdala. The grand jury hearings convened after the shootings concluded that the tumor in Whitman's brain "undoubtedly caused him much mental pain and possibly contributed to his insane actions" (W. Sullivan 1966). The most satisfying answer for Whitman's crimes wasn't to be found in his upbringing, military experience, or personal life: the most compelling explanation for a public struggling to make sense of Whitman's violence was found inside his brain.

In their 1970 book *Violence and the Brain,* neurosurgeon Vernon Mark and psychiatrist Frank Ervin suggested that Whitman's horrific act might have been prevented had he received a brain scan. Ervin and Mark were colleagues at Harvard Medical School and also practicing physicians in the Boston area: Ervin was a psychiatrist at Massachusetts General, and Mark was the head of neurosurgery at Boston City Hospital. In addition to Whitman, the doctors identified other high-profile murderers such as Richard Speck (who killed eight nurses in Chicago in 1966) and Lee Harvey Oswald as biologically violent individuals whose crimes might have been "predicted" if their brains had been examined as part of a routine public screening process (148). In a statement that clearly staked out both the understanding and the treatment of violent behavior as biomedical territory, Mark and Ervin took aim at theories that attributed violent behavior to social or political causes, arguing that these explanations made no "serious effort to understand or treat the violence-prone individual" (xi).

Three years earlier, Mark, Ervin, and William Sweet (also a colleague at Harvard) had published a letter in the *Journal of the American Medical Association* that made a similar argument about the need to study the "violence-prone individual" (1967). The racially charged examples used to frame their proposition were the recent riots in Newark and Detroit, which the authors suggested might have been the result of brain disease. The authors made no mention of the catalyzing events that had led to the days of unrest in each city: in Newark the beating of cab driver John Smith by police; in Detroit the raid on a local nightclub in an African-American neighborhood in which all patrons were arrested. Neither did the doctors put much weight on the socioeconomic factors that led to the intense dissatisfaction of Newark's and Detroit's people of color: lack of political representation; programs of "urban renewal" and gentrification that contributed to a lack of affordable housing (Governor's Select Commission 1968, 55), systematic police brutality (Fine 1989), unemployment (Sugrue 1996), and gross economic inequality. To attribute the unrest solely to social, economic, or political causes, wrote the doctors, "is to overlook some of the newer medical evidence about the personal aspects of violent behavior."

Although Mark, Ervin, and Sweet admitted that the "urban rioter" did not have a "monopoly on violence," they argued that the "the real lesson of urban rioting is that, besides the need to study the social fabric that creates the riot atmosphere, we need intensive research and clinical studies of the *individuals* committing the violence." The point of the research would be to "pinpoint, diagnose, and treat those people with low violence thresholds before they contribute to further tragedies" (1967, 895, original emphasis). Though the claim that violence might be located in the brain was itself a controversial assertion, the *JAMA* letter's racially coded focus on "urban" individuals, and Mark and Ervin's later prescription of psychosurgery for "brain diseased" people (1970, 158–159), alarmed a great many people, particularly because their research into the biology of violence was supported by nearly two million dollars annually from the National Institute of Mental Health and the Department of Justice (Trotter 1972, 175).[6]

And indeed, research was well under way in the late 1960s to use psychosurgery as a way to mitigate aggression and violence. The most well known of these experiments were conducted by Yale physiologist Jose Delgado, who implanted a "stimoceiver" in animals' brains in an area believed to elicit and inhibit aggression. In one spectacular experiment in 1963, Delgado placed one of his stimoceivers in a bull and stood in a bullfighting ring with a handheld transmitter. When the bull charged, Delgado pressed a button, the bull reared its head, and it stopped just a few short feet away. In an editorial in 1967, the *New*

York Times commented that although Delgado's experiments with animals had not been replicated in humans, and although Delgado claimed that electrical stimulation did not change the "basic characteristics" of the subject, "the mere existence of such a possibility is disturbing, and certainly merits wider public discussion and greater attention than it has received up to now" ("Push Button People" 1967). If the *Times* was disturbed by the social and political implications of the research, Delgado did little to quell those fears with his book *Physical Control of the Mind: Toward a Psychocivilized Society* (1969), in which he claimed that medical science was on its way to creating "a less cruel, happier, and better man" through a partnership between neurology and technology (232).

The research of Jose Delgado, William Sweet, Vernon Mark, and Frank Ervin might have remained a small blip on the public radar if it wasn't for Frank Ervin's former medical student Michael Crichton, who fictionalized their research in his second bestselling novel, *The Terminal Man* (1972). In the novel, Harry Benson, a patient with psychomotor epilepsy, is subjected to psychosurgery, specifically electrode stimulation, to treat his aggressive behavior. The treatment has the opposite effect: the electrodes stimulate his brain at a faster and faster rate until Benson goes on an uncontrollable killing spree. Crichton drew material for his book directly from the research of his former professor: the book's surgeon, John Ellis, even cites the three examples of Whitman, Speck, and Oswald in his explanation of the neurobiological basis of violence (248). To emphasize the timeliness of his novel, Crichton included an author's note and a bibliography in order to make sure his audience knew that *The Terminal Man* was not a futuristic work of speculative fiction, but a commentary on the present state of biomedical affairs:

> Research in neurobiology is spectacular enough to appear regularly in Sunday supplements. But the public has never really taken it seriously. There has been so much ominous talk and so much frivolous speculation for so many years that the public now regards "mind control" as a problem removed to the distant future: it might happen, but not soon, and not in a way that would affect anyone alive. (xv)

Fueled by the research of scientists like Delgado and inflamed by novels like *The Terminal Man* and Stanley Kubrick's adaptation of Anthony Burgess's 1962 novel *A Clockwork Orange* (1971), in which a young criminal is subjected to an inhumane treatment for violent tendencies, public skepticism about medical "cures" for violence intensified into alarm after it was revealed that California had developed a program to treat incarcerated violent offenders. "The fictional future" that Crichton and Kubrick had described, noted one writer for *Science News*, "seems to show some strong resemblances to a set of events that have come to public knowledge recently in California" (Trotter 1972, 174).

The California program was located within a division of the Vacaville Medical Center called the Maximum Psychiatric Diagnosis Unit, which was designed to diagnose, treat, and also experiment on prison volunteers. In 1971, doctors from Vacaville applied for five hundred thousand dollars in combined funds from the US Department of Justice's Law Enforcement Assistance Administration and the State of California to begin a program to use neurosurgery to treat some of the offenders it deemed to be biologically violent. The state rejected the proposal, and the plan was shelved ("Proposal for Surgery on Convicts" 1971; Trotter 1972, 174). However, it was later revealed that in 1968, three inmates at Vacaville had already received amygdalotomy to treat "violent" seizures (Aarons 1972)—the same violent seizures, I might add, suffered by Harry Benson in *Terminal Man*.

Shortly after the revelation about what had happened at Vacaville, a similar story again attracted national headlines: a program in Michigan that proposed to surgically rehabilitate sexual offenders. Although the prisoner in the pilot study had consented to the experimental procedure, civil rights attorney Gabe Kaimowitz filed suit on his behalf against the Michigan Department of Mental Health. Kaimowitz later wrote that when he first learned of the program in Michigan, "echoes of *Terminal Man* began to sound in my head" (1980, 516). Kaimowitz built his case on the premise that the prisoner's incarcerated status made him incapable of providing informed consent:

> A state-held inmate can hardly decide when to go to the bathroom, much less go for a walk or exercise rights of protest while under state control. How then can a prisoner voluntarily, knowingly, and competently consent to participate as a subject in a state-financed and -directed research to permanently alter his behavior? (511)

The circuit judges in Michigan agreed with Kaimowitz, concluding that "involuntarily detained mental patients cannot give informed and adequate consent to experimental psychosurgical operations on the brain" (cited in Shuman 1980, 443). Strikingly, in the middle of the trial, the prisoner changed his mind about the surgery that would have irreversibly changed his mind.

Kaimowitz's primary medical expert was Peter Breggin. Relatively young, having received his MD in 1962, Breggin had become a prominent public voice by allying himself with America's burgeoning antipsychiatry movement. Although psychiatry has faced opposition from a number of different fronts and for a host of disparate reasons, antipsychiatry activists of the 1960s, much like the conservative opponents of psychiatry in the previous chapter, were "primarily interested in the power and influence wielded by the psychiatric profession, not only over the mentally ill but over society as a whole" (Dain 1994, 416). Psychiatrist Thomas Szasz, for example, described the psychiatrist's role as a "social engineer or controller of social deviance," akin to "priest and policeman, arbitrator and judge, parent and warden" (1961, 260). Breggin operated from a similar premise, often repeating Szasz's phrase "so-called mental illnesses" in his writing. In works like *The Myth of Mental Illness* (1961), Szasz took on the entire profession of psychiatry—both psychoanalysis and biological psychiatry— while Peter Breggin focused his critique on biological psychiatry, and somatic treatments in particular.[7]

Breggin first encountered somatic psychiatry at Massachusetts's Metropolitan State Hospital in the mid-1950s, "an old-fashioned snakepit" where he worked as a student volunteer while a freshman at Harvard (1991, 3). After observing patients subjected to ECT, insulin coma, and high doses of drugs like Thorazine, Breggin concluded that somatic treatments were brutal, ineffective, and unnecessary. After becoming a leader in the student volunteer program, he convinced the superintendent of the hospital to let each student volunteer work with one of the "burnt-out schizophrenics," residents of the back wards who had been written off by the hospital administration as lost causes. During the year, student volunteers treated patients by treating them well: taking them for walks, talking with them, buying them new clothes, and having them fitted for false teeth and eyeglasses. For perhaps the first time at Metropolitan, Breggin writes, these patients were not just treated humanely— they were treated like human beings. At the end of the experiment, eleven of the students' fourteen patients were released from the hospital (Umbarger et al. 1962; Breggin 1999, 5–10).

In 1966, Breggin was appointed as a full-time consultant at the National Institute of Mental Health. At that point, he writes,

psychiatry was well on the way toward its wholesale conversion to biochemical and genetic theories and to technological interventions, such as drugs and electroshock. Ironically, the "new psychiatry" was not at all new to me, because it resembled nothing so much as the old state mental hospital psychiatry, where patients were considered biologically and genetically defective and subject to degrading, damaging treatments. Tragically, what was once the psychiatry for the poor—biopsychiatry—was now becoming the psychiatry for everyone. (1991, 10)

What Breggin describes as the turf battle between psychoanalysis and biological psychiatry was a war over professional sovereignty that had been raging since at least the 1940s. Psychoanalysis famously lost the fight, which culminated in the restructuring of the third edition of the *Diagnostic and Statistical Manual of Mental Disorders* in accordance with biological theories of mental illness in 1980.[8] Breggin refused to ally with either biological psychiatry or psychoanalysis, preferring his own brand of holistic therapy, which stressed care instead of cure. In addition to treating patients in private practice, Breggin was active in bringing his concerns about psychiatry to public attention:[9] he founded the Center for the Study of Psychiatry; he worked with the American Association for the Abolition of Involuntary Mental Hospitalization and the Citizens' Committee for Human Rights;[10] and he founded and directed a group called the Project to Examine Psychiatric Technology, the sole purpose of which was to eradicate surgery from the psychiatric armamentarium.

Breggin's campaign against psychosurgery began when he noticed an increasing number of references to surgical treatments in the psychiatric literature in the late 1960s. In an effort to collect information, Breggin sent out surveys to practicing psychosurgeons, inquiring about their methods, results, and rates of use. On the basis of these surveys, Breggin estimated that four to six hundred psychosurgeries were being performed in the United States each year. Even worse, he reported with alarm, the rate of psychosurgery appeared to be increasing (1972a, 98). Breggin writes that he first tried to mobilize his colleagues in order to "stem the 'second wave' predicted by the psychosurgeons"; yet when he brought his concerns to the psychiatric community, he found little support, even from psychiatrists who were personally opposed to psychosurgery (1980, 17). Convinced that his colleagues were neither able nor willing to resist psychosurgery's "second wave," Breggin took his campaign to the American people.

The Return of "Lobotomy"

Breggin might have fought against psychosurgery in a number of ways. He might have continued to lobby psychiatrists and other medical professionals in order to encourage internal resistance. He might have focused his public critique on somatic treatments in general and advocated for the holistic, noninvasive therapies he believed were more ethical in principle and more effective in practice. Breggin's main strategy, however, was to sound a public warning about the "return of lobotomy" in order to "rally many community and political leaders" and force federal and state intervention into psychiatric practice (1980, 468). Since Breggin's ultimate goal was to motivate the American public to take action in order to stop the resurgence of psychosurgery, it was necessary that they share both his evaluation of the new surgeries and his sense of urgency that they must be stopped. However, most of his audience would not have been familiar with procedures like amygdalotomy, thalamatomy, or bilateral cingulotomy. The term "lobotomy," however, would have been immediately recognized by any audience, and it came complete with an emotional response and a value judgment.

Lobotomy was an ideal condensation symbol for opponents of the new psychosurgeries. It was seen as an outmoded technique, made redundant by the drugs that saturated psychiatric treatment by the late 1950s. But more powerfully, as I argue in the previous two chapters, it had become politically suspect. The authoritarian associations that emerged in the 1950s were further amplified in the 1960s by representations of the operation in popular fiction like *One Flew over the Cuckoo's Nest* (1962) and films like *A Fine Madness* (1966) and *Planet of the Apes* (1968), in which psychosurgery is portrayed as a punishment with no therapeutic benefit whatsoever. In *Planet of the Apes,* psychosurgery is part of a procedure called "final disposition," which the apes attempt to use on Taylor, the human protagonist memorably played by Charlton Heston. Echoing a number of critiques of lobotomy from the 1950s, the apes' Dr. Zaius describes "final disposition" as "emasculation to begin with. Then, experimental surgery on the speech centers, on the brain . . . eventually a kind of living death." As he is dragged out of the room, Taylor resists, screaming: "All right, you can cut pieces out of me! You've got the power! But you do it out of fear, remember that! Remember that! You're afraid of me! What are you afraid of, doctor?" Only fifteen years after Egas Moniz won the Nobel Prize, lobotomy had become a brutal relic of the medical past, shelved in the American imagination somewhere between truth serums and phrenology machines.

One article Breggin coauthored with David Greenberg, "Return of the Lobotomy," published by the *Washington Post* in 1972, illustrates a number of rhetorical strategies that connected new forms of psychosurgery with lobotomy. The article begins with a narrative about a nine-year-old boy subjected to psychosurgery in order to treat what his doctors described as "hyperactive, aggressive, combative, explosive, destructive [and] sadistic" behavior. Although the boy's behavior "markedly improved" after multiple surgeries, his surgeon commented, "intellectually . . . the patient is deteriorating." Breggin and Greenberg write that this narrative "might strike some as a tasteless satire, inspired perhaps by an over-excited reaction to the film 'A Clockwork Orange.'" But they warn their readers that what they describe is not fiction: "the operations . . . are part of a second wave of psychosurgery—popularly known as lobotomy—that is now gaining momentum in the United States and around the world" (1972). Breggin and Greenberg continue the substitution of "lobotomy" for "psychosurgery" set in place by the article's title by leaving out one important qualifier: "popularly known *in the form of* lobotomy."

Breggin and Greenberg strengthen the connection by using the term "lobotomist" to refer to all psychosurgeons, a word they wield as an epithet. They describe contemporary psychosurgeons as a secret cabal of lobotomists who have laid in wait with Walter Freeman for their operation to return from limbo:

> [Although] it was apparent to even the most rabid lobotomist that carving up the frontal lobes frequently quieted the patient at the cost of turning him into a tractable vegetable . . . the lobotomists . . . did not disband. Though it was clear that surgical intervention in the human brain was on a par with firing bullets into the hood of a car to remedy a knock—with occasional success—they had experienced enough "success" to arouse the belief that less mutilating, more precisely placed interventions were what was called for. (1972)

The collapse of *all* psychosurgery to lobotomy and all psychosurgeons to "rabid" lobotomists serves one purpose in this article: to connect present medical progress to past medical ignorance and failure and to call into question the new psychosurgeons' claim that "the lobotomy era of psychosurgery is in the past" (Orlando Andy, in U.S. Congress 1973, 352). By connecting the new psychosurgeries with the old in this way, Breggin charged that medicine was not progressing; rather, it was *regressing*. This claim was intensified by the article's illustration: a woodcut of a medieval surgeon boring into a man's head with a bit and brace.

Breggin frequently and freely substituted "lobotomy" and "psychosurgery" in other pieces of writing as well. For example, in one article submitted by

Representative Cornelius Gallagher (D-NJ) to the *Congressional Record,* Breggin frequently refers to mentions of psychosurgery in medical discourse as the "lobotomy literature" (US Congress 1973, 455–456, 466). In another paragraph, Breggin decries the promotion of psychosurgery in medical journals and writes that both *JAMA* and the *American Journal of Psychiatry* have been "offering pro-lobotomy articles based upon inadequate scientific studies" (455). Later in this article, Breggin describes a case study from Mark and Ervin's *Violence and the Brain,* a woman "brought in for psychosurgery, specifically thalamatomy." Breggin then comments, again substituting the two terms, "this is the *only* detailed case report I have found in the entire current lobotomy literature" (466, original emphasis).

A comprehensive analysis of the psychosurgery literature of the 1960s led Elliot Valenstein (1973) to conclude that by 1970, "almost no" lobotomies were being performed in the United States (284). According to Valenstein's definition of lobotomy, which relied on a denotative match with the specific operations performed by lobotomists like Freeman and Watts, Breggin's claim that "lobotomy has returned" was false or at least seems a careless conflation. Yet it is highly unlikely that Breggin would have accidentally conflated lobotomy and psychosurgery. Not only was he trained as a psychiatrist, but, as his lengthy bibliographies indicate, he also was clearly familiar with the psychosurgery literature. Breggin's use of "lobotomy" therefore appears to be solely a rhetorical tactic. Condensed into syllogism, Breggin's argument reads as follows: *all psychosurgery is lobotomy; all lobotomy is bad; therefore, all psychosurgery is bad.* As a categorical argument, this fails. All psychosurgery is not lobotomy— thalamotomy and amygdalotomy are also kinds of psychosurgery. However, this argument fails only when "lobotomy" is used to denote a specific operation. A closer examination of Breggin's other uses of "lobotomy" reveals a very different definition of lobotomy than that of Elliot Valenstein or the psychosurgeons Breggin opposed.

For Peter Breggin, anything producing a similar behavioral effect to lobotomy ought to be classified as a lobotomy. In the *Congressional Record* article, for example, he references the work of one psychosurgeon, Petter Lindstrom, who used ultrasonic beams of energy in his operations:

> Lindstrom apparently balks at being called a lobotomist. He says that he has been able to titrate his doses of energy so that he can reach a point where the damage is not grossly perceptible and hence does not constitute a lobotomy. *But*

if he's getting a behavioral effect, he's done a lobotomy, even if it's merely a lobotomy by disruption of the brain chemistry. (US Congress 1973, 464, my emphasis)

Breggin couldn't be clearer. For him, "lobotomy" did not designate a particular surgical procedure, but rather a set of behavioral effects associated with that procedure. Using this definition, the new psychosurgeries, which produced similar effects, could be called "lobotomies," as could chemical treatments like Thorazine, which Breggin later disparaged as a "pharmacological lobotomy" (1980, 476).[11]

What are the behavioral effects that Breggin identifies as criteria for "lobotomy"? In an article in *Medical Opinion* entitled "Lobotomies Are Still Bad Medicine," Breggin writes that although the techniques of contemporary psychosurgeons "may be much more precise than those used by early lobotomists, who won a reputation as 'hatchet men' . . . the outcome is basically the same": "at worst, they are irreversibly damaging the patient's 'self,' the very qualities of insight, creativity, judgment, etc., that separate man from the lower species. At the very least, they are blunting the patient's emotional response" (1972b, 32). This metonymic definition of lobotomy as a set of particular effects is one of its most dominant contemporary meanings, illustrated by a swarm of contemporary popular images in which "lobotomy" stands in for something akin to "brain damaged" or sometimes just "stupid" or "dull." The use of "lobotomy" as a trope for its effects is not confined to representations in popular culture, however. Consider the meaning of lobotomy in a 2004 *Neuroscience* article entitled "Lobotomy of Genes," for instance, which isn't about lobotomy, or even psychosurgery, at all. The article describes a recently developed process to inhibit gene expression using artificial double-stranded RNA, which allows researchers to determine gene function. Here, "lobotomy" is used as a play on the word "expression." These aspects of RNA are unable to express themselves, in much the same way that lobotomy stunts emotional expression in patients (Holen and Mobbs 2004).

As one would expect, psychosurgeons were outraged by Breggin's characterization of their work, and they took special offense to his description of their practice as lobotomy. After *Medical Opinion* published an article in which Breggin repeated the conflation of lobotomy and psychosurgery, called out a number of practicing psychosurgeons by name, and concluded with the claim that "psychosurgery is a crime against humanity, a crime that cannot be condoned on medical, ethical, or legal grounds," a number of psychosurgeons wrote to the journal with strongly worded rebuttals and defenses of their field of study and mode of treatment (1972b, 36). Robert Heath, a surgeon who was experimenting with electrical stimulation, wrote that Breggin

> has never visited our laboratories, has not seen the work we have under way, and has not interviewed any of our patients. I do not share the views he has expressed in his anecdotal article. I wonder how much he knows about the subjects he has reviewed, and what his own background training and experience have been. In any event, he has a right to his opinion, regardless of how he developed it. (1972, 13)

William Beecher Scoville, president of the International Society of Psychosurgery, minced no words in his condemnation of Breggin's article and its claims. Like Heath, Scoville charged that Breggin had never studied his patients, and in an echo of Walter Freeman's critique of Roy R. Grinker Sr., discussed in chapter 1, Scoville dismissed Breggin's "emotional" tone. "As a scientist and a physician," Scoville declared, "I am disturbed by the emotional fervor with which Dr. P. R. Breggin damns an accepted form of treatment for intractable mental and emotional illness." Scoville claimed that his patients "have returned to their homes and to high executive positions, are happy and cheerful in the midst of their families. They are in no way comparable to the old lobotomy patients" (1972, 13). Scoville offers an implicit comparative history of lobotomy here, in which the "old" lobotomy patients remained in psychiatric hospitals, unemployed and depressed, with no mention of the other possible outcomes. (Remember that 1972 was the same year Walter Freeman wrote to the *American Journal of Psychiatry* trumpeting his success in "getting them home.") Peter Breggin thus was not the only one in the psychosurgery debate who used lobotomy as a condensation symbol for medical failure: Scoville, a strong proponent of psychosurgery, also drew upon lobotomy's marvelous history to make his point.

Petter Lindstrom, the surgeon Breggin tagged as a "lobotomist" for his use of ultrasonic energy, also wrote to *Medical Opinion*, charging that Breggin's article had "no significance except as a vehicle for an emotional and biased judgment of psychosurgery." Lindstrom complained that Breggin had irresponsibly collected information for the surveys on which his article was based and had used quotations from the "lobotomy literature" that were nearly thirty years old. As a whole, Lindstrom wrote, the article relied on "distortion and misinterpretation of facts and figures" that "are so striking that it is meaningless to attempt an analysis." Lindstrom also took particular offense with the description of his research as lobotomy. Referring to Breggin's psychosurgery survey, Lindstrom explained, "he received from me numerous articles and references clearly indicating that present-day procedures have little to do with the old techniques. I do not know of a single physician who in the last 10 years has performed any of the radical lobotomies of 20–30 years ago." And, he continued, "with respect to the prefrontal sonic treatment (PST) which I introduced 15 years ago, Dr. Breggin refers to it as a 'lobotomy,' which it specifically is not. It does not involve any surgery of the brain" (1972, 17). The surgeons found numerous faults with Breggin's arguments. They claimed that Breggin misrepresented their data; that he was too "emotional" in his arguments; that he hadn't done his research; that he was simply wrong. But nowhere in their rebuttals was a strong argument to counter Breggin's primary charge: *if he's getting a behavioral effect, he's done a lobotomy, even if it's merely a lobotomy by disruption of the brain chemistry.*

For these psychosurgeons, lobotomy was irrelevant to their practice except as a point of comparison of how much psychosurgery had changed. Their definition of lobotomy applied to a specific surgical procedure: we do not do *that* anymore; we do something new, something better, something more refined, something more scientific, something more ethical. Breggin, however, relied on lobotomy as a trope, defining lobotomy as anything that produced a similar *effect* in a patient. Breggin's focus on the similar effects of lobotomy and the new psychosurgeries allowed him to craft a critique in which the new knowledge, new techniques, and new anatomical targets of psychosurgery mattered little. This rhetorical strategy enabled Breggin to make potent political claims about the connection between psychosurgery and behavior control, a point that drove much of the discussion in the Senate hearings about psychosurgery in early 1973.

The Senate Hearings on Psychosurgery

The early 1970s was rife with public debate about the ethical limits of biomedical research and practice. In addition to growing public concern about psychosurgery, scandals about medical abuses of the highest order broke in successive waves in the national media. In 1972, ABC News aired Geraldo Rivera's exposé of the Willowbrook State School, an institution for children with developmental disabilities on Staten Island. The report detailed the severe overcrowding and unsanitary conditions of the facilities and reported that abuse of children by staff members was routine. Just a few years earlier, the school had provoked public outrage when it was discovered that researchers had intentionally infected newly admitted children with hepatitis in order to study the "natural history" of the disease and the immunizing effects of gamma globulin, arguing that the children would have been infected anyway. Also in 1972, the American public learned that nearly four hundred African American men in and around Tuskegee, Alabama, had been intentionally denied syphilis treatment so that researchers could study the progression of the disease over their lifetimes. And as the country deliberated along with the Supreme Court about *Roe v. Wade*, a number of public arguments expressed concern that fetuses would be used for biomedical research (Wertz 2002).

In response to growing public concern about the ethical boundaries of science and medicine, the Health Subcommittee of the Senate's Committee on Labor and Public Welfare began a series of hearings on the subject, which led to the passing of the National Research Act in 1974; the formation of the National Commission for the Protection of Subjects of Biomedical and Behavioral Research; and the drafting of the Belmont Report in 1979, the foundational document that still guides most American universities' institutional review boards with regard to human subjects research. During the second session of the hearings, the subcommittee took up the issue of psychosurgery. Much like the sparring between Breggin and the psychosurgeons I explore in the previous section, the driving topic of the hearings was a struggle over what psychosurgery *means*.

Senator Edward Kennedy, who had recently assumed the position of Health Subcommittee chair, convened the hearings on February 23. (Kennedy's sister Rosemary had received a botched lobotomy from Walter Freeman and James Watts in 1942, a point he never mentioned during the discussion.) Called to testify were Bertram Brown, director of the National Institute of Mental Health, and a number of his colleagues; psychosurgeons Orlando Andy and Robert Heath; bioethicist Willard Gaylin; psychologist B. F. Skinner; and Peter Breggin.

Bertram Brown was the first to speak. He began by providing the committee with a brief history of psychosurgery in which he explicitly separated the lobotomies of the past and the psychosurgeries of the present. "Unfortunately," Brown commented, "it is the lobotomy that the public associates with psychosurgery—a procedure in which the 'cure' was sometimes worse than the disease. And I think I can state unequivocally that no responsible scientist would condone a classical lobotomy operation" (US Congress 1973, 340). Brown then commented on the fact that psychosurgery had become controversial, which he likened to public concern over marijuana use in the late 1960s. Marijuana was more than a health issue: it had become a "lightning rod" for a host of other social and political issues, Brown explained: "the generation gap, who shall set the laws, what shall be done—a whole complex of values of concern to the society as a whole" (346). Although Brown's analogy between marijuana use and psychosurgery is a poor fit—he neglects to mention, for example, the issues of power and consent involved in each—his use of the term "lightning rod" is illuminating. Like marijuana, which became a condensation symbol of the intergenerational cultural conflicts of the late 1960s, psychosurgery had come to represent much more than a medical procedure, namely, as Brown explained, "the control of behavior, political intent, the rights of oppressed minorities, and the like." For Brown, psychosurgery's iconicity was troubling, and he urged the separation "between the lightning rod aura" and "the intrinsic problems" involved in the procedure (346).

In this comparison, psychosurgery's "aura" is implied to be cultural territory, while the "intrinsic problems" of psychosurgery are implied to be the territory of medicine. However, what Brown's comparison misses is that psychosurgery had attracted an "aura" not only because of its representation in fiction like *Planet of the Apes, A Clockwork Orange,* and *Terminal Man* but also due to public concern over the stated research goals of Jose Delgado, Frank Ervin, Vernon Mark, and William Sweet, the Vacaville inmate surgeries, and the Kaimowitz trial—cases in which medical science had directly contributed to the "lightning rod aura" Brown described.

Even further, some of the psychosurgeons' research did indeed seek to control "abnormal" behavior. Mississippi neurosurgeon Orlando Andy, for example, had investigated the use of psychosurgery on patients who behaved "abnormally" but did not necessarily meet the criteria for "psychosis." Andy defines abnormal behavior and its effects as follows:

> Behavior is defined as "the manner of conducting oneself," and the term abnormal, "deviating from the normal or average." Norm is "a principle of right action binding upon the members of a group and serving to guide, control or regulate proper and acceptable behavior." Thus, it is obvious that abnormal behavior may include patients who suffer from a very mild emotional or neurotic disturbance to patients who suffer from a severe psychosis. However, it must again be

stressed, this presentation does not include psychotic disorders. Symptoms which characterize the abnormal behavior in this treatise are emotional tension, anxiety, aggressiveness, destructiveness, agitation, distractibility, attack, suicidal tendencies, nervousness, mood oscillations, stealing, rage, negativism, combativeness, and explosive emotions. These various symptoms or syndromes contribute to a social maladjustment *for which society demands correction or appropriate control.* (1966, 232, my emphasis)

The results of his research led Andy to describe "the future of 'behavioral neurosurgery'" as "promising" (237). The social and political implications of Andy's research were further complicated by the fact that many of his subjects were African American children, one as young as six (Washington 2008, 284). Psychosurgery had indeed acquired a "lightning rod aura" by the early 1970s as a mode of social engineering and behavioral control; however, this aura was a co-creation of biomedical research and the image of that research in public culture.

Brown ultimately advocated a cautious "middle stance" on the use of psychosurgery, which is best illustrated by his response to one of Kennedy's final questions. When Kennedy asked Brown directly if he thought psychosurgery was a valid treatment for mental illness, Brown refused to either endorse or condemn the procedure: "My answer is a crisp 'maybe.' And under what conditions? I would say that only when extensive attempts have failed and the situation is very equal [*sic*] or desperate, and only under the most carefully controlled conditions" (7). For Brown, psychosurgery was neither the wave of the future nor a relic of the past; instead, Brown's crisp "maybe" reflected a permissive attitude for psychosurgery as a treatment of last resort, a position, I might add, very close to that of "classical lobotomists" like Walter Freeman.

Like Brown, the psychosurgeons who testified drew clear distinctions between the lobotomies of the past and the psychosurgery of the present. Orlando Andy provided the committee with a number of case histories in which psychosurgery had relieved his patients of their distress and drew their attention to the differences between lobotomy and his current practice (US Congress 1973, 352). (He mentioned nothing about his published comments on socially abnormal behavior or its control, cited above.) Robert Heath, the second psychosurgeon called to testify, never referenced lobotomy specifically; however, he described the aim of his practice as "the development of less-injurious—and more effective and specific—treatments for severe mental and nervous system diseases, which have been untreatable" (364), a claim in which lobotomy clearly offers the unstated point of comparison.[12]

When Breggin addressed the committee, he directly challenged the surgeons' claims that the lobotomy era was in the past. "Lobotomy is still with us," he told Kennedy bluntly. "Do not believe what you have been told today, Senator, about the demise of lobotomy. There is a great deal of lobotomy going on in this country right now" (US Congress 1973, 358–359). It likely appeared to the subcommittee that Breggin was speaking denotatively of the prefrontal lobotomy operation; however, as he continued his commentary, he once again made his argument through the metonymic association of lobotomy and its behavioral effects:

> [William] Scoville and most of the knowledgeable psychosurgeons admit that all of the newer procedures *do the same thing*: they are *partial lobotomies*. Let me review one quote, from 1972, from a very well-known psychosurgeon:
>
>> After the operation, there develops a sense of fear. In cases that are still mildly troublesome, the threat of punishment quiets them . . . the patient became more cooperative and obeyed commands.
>
> Dr. Brown is not telling you the facts when he tells you that this procedure is not *closely related* to lobotomy. Ruth Anderson . . . says that the newest operations have *the same effect as lobotomy*: emotional blunting, passivity, reduced capacity to learn. (360, my emphasis)

Breggin's primary tactic in the hearings was not just to call psychosurgery "lobotomy," but also to draw out the social and political consequences of effects like "emotional blunting" and passivity, which he described as "the real problems that we are facing today" (358). The ultimate goal of any psychosurgery, Breggin believed, was not cure, but "tampering with the brain . . . in the interest of controlling the individual" (358). Breggin then linked the research in psychosurgery to research in behaviorism, which he called "mechanistic, anti-individual . . . and anti-spiritual," in order to make his boldest claim of the day:

> The psychosurgeons here today, represent the greatest future threat that we are going to face for our traditional American values, as promoted in the Declaration of Independence and the Bill of Rights. This totalitarianism asks for social control, including social control of the individual, at the expense of life,

liberty, and the pursuit of happiness. . . . If America ever falls to totalitarianism, the dictator will be a behavioral scientist and the secret police will be armed with lobotomy and psychosurgery. (358)

Peter Breggin's claim that America would succumb to a B. F. Skinner–like dictator, armed with an army of leucotome-wielding lobotomists, is precisely the kind of hyperbole that leads many to dismiss his arguments. When paired with Breggin's critique of psychosurgery as a whole, however, the remarks begin to take shape as a deliberate rhetorical strategy supported by recent developments in biomedical research and interpretations and counterinterpretations of those developments in American public culture.

Breggin wasn't shouting into the wind, nor was his statement removed from the tenor of the day's testimony. Edward Kennedy had inaugurated the hearings by framing psychosurgery as a social and political concern:

> There are those who say the new behavioral research will enable us to realize our full potential as a nation and as a people. There are others who believe that the new technology is a threat to our most cherished freedoms. It is important for the people of this Nation to begin to understand the nature and implications of behavioral research. Scientists have developed some very powerful tools, tools that have the potential to affect, and perhaps even alter, each of our lives. We must as a society decide how these tools are to be used. (US Congress 1973, 337)

The primary issue of the day was not necessarily *does psychosurgery work?* but *what does psychosurgery mean?* when measured against American liberalism. As he questioned each of the witnesses, Kennedy frequently returned to the question of whether psychosurgery might be employed as a method of social engineering. After Bertram Brown dismissed the social and political aspects of psychosurgery as an "aura" of concern rather than a legitimate critique, Kennedy pushed back, asking if the surgery could be used for "mass behavioral control." On this point, Brown was forced to concede that he could imagine situations like the one Breggin described above: "I can picture scenarios under certain kinds of authoritarian or totalitarian situations where it could be used for such purposes. I think they would be dreadful—and un-American" (347). When Breggin later injected the image of a lobotomist army into the day's discourse, then, he was responding to the earlier comments of Kennedy (who himself might have been responding to Breggin's comments in the press).

Interviewing psychosurgeon Robert Heath, Kennedy was even more direct, pressing him to declare the difference between his practice and "behavioral control." After Heath explained that his use of psychosurgery was limited to treating people who had been diagnosed with mental illness, Kennedy was blunt, stating: "What you are really talking about is controlling behavior." Heath was equally blunt: "I am a physician and I practice the healing art. I am interested in treating sick behavior—not in controlling behavior" (US Congress 1973, 367). For Heath, like Brown, there was little similarity between his research and the applications of psychosurgery discussed in the hearings. In his response to Kennedy, Heath drew a dividing line between social and medical territories: the art of healing and the art of social control were mutually exclusive. On this point, I turn to sociologist Irving Zola, who in the year before the hearings had made this particular division the subject of a blistering essay. In recent years, American medicine had become a battleground, Zola wrote, but

> not because there are visible threats and oppressors, but because they are almost invisible; not because the perspective, tools and practitioners of medicine and the other helping professions are evil, but because they are not. It is so frightening because there are elements here of the banality of evil so uncomfortably written about by Hannah Arendt. But here the danger is greater, for not only is the process masked as a technical, scientific, objective one, but one done for one's own good. (1972, 502).

According to Zola, medicine was not just a potential *tool* of social control. By expanding the territory of human life subject to medicalization, by retaining absolute control over certain technical procedures and knowledge, and by exercising these modes of power via public trust in medical authority, medicine had become an *institution* of social control.

Although Breggin's statements in the Senate hearings might have been hyperbolic, they did precisely what his public campaign against psychosurgery accomplished: they got people talking about psychosurgery on his terms. In short, Breggin was able to shift the rhetorical terrain of the national debate over psychosurgery from a medical issue to a social issue. Much of the Senate hearings on psychosurgery focused not on surgical technique, nor patient case studies, nor the numerous differences between lobotomy and the newer psychosurgeries, but on the social and political implications of psychosurgery.

To take Breggin's role in the history of psychosurgery seriously does not mean that we need to agree with the content or conclusions of his arguments nor that we approve of the rhetorical tactics he used to get his point across. From the vantage point of medicine and conventional medical history, Breggin was wrong: no matter how much Walter Freeman might have hoped to the contrary, lobotomy had not returned to American medicine in the early 1970s. However, it is actually one of Breggin's targets, Frank Ervin, coauthor of *Violence in the Brain*, who provides one of the best arguments for why Peter Breggin is such an important figure in a rhetorical history of lobotomy. Although he disagreed with his opponent's tactics, he told *Science News* (1972), there was a "germ of truth" to what Breggin was saying:

> The whole science of behavior technology—of which surgery is only a tiny piece—is bustling along at full tilt and getting better all the time, i.e. more powerful all the time. And this is one of those technologies that we damn well better keep on top of socially and politically. People ought to know what is available and what is happening—such as who is using what tool to do which with. . . . Everybody ought to be thinking about these things. . . . Everybody ought to be involved, not just an elitist group. ("Debate over Psychosurgery" 1972, 182)

For Ervin, the lesson to take away from Breggin's campaign against psychosurgery is not that he and his colleagues were plotting to reshape the American psyche. The lesson is that any research or intervention into human brains or behavior is always already a social and political matter and, as such, it ought to be the subject of public deliberation.

In 1977, the National Commission for the Protection of Human Subjects of Biomedical and Behavioral Research released its report and recommendations on the use of psychosurgery, a document in which Peter Breggin's name is prominently featured. The first line of the report notes that the formation of the commission was "in response to widespread public concern" (26318). Later in the report, under a section entitled "Rise of Public Concern," the commission directly addressed Breggin's pivotal role in the debate:

> Coinciding with the development of refined techniques for psychosurgery, the climate of political unrest in the 1960s, general fear of behavior control and

concern about abuse of minorities provided the background against which Dr. Peter Breggin . . . began to publish articles warning about the "new wave of psychosurgery" and the "return of the lobotomy." (26319)

Breggin is mentioned a number of other times in the report, particularly his claims about psychosurgery's implications: the report states that Breggin "has voiced deep concerns that psychosurgery will be used (or misused) as a social or political tool, applying socially determined definitions of 'abnormal' behavior to justify controlling dissidents or subduing individuals whose behavior is disruptive or otherwise bothersome" (26320). The commission also highlighted the powerful role of popular fiction: *A Clockwork Orange* and *The Terminal Man* are cited specifically as adding "fuel to the fire" (26319).

The 1977 psychosurgery report echoed Bertram Brown's contention in the 1973 hearings that the answer to the question of psychosurgery was a "crisp maybe." It recommended a stricter policy with regard to peer and public review, advocated careful and consistent data collection on surgeries, suggested that psychosurgery should not be performed on children or prisoners, and requested that the practice of psychosurgery be regulated by institutional review boards. These recommendations remain only guidelines, however, and have never been implemented in any federal regulations or legislation (Valenstein 1986, 289).

Although the US government has never successfully passed legislation to control the use of psychosurgery (a 1973 House bill sponsored by members of the Congressional Black Caucus was never brought out of committee),[13] Oregon and California passed measures to regulate psychosurgery in 1973 and 1977, respectively. Although there are similarities between these pieces of legislation, there are also a number of significant differences. The Oregon statute provides for the creation of a Psychosurgery Review Board composed of a neurologist, two neurosurgeons, two psychiatrists, one clinical psychologist, one neuroscientist, one lawyer, and—significantly—one "lay" member of the public (Grimm 1980, 423). If an Oregon physician wishes to perform psychosurgery on his or her patient, it is first necessary to petition the Review Board and to successfully argue that (a) the patient or legal guardian has provided informed consent to the procedure, (b) the procedure is an appropriate treatment for the condition described, and (c) all other conventional therapies have been tried. After the initial petition, the review board then determines whether psychosurgery is warranted. Of the six cases that were brought to the review board during the 1970s, only one was approved. In the five unsuccessful cases, patients showed ambivalence about their consent, and two were reported to have recovered between the time the petition was filed and the time the case was decided. According to Robert Grimm (1980), one of the authors of the Oregon bill, it was unknown how many psychiatrists had sent their patients out of state to obtain surgery, a measure that a number of them had informally threatened in response to the regulations.[14]

In 1977, California passed similar legislation establishing regulations on psychosurgery. Like the Oregon statute, the California law demands written consent, which can be provided by a close relative or guardian. And like the Oregon statute, the treating physician's petition must demonstrate that all other therapies have been tried without success. Yet unlike the Oregon statute, which requires only the petitioning physician's medical opinion, the California law requires that an additional three physicians must examine the patient and agree that psychosurgery is warranted. While in Oregon a patient's case is heard by a review board, in California a decision is made by a court. In addition, the California law establishes a seventy-two-hour waiting period after a patient's written consent and prohibits the use of psychosurgery on minors.

According to Grimm, the regulations in Oregon and California effectively ended the practice of psychosurgery there. In Oregon, the petitioning process was a "hassle," which required dogged persistence by the petitioning physician. While many physicians saw the process as unnecessary governmental intervention into their affairs, Grimm pointed out that Oregon's lengthy "hassle" yielded a significant outcome: the chance for a patient to change his or her mind, much like what had happened in the Kaimowitz case in Michigan. By 1980, led by the legislation in Oregon and California and strengthened by the forces of public opposition I have described in this chapter, Grimm felt that "psychosurgery in the United States seems to be dying a natural or unnatural death, depending on one's point of view" (1980, 437). Grimm's last point is spot on, though it is probably not the point he had intended. In the twenty-first century, as I will show in the next chapter, psychosurgery is either dead or very much alive, depending on the words one uses.

CHAPTER 5

Not Our Father's Lobotomy

Memories of Lobotomy in the New Era of Psychosurgery

> *Primum non nocere, Melius anceps remedium quam nullum.* So long as we always guard this crucial balance, the psychiatric surgery currently in development will not be our father's lobotomy.
>
> —BRIAN KOPELL, ANDRE MACHADO, AND ALI R. REZAI, PRESENTATION TO THE CONGRESS OF NEUROLOGICAL SURGEONS (2005)

> The greatest part of disputes is more about the signification of words than a real difference in the conception of things.
>
> —JOHN LOCKE, *AN ESSAY CONCERNING HUMAN UNDERSTANDING* (1694)

As we saw in the previous chapter, while the lobotomy era of psychiatry largely came to an end by the end of the 1950s, the general practice of psychosurgery was never entirely abandoned. Today a number of forms of psychosurgery remain in use for mental illnesses for which other forms of treatment, such as psychotherapy, psychopharmacology, and electroconvulsive therapy, have failed. Anterior cingulotomy, for example, is an option for patients with severe forms of obsessive-compulsive disorder (e.g., Sheth et al. 2012), subcaudate tractotomy and cingulotomy may be recommended for patients with bipolar disorder (e.g., Cho, Lee, and Chen 2008), and amygdalotomy is offered as a treatment for some patients whose behavior has been classified as pathologically aggressive (e.g., Lee et al. 1998). These forms of ablative psychosurgery are quite rare in the United States and many other parts of the world.[1] In the last decade, however, psychosurgery has experienced something of a "resurrection" (Elliot et al. 2011) in the form of deep brain stimulation (DBS), which has been heralded as the newest frontier in the treatment of otherwise treatment resistant depression (TRD).

In the first clinical study of DBS for TRD (Mayberg et al. 2005), researchers placed electrodes in the subgenual cingulate of six patients for whom psychotherapy, electroconvulsive therapy, and at least four different antidepressants had failed. When the electrodes were turned on, "all patients spontaneously reported acute effects including 'sudden calmness or lightness,' 'disappearance of the void,' sense of heightened awareness, increased interest, 'connectedness,' and sudden brightening of the room, including a description of the sharpening of visual details and intensification of colors in response to electrical stimulation" (652). Four of the six patients experienced a "striking" and "sustained" remission of their depression, leading the researchers to conclude that DBS appears to present an "effective, novel intervention" for TRD (651).

As of the writing of this book, the US Food and Drug Administration (FDA) has not approved DBS for use in TRD. Clinical trials are under way, however, and the day when DBS will be available for patients with severe forms of depression seems to be on the horizon. In 2009, Medtronic, Inc., announced its "official entrance into psychiatric therapies" after it received an FDA humanitarian device exception for the use of its DBS stimulator (Reclaim™) in cases of treatment resistant obsessive-compulsive disorder.

According to an editorial in *Biological Psychiatry*, "commentaries on the subject of DBS in neuropsychiatry seem incomplete without some discussion of the lessons to be learned from the excesses and abuses of its distant predecessor, frontal lobotomy" (Goodman and Insel 2009, 263). Given the deep imprint of lobotomy in the American imagination, if advocates for DBS are to convince their audiences that new forms of psychosurgery are scientifically grounded, clinically effective, and ethically sound, then "the clinical and scientific community must assure the public that the kind of mistakes made before are not repeated" (Goodman and Insel 2009, 263). For DBS advocates (which include neurosurgeons, psychiatrists, neurologists, and bioethicists), to establish a relationship between these two treatments involves crafting a lineage for DBS that in some way answers the lobotomy question that hangs over any surgical attempt to alter mind, mood, or behavior. When advocates write that "careful work is needed so that DBS does not acquire the negative connotations of psychosurgery" (Sachdev and Chen, 2008, 29) the work they describe not only involves scalpels and electrodes but also words and arguments.

In this chapter, I analyze discourse about deep brain stimulation in popular and medical media in order to explore a number of strategies that stimulation advocates employ to rhetorically manage the collective memory of lobotomy. In the first section, I explore the concept of collective memory in order to show

how it may be identified in arguments that assume a shared judgment about the past. I then turn to arguments for the use of DBS in treatment resistant depression, which I group according to three rhetorical strategies that manage the relationship between DBS and the lobotomy era. In the conclusion, I revisit the concept of rhetorical management and suggest an alternative strategy of rhetorical engagement, in which the collective memory of lobotomy is employed in order to foster broader-based dialogue about the use of DBS and other forms of psychosurgery.

Memories of Medicine

The origin of the term "collective memory" is generally attributed to sociologist Maurice Halbwachs ([1925] 1980), who argued that individual memories emerge in dialectical relation with a particular social milieu. In this way, society not only forms the basis for the acquisition of individual memory, Halbwachs explained, but also enables the recall, recognition, and interpretation of those memories in the present. Recently, the academy has seen something of a "boom" in memory studies, and there are as many definitions of collective memory as there are scholars who use the term (Winter 2000).[2] My use of collective memory draws on the work of rhetorician Bruce Gronbeck (2003), who highlights the role of meaning in the formation of collective memory. "Through evocation of collective memories," Gronbeck writes, "past and present live in constant dialogue, even in a hermeneutic circle where neither can be comprehended without the other" (57). To share a memory with another does not just mean that we share knowledge about what happened in the past, in other words. It also means that we share an understanding of what that past means for the present.

Although collective memory is subject to change, once established, it acts as a common, if provisional, ground to form what Jan Assmann (1995) calls cultural memory. Cultural memory extends beyond an individual or group of individuals and becomes preserved in cultural formations: "that body of reusable texts, images, and rituals specific to each society in each epoch, whose 'cultivation' serves to stabilize and convey that society's self-image" (132). For Assmann, cultural memory serves to bind a community together in two separate but related ways: "the formative one in its educative, civilizing, and humanizing functions and the normative one in its function of providing rules of conduct" (132). This latter role is the rationale behind monuments and other visible mnemonics that honor people and events from the past. In so doing, they inculcate a community's normative boundaries in the present so that they, and by extension the community, may persist into the future. In this way, because they selectively remember, interpret, and preserve a past according to present needs and values, collective and cultural memory might be categorized as forms of epideictic discourse (Gronbeck 2003).

Epideictic, writes Judy Segal (2005), "is a culture's most telling rhetoric, because, in general, we praise people for embodying what we value and we blame them for embodying what we deplore" (61). Like any other culture, medicine erects monuments to its heroes and heroines (Thomas Hodgkin, Louis Pasteur, Christiaan Barnard, Elizabeth Blackwell), whom the profession remembers for scientific, technical, or ethical contributions and also because they embody values that medical professionals are encouraged to emulate. However, medicine remembers its thalidomides as well as its penicillins; it remembers its Mengeles as well as its Salks. Just as a nation constructs the virtue of patriotism in relief by remembering its traitors, by remembering heroes *and* villains, successes *and* failures, medicine develops a reflexive attitude toward its past in order to guide its present and future. As Jack Pressman (1999) points out, however, medicine's memories of failure do not displace "cheery illusions about biomedical progress"; in fact, condemnation of actors and events in medicine's past as failures, errors, and mistakes only reinforces teleological notions of biomedical progress (44). When doctors tell the story of lobotomy to each other, as we shall see shortly, it is often to blame the lobotomists as unethical doctors and bad scientists. However, Pressman maintains,

> there is no simple way to separate past villains from heroes without extensive historical investigation; this is not something that can be directly deduced from current perceptions. Any practitioner, regardless of his or her medical or scientific virtues, can one day end up looking quite foolish indeed, . . . Scapegoating our predecessors by presuming, whenever they engaged in medical practices that look dubious to us today, that such conduct must have resulted from bad science or immorality is not a helpful policy. Not only is it egregiously unfair to the original actors, but it instills a false sense of security and draws our attention even further away from dangers that are actually present. (441–442)

For Pressman, the tension between the history of lobotomy and the memory of lobotomy—preserved in popular culture as well as medicine's interpretation of its past—is largely a fight over what lobotomy is supposed to teach and to whom. But it is also a fight over the medical profession, at least as far as its diachronic identity is concerned. For Pressman, medicine's tendency to disavow lobotomy and disown lobotomists reflects an image of the profession in which knowledge, practices, and ethics are assumed to be consistent from one era to the next.

Although I heartily agree with Pressman's conclusion, which has significant implications for history and medicine alike, I want to complicate his assertion that discerning heroes and villains can only be accomplished by "extensive historical investigation," which positions history as a kind of therapy for memorial ills. Heroes and villains are not static figures we discover in the past. They are a dynamic creation of the present. As the result of their precarious dependence on the ever-changing needs and values of the present, these subject positions are highly contingent: heroes can be tarnished and villains redeemed in different times and places. (The memorial to Julius and Ethel Rosenberg in Cuba springs to mind.)

Perhaps nowhere is the contingency of medical heroism and villainy more vividly illustrated than by the case of J. Marion Sims, the nineteenth-century American surgeon often called the "father" of modern gynecology. Many medical schools feature busts of Sims, and he is lauded in many textbooks for his work on fistula surgery and the development of the speculum. However, in the last few decades, Sims has become a deeply controversial figure because he developed the fistula operation by operating on enslaved black women without anesthesia before trying it on white women. One enslaved woman, Anarcha, was subjected to thirty such surgeries as Sims tried to perfect the procedure. There is a large monument to Sims in New York City, where he founded Woman's Hospital in 1855, the first hospital of its kind in the United States. In recent years, many residents of New York City have protested that the Sims memorial is inappropriate and disrespectful, and they have requested that if the city is not willing to tear it down, they should at least amend the history carved into its base with a disclaimer. In this case, the primary historical facts of Sims are not under dispute. Scholars debate whether present or past ethical standards should be used to evaluate Sims's contribution to medicine and whether he hurt or helped the enslaved women he treated (Barker-Benfield 2000; Sartin 2004; O'Leary 2004; Wall 2006). However, the controversy over the memorial in Central Park concerns the meaning of the statue in the present and the community it invokes. Should we praise or blame J. Marion Sims? Is he a hero or villain? How we go about answering those questions reveals as much about who *we* are and the world we want to live in as it reveals about who Sims was or what he did.[3]

Although collective memory and countermemory take their most recognizable rhetorical shape in statues, monuments, landmarks, and commemorative speeches, in this chapter I examine memory in a more subtle manifestation: in enthymematic arguments that assume a common evaluation of the past. Rhetorical tradition defines the enthymeme as a logical syllogism in which one of the premises is suppressed.[4] As Jeffrey Walker (1994) argues, the enthymeme "invokes not only a premise (or warrant) as justification but [also] a 'chord' of value-charged, emotively significant ideas to motivate a passional adherence or identification with its stance" (63). For example, when I wrote above that medicine "remembers its Mengeles as well as its Salks," I clearly assumed that as a reader interested in medicine, you are familiar with Josef Mengele's experiments at Auschwitz-Birkenau, and I also assumed that we share the judgment that he acted unethically. The stronger a memory is, the less it needs to be articulated explicitly and—this is a very important point—the more potent its rhetorical force.

In the arguments for DBS I will analyze below, advocates manage the collective memory of lobotomy by first crafting a distinction between the psychosurgery of the past and the psychosurgery of the present and then presenting a particular relationship between the two.[5] In the next section, I identify three such strategies of memory management: the *evolutionary* strategy, in which DBS is presented as an improvement upon lobotomy; the *genealogical* strategy, in which the neurological, not the psychiatric, lineage of DBS is foregrounded; and the *semantic* strategy, which asserts that DBS is not a form of psychosurgery and severs the relationship altogether. The strategies employed by DBS advocates to contrast the new era of psychosurgery with the old are not mutually exclusive. Arguments often employ multiple strategies, often in the same paragraph and sometimes in the same sentence, yet they all in some way seek to answer the lobotomy question that hangs heavy over any argument for contemporary psychosurgery.

Not Our Father's Lobotomy: The Evolutionary Strategy

In arguments that employ an evolutionary strategy, the audience's memory of lobotomy is explicitly or implicitly referenced in order to highlight how contemporary psychosurgery has changed since the lobotomies of the mid-twentieth century. The evolutionary strategy reinforces a vision of biomedical progress as the continuous refinement of knowledge, technique, technology, and ethics in order to maximize human health and minimize human suffering.

Ethicist Joseph Fins (2009), for example, writes that "neuromodulation has evolved beyond the primitive—even barbaric—sweep of the lobotomy, and with this advance, categorical resistance to this work has dissipated. And that is all to the good" (1). In this brief sentence, lobotomy is characterized as an atavistic throwback to a different time and place and positioned outside the boundaries of modern medicine. Mashour and his coauthors (2004) also use the word "evolve" directly, noting that "psychosurgery has a complex and controversial history dating back to antiquity, and continues to evolve in the present era of neurosurgery" (216). It is clear in these examples that "evolve" is not used as a value-neutral term to describe a gradual change in biomedical technology; neither is it used to describe a procedure's "reproductive fitness," perhaps as a way to account for the path dependence of certain biomedical techniques and technologies. Rather, "evolve" is employed to describe a positive change that hints at teleology. If surgery "evolves," in other words, it evolves in the popular, not scientific, sense of the term: biomedical change is always progress, and it is progress toward a known goal with a positive outcome.

Others express the evolutionary strategy through comparison. For example, Abosch and Cosgrove (2008) advocate for DBS based on new models of depression as a systems-level disorder and emphasize a litany of improvements that distinguish the new era from the old:

> Although the field of psychosurgery has its roots in anecdotal experience as opposed to hypothesis-driven experimentation assessed with validated outcome measures, a new era is fortunately emerging. Advances in the field of neuroimaging have allowed the use of human participants for testing hypotheses about the mechanisms that underlie these disorders. In addition to higher expectations and greater scrutiny placed on investigations in this arena, the advent of DBS technology has provided investigators with a tool that is nondestructive, modifiable, capable of being turned on or off, and more focal in its effects. (1)

In this argument, DBS represents biomedical progress at nearly every point of comparison: more rigorous testing based on controlled experimentation, better theories of mental illness, keener imaging technology, greater regulations and oversight, less destruction, refined precision, reversibility. Contemporary psychosurgery is thus argued to be an improvement on lobotomy in nearly every way. Note that the history of psychosurgery is not told here. Instead, it appears in enthymematic relief as the unstated point of comparison. No history is offered for lobotomy because that history is assumed to be obvious, as is the negative evaluation that the suppressed history presupposes. A history is told because the audience needs to know. Memory provides a reference point for something *the audience already believes*. There is no need to tell this story nor to make an explicit, expansive, evaluative argument about why psychosurgeries in the past may have been erroneous or became subject to "appropriate public and governmental concern" (2) because the authors can count on the audience's judgment—their memory of lobotomy—to assist their argument. To close the article, the authors state their wish for properly regulated and controlled clinical studies "so as not to repeat the errors of the past" (8). In this last phrase, lobotomy is invoked as an "error," a deviation from what should have been.

In the evolutionary strategy, advocates note a number of changes in scientific knowledge, technology, and surgical technique, but they also highlight the ethical environment in which DBS is researched and therapeutically applied. An article from *Psychiatric News* (Moran 2004) brings ethicists Joseph Fins and Benjamin Greenberg together to claim that the "appreciation of the importance of informed consent and other ethical considerations—make the current environment vastly different and more conducive to safe investigation." Other contemporary ethical issues pertinent to the development of DBS, Hardesty and Sackheim (2007) suggest, "include patient selection, patients' rights, adverse event reporting, and a commitment to long-term care" (834). Again, in these examples, the lobotomy era haunts these arguments as the unstated point of comparison ("vastly different," "more conducive").

In addition, some DBS advocates will point to the development of neuroethics, an emergent subfield of bioethics, as evidence of an evolved ethical environment in which neuromodulation is developing. Although the field is still in the nascent stages of theoretical development, neuroethicists tend to focus on two related sets of issues first identified by Adina Roskies (2002). The *ethics of neuroscience* addresses familiar bioethical concerns about research design and implementation, as well as the impact of that research on "existing social, ethical, and legal structures." The *neuroscience of ethics* investigates how a neurological substrate of morality, if discovered, might impact traditional notions of ethics and human behavior (21–22). Although these two strands of inquiry are clearly related (which raises questions about the logic of their division), they both find exigency in psychosurgery, which raises traditional concerns about research design and treatment practices and also provokes discussion about larger ethical issues, such as what morality means if it can be modified by the flip of a switch.[6] Exploring the impact of neuroethics on contemporary psychosurgery, Wind and Anderson (2008) reference the lobotomy era a number of times, most strikingly in the conclusion:

> In retrospect, it is interesting to ponder whether Egas Moniz would have traveled down the road of the leucotomy had he known the implications of his actions. If Moniz had known that he was not simply searching for a treatment for psychosis, but rather traveling towards technology that could shake the concept of human personhood, would he have continued? One can only speculate. But the questions left to be answered, the therapies still to be developed, and the ethical lines yet to be drawn will be some of the great challenges of medicine in the near future. (4)

The authors "only speculate" that Egas Moniz may not have conducted research on psychosurgery had he known the implications of his actions; however, as we saw in chapters 2 and 3, questions of personhood and agency were swirling around lobotomy when it was still in practice, albeit primarily in public culture.

Given the history, then, of what we might call "vernacular neuroethics," to modify an idea from Tod Chambers (2009), in lobotomy's rhetorical history, it seems appropriate that the term "neuroethics" originated not in the pages of a bioethics journal, but in a *New York Times* editorial written by columnist William Safire (2002). Writing against the enthusiasm that accompanied the "decade of the brain," Safire worries about the dangers that accompany the "unbridled science" of mind and mood and recommends that the "soul-searching debate" neuroscience provokes should "get out of the ivory tower, onto the floor, onto the tube and into print until it penetrates every sentient being's consciousness." For Safire, in an echo of Frank Ervin's comments at the close of the previous chapter, the discussion surrounding current research in neuroscience, intertwined as it is with some of the deepest ethical, social, and political questions of our—or any—time, ought to be subject to careful deliberation and intense public debate.

In an echo of media enthusiasm I explore in chapter 2, the popular press has reported on DBS with gusto, and in another echo, they have mostly taken a positive stance on the procedure largely "without reference to ethical debates" within biomedicine and bioethics (Gilbert and Ovadia 2011). When the specter of lobotomy is raised in these press stories, it is nearly always managed via the evolutionary strategy. In an interview with the *Washington Post* (Stein 2004), for example, Joseph Fins claims that "today's [psychosurgery] is far more discreet, less toxic and easier to study than its predecessor." An article in *Slate* (Richards 2008) comments that DBS is a "far cry from the days when lobotomies robbed patients of the ability to feel emotions like love and compassion." An article on DBS in *Time* (Song 2006) employs the memory of lobotomy in much the same way: "the practice of psychosurgery has long been dormant—tarnished by the notorious brain-scrambling lobotomies of the 1940s and '50s—but it has recently reclaimed a bit of its luster, thanks to a relatively new and much more benign technique called deep-brain stimulation." When compared to psychosurgery of the past, DBS finds validation. "New" psychosurgery is "much more benign." Changes are "dramatic." The regulative environment is "vastly different" and "safer" than that of the days of the lobotomy. These arguments invoke the memory of lobotomy as a comforting touchstone of biomedical progress, and in so doing, they preemptively settle the ethical debates that such memories might provoke.

It is rare to encounter newspaper articles that worry about the removal of a brain tumor on principle. As Safire succinctly puts it, "no ethical problem exists with a pacemaker to protect the heart" (2002). Although ethical issues clearly accompany cardiac pacemakers (such as which patients can financial access to them), what we might take Safire to mean is that the ethical issues raised by surgery for psychiatric conditions provoke (Safire might say "merit") public concern in a way, and at a level of intensity, that surgery for neurological disorders does not. As Nikolas Rose (2007) comments, in an age in which bioethics helps to create markets for biotechnological products, "products that do not come with appropriate ethical guarantees . . . will not find it easy to travel around the circuits of biocapital" (30). In a time when health and illness are big business, ethical questions are also economic questions. It is worth pointing out that biotechnology corporations that manufacture DBS devices will see significant profits if the procedure is approved for psychiatric applications.

According to neuropsychiatrist Perminder Sachdev (2007), "if [deep brain stimulation] was only restricted to neurological disorders, it would not be a topic of ethical debate" (97). If anything, neurosurgery for neurological disorders is hailed in the popular imagination as the apex of medical achievement, and we behold neurosurgeons with the kind of awe reserved for that echelon of humanity that includes astronauts and summiters of Everest. There is something about surgical intervention into *psychiatric* conditions, however, that provokes immediate ethical concern—an admixture of our trust in neurosurgery, our perpetual wariness of psychiatry, our tendency to locate personhood and subjectivity in the brain (Dumit 2004; Vidal 2009), and our persistent memory of the lobotomy era. If we revere neurosurgeons as demigods, we revile psychosurgeons as their demonic counterparts—a perversion of everything we value about surgery on the brain. Another effective strategy to manage memories of the lobotomy era, then, is to redraw DBS's family tree in order to highlight its respectable ancestors (neurosurgery for neurological disorders) and favorable relatives (cardiac pacemakers), while downplaying its lineage in the lobotomy era, a strategy that might best be termed *genealogical*.

Not Our Father: The Genealogical Strategy

Nearly every discussion of DBS in biomedical and popular literature references its initial application to manage the tremor and dystonia associated with Parkinson's disease. In the genealogical strategy, the progenitors of DBS patients are not lobotomy patients but Parkinson's patients, a difference as stark as that between the horror of *Asylum* and the wonder of *Awakenings*. In most biomedical discourse about DBS, this genealogy is stated briefly at the start before moving into the current applications for psychiatric disorders. Discussions of DBS in the popular press, however, spend much more time describing its neurological lineage.

In an interview with *Time* (Song 2006), for example, neurologist Michael Okun explains, "we can thank the patients with Parkinson's disease for helping us develop these therapies because what we learned from them we're applying to other disorders." The *Time* article provides a brief narrative common to many popular articles about DBS, which enmeshes the evolutionary and genealogical strategies:

> Deep-brain stimulation (DBS) was first developed in France in 1987 and evolved out of the so-called ablative, or lesioning, surgeries in which doctors use heat probes to burn and permanently damage small regions of the brain—in the case of Parkinson's, regions where patients' tremors and quakes are known to arise. These same brain areas are targeted with DBS, but instead of destroying tissue, doctors implant slender electrodes that pump steady pulses of electricity— think of it as a sort of pacemaker for the brain.

The article's description of DBS as a "sort of" pacemaker for the brain is one of the most frequent ways in which DBS is rhetorically connected to nonpsychiatric conditions, and it draws a genealogy for the procedure that extends outside of the brain and into the heart.

Ali Rezai, former head of the Cleveland Clinic's Center for Neurological Restoration and one of the most visible and vocal advocates for neurostimulation, compares DBS's medical moment in the early twenty-first century to

> where heart pacemakers were in the 1950s. Back then, you would tell someone, "I'm having a pacemaker put in," and people would go, "What's that?" Now everyone knows what a heart pacemaker is. I think that it will be a similar situation for brain pacemakers in 10 or 20 years. (quoted in Stephen Hall 2001)

The pacemaker analogy has become so common that it often loses its analogical quality. In the Rezai quote above, the DBS device is not said to be *like* a pacemaker. It *is* a pacemaker. Another article about DBS in *Discovery Magazine* that quotes Rezai is entitled "Brain Pacemakers Tackle Depression," a headline in which the analogy-invoking quotation marks are also dropped (Neergaard 2008). The headline of an article about DBS in *Wired* magazine claims that the "Brain 'Pacemaker' Tickles Your Happy Nerve" (Graham 2007). The *Washington Post* writes: "modeled on heart pacemakers routinely implanted in people's chests to automatically regulate heart rhythms, brain pacemakers were first developed in the late 1980s to treat Parkinson's, a devastating brain disorder in which victims inexorably lose control of their muscles" (Stein 2004). And perhaps most striking, the Cleveland Clinic and the US Department of Health and Human Services Office on Disability cosponsored a conference on DBS in May 2008 using the analogy as the title: "Brain Pacemakers: A Promising Approach and a New Era of Hope for Neurological Disorders."

The pacemaker analogy is rhetorically effective for two primary reasons. First, the pacemaker is a device well known to the public: many Americans know at least one person with a cardiac pacemaker personally. Second, as William Safire observes, the cardiac pacemaker is a prime example of a noncontroversial medical technology. The pacemaker analogy works, like all analogies, by associating something the audience doesn't know with something they do know and that, importantly, is ethically neutral. Emphasizing the initial use of DBS for neurological conditions, in other words, rhetorically sites the surgery's origin in a medical lineage far less likely to provoke an ethical maelstrom.

I want to emphasize that describing these strategies of memory management as rhetorical is *not* to suggest that they are fallacious or specious or that their authors are somehow unethical or have malevolent motives. It is true that DBS was developed to treat Parkinson's disease, and the stimulator clearly resembles the cardiac pacemaker in many respects. It is true that contemporary neurosurgical techniques are more precise than those of the 1940s, and the effects of contemporary psychosurgery are different from the effects of prefrontal and transorbital lobotomies. It is not untruthful to call a neurostimulator a brain pacemaker or more truthful to call DBS a form of psychosurgery. Rhetoric is an "art of emphasis" (Weaver 1970, 211), but it is equally an art of deemphasis. What I am interested in here are the language and arguments used to manage memory in order to position an audience in a certain way: the making-present of one lineage, the making-absent of another (e.g., Perelman 1982, 33–40). And nowhere is the rhetorical strategy of making-absent more evident than in what I call the "semantic strategy," which attempts to avoid controversy and debate by severing DBS's lineage with psychosurgery altogether.

Not Our Father, Not Our Lobotomy: The Semantic Strategy

"Perhaps no other word in the field of neurosurgery, or medicine for that matter, conjures up a more negative connotation than the word 'psychosurgery,'" writes surgeon Paul Larson (2008, 50). Faced with the rhetorical burden of lobotomy, some DBS advocates have argued that the field should abandon "psychosurgery" in favor of another term. Some alternatives include "psychiatric neurosurgery," "neurosurgery for psychiatric disorders," "neurosurgery for mental disorders," and "limbic system surgery." Although a phrase like "limbic system surgery" denotes the same class of procedures as "psychosurgery," it simply does not bear its connotative weight. To put it another way, *we do not remember* the phrase "limbic system surgery." There is a history of limbic system surgery familiar to a few surgeons and historians of medicine, of course, but there is no cultural memory, and thus no collective memory, of the term "limbic system surgery," which is precisely why it is preferred.

Some DBS advocates, such as Sachdev and Chen (2008), argue that the name change is warranted because psychosurgery and neuromodulation are categorically distinct procedures: "DBS is not 'psychosurgery' even though it involves neurosurgery for the treatment of psychiatric illness. This is because no brain lesion is created, except for any inadvertent damage produced by the insertion of electrodes" (28). For the authors, the distinction between psychosurgery and DBS lies in the function of ablation. While they admit that every operation requires some amount of damage to brain tissue, they do not classify DBS as "psychosurgery" because lesions are means rather than ends (as is the case in ablative surgeries like lobotomy or cingulotomy).[7] To further their argument, Sachdev and Chen turn to the pacemaker analogy: "The insertion of a cardiac pacemaker is not 'cardiac surgery.' Although this may be a trivial distinction, *it is important so as not to tar DBS with the lobotomy brush*" (28, my emphasis). Intriguingly, the authors describe the difference between ablation-as-ends and ablation-as-means as trivial: what is important in the name change is not semantic precision, but the rhetorical management of memory—a clear anxiety that DBS, if regarded as psychosurgery, will be "tarred with the lobotomy brush."

Sachdev (2007) speaks directly to these concerns in another article in which he argues that "the bad press for psychosurgery originated from the period of 'lobotomy,' which involved the removing or lesioning of large parts of the frontal lobes and which is thankfully behind us" (97). Although Sachdev again focuses his attention on the different functions of ablation in order to make the case for the name change, he also makes it clear that the primary force driving the name change is the "pejorative connotations" affixed to psychosurgery during the lobotomy era. Because of "the emotive nature of the term" (97), Sachdev recommends that the term "psychosurgery" be "firmly replaced by 'neurosurgery for psychiatric disorders'" (98). The name change is not just advocated for DBS. Rosenfeld and Lloyd (1999) also strongly favor a name change for other forms of ablative psychosurgery: "the term psychosurgery is imprecise and is burdened with the connotation of destructive lobotomy operations," they write, and "should be replaced with the phrase 'Neurosurgery for Mental Disorder' (NMD); 'Limbic System Surgery' is another alternative" (106). Again, the authors express concern that the term "psychosurgery" is "imprecise"; however, the primary motivation underlying the name change is to unload the heavy burden of connotation.

Stuart Yudofsky (2008) also strongly advocates for a change in terminology in an editorial in the *American Journal of Psychiatry*. Like Sachdev and Chen, Yudofsky is concerned with the precision of the term "psychosurgery." For Yudofsky, however, precision refers to the first part of the term ("psycho") rather than the latter ("surgery"), since surgeons are "unable to perform surgery on the mind" (672). Yet far more important to his argument to abandon "psychosurgery" are the connections that the term makes between DBS and the lobotomy era:

> The use and misuse of lobotomy for psychiatric disorders in the twentieth century led to so-called psychosurgery becoming synonymous with the nefarious exploitation of people with psychiatric disorders by callous, unethical, and unchecked mental health professionals. In the minds of the general public and even of psychiatrists and neurologists, the "good" of such procedures became submerged in the murky, lowering tides of the "evil" of their abuses. In the 1975 Academy Award–winning best picture based on Ken Kesey's *One Flew Over the Cuckoo's Nest,* lobotomy was used to transform the willful, cantankerous, and captivating protagonist, played by Jack Nicholson, into an obedient, zombie-like, tragic character. (672)

For Yudofsky, the representation of lobotomy in *One Flew over the Cuckoo's Nest* was so powerful that future research in psychosurgery is stuck in the muck its memory disturbs. This "evil" image of psychosurgery is firmly imprinted not only in the mind of the "general public" but in the minds of psychiatrists and neurologists too, and the author's use of the term "even" suggests that medical professionals ought to know better. Yudofsky recommends the rather unfortunate phrase "neurosurgical and related interventions for the treatment of patients with psychiatric disorders" as a "more neutral" replacement (673). In an earlier article on ablative psychosurgery, Yudofsky and Ovsiew (1990) also recommend that colleagues avoid the term "psychosurgery," which they believe has become a "stigmatizing" word in the "common parlance" and is "burdened by unfortunate associations with punishment and other social or political misuses" (253). The consequence of these associations, they explain, is the development of "attitudinal barriers" in both medical professionals and the general public (255). Whether DBS is termed "psychosurgery" or "neurosurgical and related interventions for the treatment of patients with psychiatric disorders" seems to have little impact in the day-to-day treatment of patients. Where the name matters a great deal, however, is in public attitudes toward the surgery and in the barriers such attitudes erect. Indeed, as we saw in the previous chapter, public concern can have significant consequences, particularly when public concern transforms into political and juridical action.

"Words can have great power," Sachdev (2007) observes, sounding very much like a rhetorician, and "because of the prohibition on psychosurgery in many jurisdictions, the development of DBS as a new therapeutic technique would be severely thwarted" (98). In other words, in places where "psychosurgery" is specifically prohibited, DBS advocates are advised not to petition officials to create an exemption for DBS, but to change the name in order to avoid any hindrance to research or treatment. However, the distinction Sachdev draws above between ablation-as-means and ablation-as-end is already written into a number of regulations about psychosurgery. The Oregon statute against psychosurgery discussed in chapter 4, for example, defines "psychosurgery" as "any operation designed to irreversibly lesion or destroy brain tissue for the *primary purpose* of altering the thoughts, emotions or behavior of a human being. 'Psychosurgery' does not include procedures which may irreversibly lesion or destroy brain tissues when undertaken to cure well defined disease states such as a brain tumor, epileptic foci and certain chronic pain syndromes" (Oregon Senate 1973, my emphasis). The language of the Oregon statute is also cited by the Psychosurgery Review Board in Melbourne, Australia, the country in which Sachdev practices. Given this distinction, which clearly uses the purpose of ablation to delimit the definitional boundaries of psychosurgery, it would seem as though regulations like these would already make an exception for procedures like DBS. The chief concern, then, appears to be the public perception of DBS. *Words can have great power* indeed.

Definitions, as rhetoricians have argued for millennia, involve much more than correct or incorrect usage. Definitions are not facts about the world, but value-laden ways of knowing the world (Schiappa 2003). As Douglas N. Walton (2001) observes,

> popular opinions tend to take certain assumptions about definitions for granted, without reflecting on them too deeply. It is taken for granted that words, *especially scientific terms and terms used in legal statutes and government regulations, have an objective meaning*. On the other hand, it is often assumed that when there are verbal disputes about the definitions of words, that such disputes are relatively trivial, and can easily be resolved by simply clarifying the meanings of the words. (117, my emphasis)

There is no objective meaning of "psychosurgery" that can be appealed to in the debate over DBS terminology. Whether DBS is "really" psychosurgery is not a matter to be resolved by an appeal to reality or the dictionary.[8] Ultimately, debates over a word's "real" meaning are unproductive, because a word's meaning emerges from its use in a particular linguistic context. This is why dictionaries change. Since any definition of a term involves "claims of 'ought' instead of 'is'" (Schiappa 2003, 5), far more significant than whether DBS is *really* psychosurgery is the question of why this question matters, to whom, and for what reasons. The semantic strategy is thus a rhetorical issue that goes far beyond "mere semantics." As Sachdev (2007) points out, if DBS is called "psychosurgery" in certain jurisdictions, regulations will prohibit research and treatment. For clinical researchers who strongly believe in the therapeutic potential of DBS, as Sachdev clearly does, a "careless approach with our terminology can have adverse consequences" on the lives of people suffering from intractable forms of depression (98).

Although some DBS advocates seek to avoid controversy by abandoning the term "psychosurgery" or to proactively ameliorate public concern by positioning the lobotomy era within evolutionary and genealogical strategies, many advocates also use the powerful memory of lobotomy as a point of critical reflection on the past in order to stimulate dialogue about the best practices for the future. This move is illustrated by a proliferation of psychosurgery histories in biomedical literature in the last decade (Feldman and Goodrich 2001; Mashour, Walker, and Martuza 2004; Fins, Rezai, and Greenberg 2006; Stone 2008; Wind and Anderson 2008). Ali Rezai and his colleagues (2006) praise this renewed professional interest in psychosurgery's history because it provides

> a good opportunity for us to reflect on the legacy of psychosurgery and its modern iteration under the guise of neuromodulation. The seriousness of their scholarship allow a dialogue for which all . . . should be appreciative, whether or not one agrees with the piece. In consideration of the complexity of the topic, a diversity of views should be welcomed and open debate encouraged. Nothing less will provide the ethical justification for achieving a therapeutic future for neuromodulation. (713)

The authors suggest an alternate method to work with the collective memory ("legacy") of lobotomy—not as a burden but as an opportunity to stimulate further dialogue and "open" debate. The authors here do not advocate the rhetorical management of memory; instead, what Rezai and his colleagues recommend is rhetorical *engagement*.

Although rhetorical engagement with the lobotomy era is encouraged within the medical profession (what I assume Rezai and his coauthors mean by "us"), similar open debate in public and cultural arenas has been discouraged. DBS advocates Matthis Synofzik and Thomas Schlaepfer (2008), for example, direct that "societal discussion about the legitimation of psychiatric DBS should abandon any historic allusion to the infamous term of psychosurgery," because the term "is associated with misleading, negative historical and cultural biases and rather blurs than clarifies ethical and factual issues at stake" (1512). But what are the "cultural biases" that the authors wish that public discussion ought to avoid, and how do such biases "blur" the factual and ethical issues surrounding DBS? The authors do not say. Wary (and understandably weary) of the negative connotations associated with "the infamous term," the authors avoid it and, by extension, shut down potentially productive public engagement.

The public engagement approach now favored by many science and health communication scholars "recognizes that science is part of culture and that societies are increasingly multicultural" and also envisions "lay" and "expert" roles as points along a continuum rather than discrete identities (Racine, Bar-Ilan, and Illes 2005, 162). An engaged approach seeks dialogue rather than monologue, and this dialogue is enabled by carefully attending to the power/knowledge dynamics that charge any engagement between "lay" and "expert."

As Susan Reverby (2001) argues in her analysis of African American collective memory of the Tuskegee syphilis experiment (which holds fast to the idea that the men were deliberately infected), even "wrong" memories of medicine might serve a valuable role in engagement. Many historians and health professionals dismiss this collective memory of Tuskegee as incorrect and in need of correction and remediation. Reverby agrees that no deliberate infection took place. However, she recommends that scholars and health professionals ought to appreciate the rhetorical function such memories serve in the present. Engaging with collective and cultural memory of the Tuskegee study allows for rich discussion about important issues surrounding race, medicine, knowledge, and power. By rhetorically engaging these memories, historians and medical professionals open forums for dialogue, debate, and deliberation about the future. Managing memory, in contrast, through avoidance or correction, shuts those forums down.

The power dynamic that constructs a hierarchy between lay and expert deliberation might also be extended to popular discourse about science and medicine—particularly discourse dismissed as fictive and, as such, illegitimate.

Susan Squier (2004) has also argued for rhetorical engagement with science and medicine through literature, which provides "a *thick description* that can provide a ground on which to debate moral questions in this era of cultural pluralism, [and] can also provide a richer, more complex approach to bioethics" (264, original emphasis). What Squier calls the "ecosystem of fiction" embraces ambiguity, complexity, and open-ended discussion, while the "law of fact values clarity, simplicity, and closure" (263). The deliberative value Squier claims for fiction can be applied to memory as well, particularly since many collective memories of medicine have their origins in literature, film, and other forms of popular culture (Lipsitz 1990). With that value in mind, in closing I want to return to the "cultural and historical biases" Synofzik, Schlaepfer, and DBS advocates wish to avoid by so carefully managing the distinction between the past and present.

I assume that by "cultural and historical biases," Synofzik and Schlaepfer are referring to psychosurgery's use as punishment, its connection to social and political issues, and its portrayal as a force to transform humans into docile robots and zombies. As I have shown in the previous three chapters, these images have a complex, hybrid history: they emerge from the hazy space between fact and fiction and between what happened in the past and claims on that past by the present. However, even if such images originated *entirely* from fiction, they nonetheless raise salient critiques of science and medicine that are well worth attending to: doctor/patient power dynamics; the medicalization and control of social deviance; the relationship between research and treatment; state and corporate investments in medicine and biomedical technology; the intersections of medicine, and particularly psychiatry, with gender, race, class, ability, and sexuality; the scientific and social implications of cerebral sacralization and subjectivity—all issues well worth further discussion. As such, the American memory of lobotomy—a pastiche of the many images I have been exploring throughout this book—should not be dismissed out of hand as merely wrong; instead, this memory, and the intersection of medicine and culture from which it is constructed, should be valued as a rich resource for rhetorical engagement.

CHAPTER 6

How Weston State Hospital Became the Trans-Allegheny Lunatic Asylum;

or,

The Birth of Dr. Monster

Tour a living monument!

—PROMOTIONAL MATERIALS FOR THE TRANS-ALLEGHENY
   LUNATIC ASYLUM (2011)

Every monster is . . . a double narrative, two living stories: one that describes
how the monster came to be and another, its testimony, detailing what
cultural use the monster serves.

—JEFFREY J. COHEN, "MONSTER CULTURE (SEVEN THESES)" (1996)

As I wait to be "committed" to the Trans-Allegheny Lunatic Asylum (TALA) in
Weston, West Virginia, a man closes the front doors with an ominous *thud* that
echoes down the high-ceilinged hallway. As the doors slam shut, a group of West
Virginia University students standing behind me jump and then laugh nervously
as the man locks us in. *I'm gonna lose reception soon,* one girl whispers into her
cell phone before huddling close to one of her friends and gripping her arm.
There are fifty of us in line, and we have paid forty dollars each for a place on one
of TALA's paranormal tours, which are led by tour guides who double as ghost
hunters. When I reach the check-in desk, a guide crosses my name off her roster
and presents me with a souvenir "Certificate of Committal." Standing in the
corridor ringing with laughter and shrieks, holding my admission "papers" and
waiting for the tour to start, the full irony of this place hits me. This crumbling
building was once the largest psychiatric facility in the state of West Virginia.
Many women, men, and children were brought to these buildings against their

will because they experienced intense fear and anxiety. Some heard voices from speakers no one else could see. Tonight my fellow tourists and I have paid to be locked in the same hospital in order to experience intense fear and anxiety, and we all want to hear voices. It is, after all, why we are here.

The Trans-Allegheny Lunatic Asylum is promoted as one of the best places in the United States to experience paranormal activity. The asylum has been featured on a number of reality television shows devoted to ghost hunting, including the SyFy Channel's *Ghost Hunters* and the Travel Channel's *Ghost Adventures*, which broadcast a seven-hour live show from the asylum on October 30, 2009. This is how I learned about the TALA. That night I was dividing my attention between a book, the neighborhood trick-or-treaters, and the television, and I was only half listening as the host, a burly former wedding DJ named Zac Bagans, described every faint drip and creak for the camera. When one of Bagans's fellow ghost hunters suddenly placed his hand over his eye and claimed that a ghost-lobotomist had touched him, however, I started paying attention. An Internet search revealed that before the TALA became one of the nation's premier paranormal tourist attractions, it was known as Weston State Hospital—a name I knew well. In the early 1950s, Weston State Hospital was home to the West Virginia Lobotomy Project, a joint effort between Walter Freeman and the state of West Virginia to use transorbital lobotomy on a massive scale.

In this chapter, I analyze the TALA as a monstrous site and explore lobotomy's role in its affective economy. The monster, writes Jeffrey J. Cohen (1996), is "a breaker of category" (x). A hybrid creature by definition, the monster emerges from the betwixt and the between as a figure of "ontological liminality" (6). For Cohen, since the monster resists classification and order, to give an account of it one must abandon hopes for a neat "dissection-table analysis" and the comforts of teleological argument and diachronic narrative. The analysis of monsters must instead "content itself with fragments" (x). To practice monster theory is to investigate "strings of cultural moments," an approach that "is as much process as epiphany" (6). As such, this chapter focuses on movement rather than stasis, and it is more tour than lecture—or if it is a lecture, then it is a lecture in the spirit of the wandering Peripatetics of ancient Athens.[1] In the first section, I present an account of the hospital's transformation from a place of refuge and healing to a place of squalor and abject misery, situating this shift within the financial and political conditions in which West Virginia turned to mass lobotomy as a solution for hospital overcrowding. I then analyze contemporary tours offered there, with special attention to their representations of lobotomy's history. In the conclusion, building on a reference to Walter Freeman as a "monster" in the TALA museum, I consider the cultural function of the monstrous lobotomist.

The lobotomist was not always a monster, even in popular culture. In 1959, for instance, director Joseph L. Mankiewicz cast Montgomery Clift as the conflicted Dr. Sugar in the adaptation of Tennessee Williams's *Suddenly, Last Summer*, following Williams's original stage directions that the character should be young and "very, very good looking" ([1958] 1998, 5). [2] Fifty years later, in the horror film *Asylum* (2008), the lobotomist has become a decomposing, dead-eyed ghoul who wields leucotomes nearly two feet long, a perfect metaphor for how much the fear of lobotomy has grown in the American imagination. Between the poles of these two characters are the mad scientist Dr. Menken of *A Fine Madness* (1966); Dr. Zaius of *Planet of the Apes* (1968); the invisible hand of matriarchal law in *One Flew over the Cuckoo's Nest* (1975); and even the serial killer Jeffrey Dahmer, who reportedly injected alcohol into the frontal lobes of some of his victims in an effort to create "zombie sex slaves" ("Dahmer Lobotomies" 1992). [3] The lobotomist has become such a familiar monster in the American imagination, in fact, that he is a perennial character in the haunted houses that spring up across the country each October. In 2011, for example, a haunted house in a small Maine town featured a lobotomy room in which a sixteen-year-old lobotomist lurched toward the audience with a power drill and a "menacing smile" (Washuk 2011).

And yet there is nothing *intrinsically* fearful about lobotomies or the doctors who performed them, just as there is nothing intrinsically fearful about the hallways of an empty hospital, even after the sun goes down. Emotions do not reside in objects, people, practices, or places, argues Sarah Ahmed (2004). Emotions become attached to certain objects, people, practices, and places through the circulation of signifiers, which accrue meaning through historicity. Emotions have a "rippling effect": "they move sideways (through 'sticky' associations between signs, figures, and objects) as well as backward . . . 'what sticks' is also bound up with the 'absent presence' of historicity" (Ahmed 2004, 120). The renovation of a decaying psychiatric hospital into a tourist attraction thus involves much more than an expensive piece of real estate and a clever marketing plan. Such a transformation is made possible by a complex network of histories, signs, and affects that lead tourists to pay forty dollars in order to be entertained by their own fear.

There are no naïve tourists, writes anthropologist Edward Bruner (2005). [4] In addition to comfortable shoes, each tourist packs a "pretour narrative" composed of expectations and preconceptions of what a particular site will be like (Bruner 2005; Popp 2010). A pretour narrative is assembled from pieces of cultural texts, like travel shows, guidebooks, brochures, advertisements, television, literature, and film, in which places accrue meaning within larger "master stories" (Bruner 2005, 22). Las Vegas, for example, is familiar to many Americans as a place where sordid good times may be had and concealed from those back home; Australia is portrayed as the exotic outback, jumping with kangaroos. The tourism industry does not create the new. It recreates the familiar. It seeks "new locations in which to tell old stories, possibly because those stories are the ones that the tourist consumer is willing to buy" (Bruner 2005, 22).

Few tourists would be willing to pay forty dollars to walk through an empty hospital in order to look at broken dialysis machines and rusty wheelchairs. The asylum, however—the asylum has its own master story, which has emerged from two centuries of representation in American culture. The asylum exposé, for instance, has become something of a journalistic rite of passage since Nellie Bly spent "Ten Days in a Madhouse" for the *New York World* in 1887. Similar narratives of abuse and neglect flare up every few years it seems, provoke public outrage, and are quickly forgotten. There is a reason that the film *Asylum* is called *Asylum* and not *Hospital*, and it is related to the reason that "Weston State Hospital" became "The Trans-Allegheny Lunatic Asylum" when it reopened in 2008 as a tourist attraction. The asylum is more than just the setting of a narrative—it has become a genre, with conventional plots (the individual versus the institution), themes (the camaraderie of outcasts), characters (the head nurse, the "sane" observer), and props: sedatives, restraints, straitjackets, shock treatments, and, of course, lobotomy (*The Snake Pit; The Bell Jar; One Flew over the Cuckoo's Nest; Girl, Interrupted; Asylum; American Horror Story: Asylum*). Broken hospital beds, abandoned wheelchairs, peeling paint, and the smell of decay only serve to tighten the connection between the TALA and the master narrative in which it finds meaning, bolstering the site's perceived authenticity and satisfying touristic expectations (MacCannell 1999, 100).

"Tourist tales are not fixed, self-contained entities," Bruner explains. "Our stories merge with theirs, genres become blurred, the border between tourism and ethnography becomes porous, and the line between subject and object becomes obscure" (2005, 23). Gathering material for tales is a primary objective of most tourists, whose photographs and souvenirs function as mnemonics for stories later told to others (24). I am no exception. Although I visited the

TALA as a researcher, I was also a tourist, and this chapter is my tourist tale. If postmodernism has taught us anything, it is that one does not choose one's subject position. This does not mean that the TALA, the tours, and the tourists who visit cannot be subject to critique. What it means is that if I criticize the TALA and its tourists, then I am also implicated in that critique. There are no naïve tourists.

Weston State Hospital

> A hospital for the insane should have a cheerful and comfortable appearance, every thing repulsive and prison-like should be carefully avoided. . . . No one can tell how important all of these may prove in the treatment of patients, nor what good effects may result from first impressions thus made upon an invalid on reaching a hospital,—one who perhaps had left home for the first time, and was looking forward to a gloomy, cheerless mansion, surrounded by barren, uncultivated grounds for his future residence, but on his arrival finds every thing neat, tasteful and comfortable.
>
> —THOMAS STORY KIRKBRIDE, *ON THE CONSTRUCTION, ORGANIZATION, AND GENERAL ARRANGEMENTS OF HOSPITALS FOR THE INSANE* (1854)

There are a number of dates, places, events, or people with which a history of Weston State Hospital might begin, but most accounts would place the ideas of the American physician Thomas Story Kirkbride near the beginning of the narrative. Inspired by the moral treatment of Philippe Pinel and Samuel Tuke's Quaker-inspired York Retreat, Kirkbride (also a Quaker) focused his attention on caring for people with mental illness rather than confining them (Tomes 1994).[5] In 1840, Kirkbride became superintendent of the Pennsylvania Hospital for the Insane, and his commitment to moral treatment could be seen in the design of the hospital to its choice of employees, whom Kirkbride described as "attendants" instead of keepers (Whitaker 2002, 32). Kirkbride's influential philosophy of asylum management materialized in a style of asylum architecture in nineteenth-century America known as the Kirkbride Plan, which envisioned the hospital building and grounds as an essential element of a patient's healing. Kirkbride buildings, ornately designed on the outside and opulently furnished on the inside, were constructed to maximize space, sunlight, and fresh air. Unlike asylums that warehoused patients in massive shared dormitories, Kirkbride buildings featured a combination of common and private spaces:

ideally, asylums built according to the Kirkbride plan were to house no more than 250 patients (Kirkbride 1854).

In 1858, the antebellum state of Virginia commissioned a Kirkbride asylum to be built at Weston and chose the idyllic site on the Monongahela River for its easy access to water, coal, and building materials. When the hospital opened its doors to patients in 1863 under the government of the new state of West Virginia, it was known as the "West Virginia Hospital for the Insane," a name it kept until 1915, when it became known as "Weston State Hospital" (Jacks 2008, 13–15).[6] In keeping with the Kirkbride plan, the hospital offered a variety of activities such as billiards and dominoes, and on Friday nights it hosted dances in its ballroom. (During the history tour, our guide noted that Weston's local high school held its prom in the ballroom while the hospital was still in operation.) Patients were encouraged to sew, knit, cook, bake, and work with their hands as forms of occupational therapy, and in good weather, women toured the grounds in a pony-drawn carriage each evening. Photographs of the wards from the late nineteenth and early twentieth centuries depict a place that feels more like a hotel than a hospital. There are plush oriental rugs covering the floors, gauzy curtains on the windows, couches with plumped pillows, vases bursting with freshly cut flowers, and pianos covered in sheet music (see Jacks 2008, 24–25).

As a means of social reform, the Kirkbride plan reflected the "best traits of the American people. It required compassion toward the mentally ill, and a willingness to pay for generous care to help them get well" (Whitaker 2002, 34). The sentiment and, more important, the money, that fueled asylum reform in the nineteenth century, however, did not carry over into the twentieth, as the nation's hospitals began to admit more and more patients without a concomitant increase in state funding. By 1881, the hospital held close to five hundred people (Jacks 2008, 29). By 1921, thirteen hundred patients were crowded into private rooms and common spaces alike. A photograph of a men's ward in 1924 shows a room crowded with at least fifty-five beds, jammed head to foot, with barely enough room to walk between them (Jacks 2008, 72). By 1949, Weston State Hospital's population had swollen to nearly two thousand, and without adequate funding from the state, conditions deteriorated into almost unimaginable suffering for the people who lived there.

In early 1949, the *Charleston Gazette* published an exposé of the West Virginia state hospital system that ran for seventeen straight days on the front page above the fold. The series, researched and written by reporter Charles

Armentrout, revealed the appalling treatment of West Virginia's mentally ill citizens at the hands of their caregivers, and by caregivers, Armentrout clearly meant West Virginians and their elected representatives. The hand-hewn stone walls and well-tended grounds of Weston State Hospital may have been lovely to look at from the outside, Armentrout told his readers, but they also "spared [West Virginians] the sight of what goes on inside" (1949a). Armentrout's tour guide was Weston's superintendent, Joseph L. Knapp, who clearly desired to make the deteriorated state of the hospital known to the residents of the state. "This place is just as good or just as bad as the people of West Virginia want it to be," Knapp told Armentrout, and he "pulled no punches" showing the reporter the worst of the hospital's conditions in order to stimulate reform (1949c).

"'Shocking' is an inadequate word to describe the conditions—or the nauseous smells—in every one of the hospitals," Armentrout wrote in the first story of the series, and the scenes he witnessed were enough to "wring the emotions dry" (1949a). In the ward for "disturbed" women, Superintendent Knapp directed Armentrout to peer inside the room that held the ward's "incontinents." In one six-by-twelve-foot room with concrete floors lit by a single uncovered light bulb, Armentrout observed fifteen women, clad only in shirts, sitting "haunch to haunch." There were no chairs. There was no toilet. "By no stretch of the imagination," Armentrout wrote, could a room like this "be connected with the respectful description of a hospital." Knapp had recently installed tables on this ward; before that, the women had been forced to eat on the floor. Shoeless women wandered across the splintering and rotting floorboards of the hallways, which "oozed up [a] horrible odor" after years of human waste had soaked them through. There was no occupational therapy offered to the women of the disturbed ward nor any therapy at all. The women spent their days doing nothing but pacing the dimly lit, fetid corridors or rocking in the few chairs that weren't broken (1949b).

By 1949, the hospital designed with comfort and privacy in mind had become "crowded beyond the point of human decency," lamented Joseph Terell, president of West Virginia's Board of Control, the state agency charged with overseeing the state's hospitals and penal institutions (Armentrout 1949a). There were seventy patients for every attendant. Children ate and slept with adults. One lavatory serviced sixty-five patients. Hundreds of men and women spent their days confined in straitjackets or chained by their hands, feet, and waist to the walls in "seclusion" rooms. Dozens of patients were housed in a building that the state had condemned five years prior. Bedpans were stacked just a few feet from the dining room. The hospital grounds, envisioned by Thomas Kirkbride as an essential element of a patient's therapy, and that Armentrout suggested "could be used by patients for walks and play in the health-building sunshine," were rarely used—"there just isn't enough trained personnel to guard and supervise them" (1949a). Since the institution was designed to be self-sufficient, the hospital grounds included a dairy barn that supplied the kitchen with its milk. Armentrout commented that the cows appeared well fed and "seem to have the best of everything." "Of course," Superintendent Knapp replied dryly. "If we didn't meet standards, the health department would condemn our milk" (1949c).

After focusing on Weston for four days, on the fifth day of the series, Armentrout turned his attention to the wards for patients deemed "criminally insane" and intensified the power of his rhetorical tour (1949d). If the previous four articles had attempted to sway public sentiment by arousing sympathy for Weston's patients and horror at the conditions in which they lived, the fifth clearly sought to make the condition of state institutions a matter of public safety. The headline reads, "Criminally Insane Roam, Sit—and Plot to Escape," and the piece ominously begins with the image of a door swinging shut and locking. Noting again the lack of resources for these patients, offered no therapy of any kind, Armentrout argued that inadequate funding translated into inadequate staff, which meant that a number of "dangerous mental cases" often managed to escape into the neighboring communities (1949e). Armentrout offered no example of crimes actually committed by patients; instead, he relied on the stereotype of the violent, vicious mental patient to make his case.

On the sixth day of the series, Knapp turned his attention away from Weston to Lakin, a tiny, unincorporated community on the border between West Virginia and Ohio where the small hospital that housed the state's African American patients was located. The conditions at Lakin were as awful as the state's other institutions: poor toilet facilities, inadequate staffing, no therapy, crowded dormitories, and the mingling of children and adults in the same wards. Julius McLeod, a former attendant at Lakin, remembers that at the hospital

[the] budget was a real problem, supplies were a problem—didn't have towels for patients, didn't have clothing for patients. We did not have sheets to cover, to give every person a sheet. Poor folks are the ones end up in most of the mental institutions. If you can afford other kinds of treatments, you don't end up there. (Goodman and Maggio 2008)

As a black institution in the Jim Crow era, Lakin faced a number of additional hardships. One was a stark difference with regard to the appropriation of state funds. In white institutions like Weston, attendants were paid ninety dollars a month. At Lakin, African American attendants were paid seventy-five dollars a month. If the ninety-seven cents allocated per patient per day in white institutions was shockingly low, then the scant seventy-eight cents devoted to the care of patients in Lakin was beyond inhumane. In addition, although Weston State Hospital had a separate building in which patients with tuberculosis were housed, Lakin's patients with tuberculosis lived with the others, and there were no preventative measures taken to stop the spread of the disease.

Armentrout presented these stark inequalities without comment or critique. In fact, just as he relied on the trope of the dangerous mental patient to make the argument that funding Weston was a matter of public safety, he employed racial fear in order to make his case for reform at Lakin. Weaving stereotypes about race and mental illness, the Lakin story is entitled "Escape Is Easy at Lakin for Mentally-Ill Negroes," and it begins with an image of a locked door—the same image as in the story about criminals the day prior. "By failing to furnish Lakin enough money," Armentrout warned his readers, the state not only failed to provide care for its patients but also gave "reason for every free citizen of West Virginia to feel equally apprehensive" (1949e).

Armentrout's exposé appeared at a particularly fortuitous time. Based on advertisements in the paper, the series ran at the same time as *The Snake Pit,* the adaptation of Mary Jane Ward's novel, which electrified audiences with its shocking picture of the miseries of hospital life. More important, the exposé coincided with the first legislative session of the year. Although it is often difficult to find direct evidence for rhetorical efficacy, there is no question that Armentrout's series had its desired effect on the West Virginia legislature. In the middle of the series, the *Gazette* announced that the West Virginia legislature had created a new "humane institutions" subcommittee, which was tasked to investigate the condition of the state's hospitals. After members of the committee "saw, smelled, and were sickened at the depreciation of Weston State hospital and the misery of its inmates," they vowed to take action. "I just hope that those who vote against us will have to come up here and live," declared one representative, who stoutly stated he "would rather help these unfortunate people than be elected president" ("Probers Made Ill" 1949).[7] Eventually, the legislature voted to acquire a 3,500-bed hospital in Martinsburg to ease the crowded conditions in the other institutions (Countian 1949).[8]

Five months after the exposé appeared in the *Gazette*, West Virginia took unprecedented and unparalleled action to deal with the overcrowded conditions of its psychiatric facilities and the resulting strain on the state's finances: it instituted a program of mass transorbital lobotomy. In 1950, Lakin superintendent Simon Johnson invited Walter Freeman to demonstrate the procedure for the hospital staff, an event witnessed by administrators from the Board of Control ("Noted 'Ice Pick' Operation" 1950). Impressed by what they saw, the Board of Control commissioned Freeman to begin a project of what can only be described as the nation's first and only attempt at surgical deinstitutionalization.

The West Virginia Lobotomy Project

Between 1946 and 1960, Walter Freeman toured the hospitals of the United States, performing and demonstrating transorbital lobotomy for psychiatrists and hospital superintendents. In his autobiography, Freeman provided a detailed itinerary for these years, noting that he "put 86,420 miles on my 1954 car, and turned it in August 1956. My Ford 1961 had gone over 200,000 miles in 6 years" (1970, 18–3). On these trips, Freeman made a project of tracking down and cataloging the condition of his previous patients, and he eventually added "several thousand patient-years of follow-up" for thirty-five hundred of his former patients.[9] In reference to his practice of photographing patients from the chest up, Freeman called these trips "head-and-shoulder hunting," recalling that when transorbital lobotomy was at its peak, he "returned with many trophies" (18–2).

The West Virginia Lobotomy Project began in the summer of 1952. In the span of only twelve days, Freeman operated upon 228 patients in the hospitals at Lakin, Huntington, Spencer, and Weston, leading his daughter to quip that one day he would become known as "The Henry Ford of Psychiatry." On one day alone, Freeman operated upon "22 patients in a total of 135 minutes, about six minutes per operation. All of these survived."[10] Perhaps a better term for the project may have been the "West Virginia Lobotomy Experiment," since many of the patients in the West Virginia hospitals did not appear to meet Freeman's own criteria for the operation. The majority of the West Virginia patients appeared to be what Freeman referred to as "deteriorated." Some had lived in West Virginia hospitals for over a decade. Freeman also operated on people with epilepsy, senility, and "mental deficiency," and he noted without comment that "pregnant patients presented no complications" (Freeman et al. 1954, 940).[11]

In an interview with the *Charleston Gazette* in 2009, aide Julius McCleod, who was present during one of Freeman's trips to Lakin, described his feelings about the lobotomist: "I still can't put into words what I felt other than anger and disgust. These people were human, not cattle." As for Freeman, McLeod remembered him as "one of the coldest individuals I've ever met, like ice water. He was mechanical, like he wasn't even human" (quoted in Wells 2009). McCleod does not mention whether he expressed these reservations about Walter Freeman and the operation to hospital administrators.

Of the 228 patients subjected to transorbital lobotomy, 4 died of complications from the surgery. Eighty-five of the surviving patients were able to return home, which led Freeman to claim in a *JAMA* article that he had saved the state of West Virginia nearly forty eight thousand dollars (Freeman et al. 1954, 942). Considering that the cost of the entire project amounted to a mere twenty-three hundred dollars, Freeman presented transorbital lobotomy as an innovative solution to the financial constraints on state hospitals like Weston. Freeman's results once again impressed the West Virginia Board of Control, which funded the project for an additional two years. In total, Freeman performed transorbital lobotomy on 787 patients in West Virginia Hospitals (942). "All in all," as Freeman later wrote to Egas Moniz, he found the West Virginia Lobotomy Project to be a "gratifying experience."[12]

What Freeman did not tell Moniz is that many patients' families did not want their lobotomized family members returned to them. In a particularly troubling article in the *Gazette* in 1952, Charles Armentrout explained that although institution doctors and superintendents deemed a number of men and women to be "much improved" enough to be released, many of their families sent them back. Simon Johnson, Lakin's superintendent, told Armentrout that "it is not an easy task to interest the families of patients who have been hospitalized in a state mental hospital for 10 years or more in having the patient released into their custody, especially since many of them had not visited or written the patients or the hospital for years and when they actually saw the patient, [they] were bewildered" (1952, 4). Although he never directly condemned the state's transorbital lobotomy program, Armentrout made his feelings clear. The tragic situation of patients turned away by their families was only part of what he called the West Virginia Lobotomy Project's "aftermath." Yet unlike Armentrout's exposé three years earlier, which was trumpeted for seventeen days on the front page, this story ran quietly on page 4. I will add that one month before the West Virginia Lobotomy Project began, the *Gazette* ran a wire story entitled "Leading Surgeon Urges Caution in Okaying Lobotomy Operation." In the article, the eminent neurosurgeon Ernest Sachs decried the use of lobotomy as a "vogue" and stated that he believed that the surgery was being "greatly overdone." This story ran on page 40, quietly tucked between advertisements for bourbon and typewriters.

The Trans-Allegheny Lunatic Asylum

In 2007, the sprawling grounds and deteriorating buildings of Weston Hospital were purchased for one and a half million dollars by Joe Jordan, a Morgantown building contractor who specializes in asbestos removal. When the Jordan family announced their intention to reopen the hospital as a tourist attraction called the Trans-Allegheny Lunatic Asylum, a number of disability advocacy organizations, including the Morgantown Center for Independent Living, the West Virginia Mental Health Consumers Association, and WV-ADAPT, were outraged, and they picketed the TALA in protest. The groups objected to a motorcycle event called "Psycho Path"; the frightening images of mental illness featured in the TALA's promotional materials; and the family's decision to hold ghost hunts, paranormal tours, and annual haunted houses on the premises (Wickline 2008; Finn 2008).

Disability groups also protested the site's name change. Although Virginia had initially commissioned the hospital as the "Trans-Allegheny Lunatic Asylum" in the nineteenth century, the name was never used when patients actually lived there. "It's one thing to say yes, that was the name of it when it was built," commented disability activist Scott Miller, "but to call it [the Trans-Allegheny Lunatic Asylum] now is saying, all of the reasons why it was changed are flushed down the toilet" (quoted in Finn 2008). According to the owners and operators of the TALA, the name change reflects their desire to accurately depict the institution's history, a form of discursive preservation in line with their intention to preserve the hospital, which likely would have been torn down had they not intervened. (Proposals to turn the hospital grounds into a casino, hotel, or convention center were determined to be expensive and unrealistic, particularly since Weston is located hours from West Virginia's largest cities.) According to the TALA's critics, however, the name change capitalizes on negative connotations of the term "lunatic," which they feel reinforces the stigma of mental illness. In response to these objections, Rebecca Jordan-Gleason, the TALA's operations manager, has encouraged disability activists to attend their public preservation meetings and to take one of the TALA's historical tours:

"when they come and visit and see what we're doing, they don't have a problem" (quoted in Ward 2008).

The Historical Tour

As I drive onto the grounds of the TALA, the first thing that catches my eye is a trailer with brightly colored lights, which offers French fries and cheese steaks in front of the building that once housed Weston's patients with tuberculosis (fig. 5). It is the kind of food truck one usually finds on a carnival midway. The main building, now simply called "the Kirkbride" by tour guides, is a massive and beautiful building, beautiful, that is, despite the fact that many of the windows have at least one hole, courtesy of Weston's teenagers. Later, one of the tour guides explains that it is difficult to keep curious thrill seekers out of the building, which has no security system. I am struck again by irony: an institution that once worked diligently to keep people in was now having a hard time keeping them out.

Entering the building through the main door of the Kirkbride, one passes by the former office of the hospital superintendent. On a table outside the admissions desk-*cum*-ticket office sits a stack of legal forms that release the TALA's owners from liability (considering the peeling sheets of ancient paint and crumbling floor tiles, ghosts are the least frightening unseen entities floating around the hospital). On the table is an emergency room register-*cum*-guestbook. Taped on the wall above the table is a slightly wrinkled, laser-printed sheet of pink paper entitled "People with Mental Illness Enrich Our Lives," which lists a number of historical figures and celebrities next to their diagnoses in no particular chronological order: Janet Jackson, Edgar Allen Poe, Sarah McLachlan, Ezra Pound. There is also a large professionally printed placard with photographs of "Famous People with Mental Illness," which seconds the pink paper's point that people with mental illness are among our most celebrated. The poster adheres to the same categorical illogic as the pink paper: next to a famous photograph of Kurt Cobain is a picture of Rodney Dangerfield holding a boom box, hat cocked to the side, with the words "Rappin' Rodney." These lists and pictures appear to function as a preemptive answer to ethical questions that hang heavy in the air, but the answer they provide is not particularly persuasive.

On historical tours of the hospital grounds, visitors are invited to learn "about the pioneers of humane treatment for the mentally ill" and "the history

Fig. 5. The Trans-Allegheny Lunatic Asylum, 2012. (Photograph by the author.)

of medical treatments performed in asylums" (tala.com). Historical tours of the TALA are offered on Tuesday through Sunday from the end of March to the last day in October. For ten dollars, visitors may take the shorter tour of the first floor of the Kirkbride building, and for thirty dollars, visitors may take an extended tour, which covers all four floors of the Kirkbride, doctors' and nurses' private apartments, and the first floor of the Medical Center, which includes the hospital's morgue and operating room.

As I wait for the historical tour to begin (I opt for the longest version), I explore a number of rooms on the first floor of the Kirkbride that function as the TALA's museum. One room features drawings, paintings, and poetry created by patients in art therapy programs in the late twentieth century. Some pictures are cheery; some are cheeky (one pencil drawing depicts a man with veined eyes, a wry smile, and the words "don't annoy the crazy person"); and some are unbearably sad, like an embroidery sample with the words "Home Is Where the Heart Is." The ambiance of the art room is enhanced by a small portable stereo, which broadcasts the soft tinkling of a piano and the distinctive voice of Daniel Johnston, a musician involuntarily committed to Weston Hospital shortly before it closed.

Next to the art room is a space devoted to medical treatments and restraints, including a number of artifacts: an antique electroconvulsive therapy machine, a restraint chair, a straitjacket, and a large hydrotherapy tub in which a full-sized mannequin, covered with cloths and towels, grimaces at visitors. The mannequin looks as though it could double as a prop in the haunted house in the adjoining building, and I am warned by a tour guide not to "freak out" when I see it. In this room, there are two placards that tell the story of lobotomy and the biography of Walter Freeman, and the latter is positioned next to a small television that plays the 2009 PBS documentary *The Lobotomist* on repeat. Underneath the placards is a hospital gurney. In a Plexiglas box on the gurney's tray is an ice pick, which a card notes was purchased from an asylum in Massachusetts. Above the ice pick are the words "PLEASE DO NOT TOUCH!" The display clearly implies that the ice pick was used as a lobotomy tool; however, considering that the only patient documented to have received an ice pick lobotomy was Sallie Ellen Ionesco, I am fairly certain that the pick on display was used for ice only. There is neither a leucotome nor a scalpel on display.

The historical tour commences at noon, and it lasts for nearly two hours. Our guide is in her early twenties.[13] Like all TALA historical tour guides, she wears a reproduction of a nineteenth-century nurse's outfit, which consists of a blue dress covered by a white apron and a matching white cap. As we enter the patient wards, I notice that the walls of the men's ward are blue and the women's are pink, and each features hundreds of tiny, stenciled designs that give the effect of wallpaper. After learning the walls were painstakingly stenciled by residents, I find myself hunting for traces of the people who once called the TALA home. On the empty nameplate next to one room, I find small stickers of animals. In another room, I locate a man's sleeping schedule still tacked to the wall. The blue and pink paint peels in strips from the plaster, which is crumbling due to substantial water infiltration. It is raining on the day I visit, and the sound of dripping water echoes throughout the buildings. The loneliness of the place is overwhelming.

As she walks, our guide tells us stories about the hospital's connection to the Civil War and the splitting of the state into Virginia and West Virginia; she directs our attention to architectural features unique to the Kirkbride plan; she points out marks on the stairways where patients dragged their feet in a "Thorazine shuffle" as they moved from floor to floor; she explains the typical living situations for staff and patients and details about the hospital's daily operation; and she tells us stories about murders and arsons that took place within the hospital's walls. Our guide is herself guided by laminated signs that serve as partial scripts for the tour stories: "Self-Sufficient," "Thomas Kirkbride," "Dorothea Dix," and then, as we reach the end of the "violent" men's ward, I see "Lobotomies—Ice Pick—Walter Freeman—18,000 lobotomies performed from 1938–1951—Thousands in Europe last in 1967." I make a note: "explains the ice pick in the museum."

At this point, our guide pauses for our longest stop on the tour. In a rough chronology, she details a number of treatments used in the hospital, beginning with hydrotherapy, a brief description of insulin shock therapy, and a more lengthy description of electroconvulsive therapy. And then she takes a deep breath. "In my opinion," she explains, "the worst treatment was the transorbital, or ice pick lobotomy, which would take violent people and . . . turn them into vegetables." She briefly describes Walter Freeman and the prefrontal operation and explains that the transorbital lobotomy decreased operating time from two hours to "between two to five minutes." After telling the group that Freeman toured the state of West Virginia, she notes, in a statement that feels uncomfortably close to pride, that Weston "holds the record for the most lobotomies performed in a single day."[14] She asks the group to imagine the hallway crowded with people who would "attack you the minute you turned your back on them," who, after surgery, would spend their days quietly sitting in their rooms. Although this might sound like a good thing, she explains, after lobotomy "they weren't anyone anymore. Everything unique, everything different about them, [had been] taken away in seconds" (field notes).[15] In line with most historians, our guide explains that lobotomy disappeared with the introduction of Thorazine.

To close her history, our guide ends with a practiced aside. Although she has "repeated these stories hundreds of times," she tells us, she tries to stay "optimistic" and asks that before judging the doctors who performed lobotomy, we should keep in mind that this "was all they knew back then." She wonders if future generations will remember chemotherapy in the same way that we now remember lobotomy. "Now I will get off my soapbox," she concludes and continues the tour.

We continue walking through the Kirkbride, through the seclusion rooms (one of which still has anchors in the wall to which patients were chained by their hands and feet) and day rooms, through the cafeteria (which doubled as the pharmacy, with labels for Thorazine and Haldol still visible on the shelves), through the courtyard (where I notice the rusty remains of a swing set for residents' children), and into the building with the hospital's medical center. The medical center once housed an operating room, a morgue, and, in what feels like a nod to the history of surgery, the hospital's barbershop. The medical center is even more deteriorated than the Kirkbride. It is dark and smells strongly of mildew. After visiting the morgue, we walk to the operating room, where, our guide explains, the lobotomies at the hospital were performed. Since the room is covered by an inch of water, our guide gives us the option of remaining in the hallway. I hike my pants to the ankle and step inside the room in which Walter Freeman once worked.

The room is empty, save an overturned stool. Yellow paint has peeled away to reveal bricks and mortar. There are a number of large windows, and it is by far the brightest room on the first floor of the medical center. I notice that a curtain frames each window, and, although faded by age and water damage, tiny flowers are still visible on each of them. I have no idea (nor does our guide, who seems confused by the question) how old the curtains are. These curtains are etched in my memory of the TALA, not as a visible reminder of the failed promise of the Kirkbride plan; not as a "beauty in the ruins" cliché; not as a metaphor for anything. I remember them simply because they were so unexpected as to be jarring. The delicately curtained windows of the lobotomy room simply were not part of my pretour narrative.

Edward Bruner writes that one of the limitations of the pretour narrative is that like any story, there are elements that are omitted—what he calls the "touristic untold" (2005, 23). The touristic untold are those people, things, and places that remain in the background (exploited labor, for example) but also stories about a site that remain unsaid. The absent, the silent, the suppressed, the untold: these elements are as important to understanding a site's meaning as the elements made present for the tourist audience. Phaedra Pezzullo (2007) applies this dialectic between absent and present to the tourist site's function as a cultural mnemonic. By presenting elements as significant enough to be remembered, Pezzullo argues, the tour also makes absent those aspects "that are acceptable to forget" (41).

I notice, then, those persons and things in Weston State Hospital's history that are absent on the historical tour of the TALA. Although Thorazine is mentioned, Haldol and lithium are not, even though these drugs were prescribed at the hospital. Although electroconvulsive therapy is worthy of remembrance, Metrazol shock—by many accounts one of the most feared and painful somatic treatments in asylum psychiatry—is not. Nor is psychotherapy mentioned during the discussion of medical treatments, although many more patients received talk therapy and group therapy over the course of the hospital's history than received lobotomies. Although Robert Byrd—a hero to many West Virginians—is described as a key figure in our guide's brief discussion of the hospital reforms of the early 1950s, Charles Armentrout is not. And while Walter Freeman features prominently in the history of lobotomy at the TALA, Joseph Knapp does not, even though he performed a number of transorbital operations at Weston State Hospital before Freeman began his work on the West Virginia Lobotomy Project. It was Knapp, in fact, who introduced transorbital lobotomy to West Virginia hospitals in 1948 after Freeman persuaded him to do so (Freeman 1970, 14–14). Knapp became so proficient at the procedure that he gave the first demonstration of transorbital lobotomy in Texas during the 1948 meeting of the Southern Psychiatric Association, where he performed more than twenty operations.[16]

The historical tour highlights features of the TALA's history that visitors clearly have heard about and focuses on the medical marvels (lobotomy, electroconvulsive therapy, straitjackets, Thorazine) that populate the American imagination of the asylum. Although other treatments at the hospital may have been used with greater frequency, it is lobotomy that is elevated to prominence in our guide's history of medical treatments, not only because lobotomy's history in the United States significantly intersects with the history of the TALA but also because lobotomy looms large in any asylum pretour narrative.

The Paranormal Tours

As one would expect, the TALA paranormal tours begin once the sun begins to set behind the West Virginia hills. At dusk, workers switch on large sodium lights not unlike those you would find on a football field, and their ghostly glow can be seen from across town. They are assisted by the blinking colored lights of the food trucks, which serve a variety of fried delicacies to those waiting for their tours to begin. On paranormal tours of the hospital, visitors are invited to "step back in time and see how the mentally insane lived, and died, within these walls. . . . Decide for yourself if they're still occupying the historic wards and treatment rooms" (tala.com). The primary paranormal tour lasts for two to three hours and combines a walking tour of the Kirkbride building by flashlight with ghost stories and attempts at what might loosely be called séances. There are options for overnight stays in the building, and one may also hire a tour guide in order to conduct a private ghost hunt. Because of the demand for the paranormal tours, particularly during the month of October, one must purchase tickets well in advance. In October, the TALA also features a haunted house in the tuberculosis building, which changes themes each year. In 2011, it is entitled "Bedlam." The poster (available for purchase in the gift shop next to t-shirts, coffee mugs, and local beef jerky) features a large man in a bloody butcher's outfit who menaces the viewer with an oversized meat cleaver.

As I retrieve the tickets for the first of my two paranormal tours, my eye is drawn to the three-by-five-foot poster board that screams WARNING in a blood-red, dripping font and lists a number of medical conditions that would prompt the TALA to refuse admission to "Bedlam." Heart conditions, respiratory conditions (including asthma), and seizure disorders are all disqualifying conditions for entry, as are "physical limitations" (including crutches and casts). There is no mention of tuberculosis. And in yet another of the many ironies of the TALA, one is denied admission to what was once West Virginia's largest psychiatric facility if one is currently suffering from "any form of mental illness."

The first paranormal tour I take is the "lobotomy flashlight tour," which lasts for forty minutes and is advertised as "half historic/half paranormal." Waiting for the tour to start, I wait outside the Kirkbride building with a group of five other people. My fellow tourists largely hail from neighboring towns in West Virginia (a large map close to the ticket desk indicates that visitors have come to the TALA from across the United States). As I chat with the people in line, I learn that none attended the historical tours, but most have visited "Bedlam."

When the doors open at seven p.m., our tour guide, Greg Graham, a forty-something white man with long red hair who goes by the name "Copperhead," invites us into the Kirkbride building, which by now is completely dark, save the light that filters in through the windows from the sodium lights outside. Copperhead walks our group of six through the hallways of the Kirkbride wards with a flashlight as he recounts experiences with ghosts he has encountered here, and it soon becomes clear that the lobotomy flashlight tour is more paranormal than historical. In one room Copperhead tells us about the ghost of a little girl the TALA guides call "Lilly." In the time between the history tour and the paranormal tour, guides have placed a number of rubber balls in this room for Lilly's ghost to move around. We wait for a few minutes, eyes fixed on the

Fig. 6. The Trans-Allegheny Lunatic Asylum, 2012. (Photograph by the author.)

balls, but they do not move. We leave and continue walking through the wards, stopping in one room where Copperhead recounts a particularly gruesome story of the murder of one patient by two others. And then we reach a large open room. Here, Copperhead stops:

> This area here would have been the lobotomy recovery room. Beds would have been lying down through here, and rows and rows of beds up through here and against the wall. And Doctor Walter Freeman, do you know who he was? Well, the lobotomy was about a thirty-second procedure. They'd either come in through the eye, right beside the eye, or they'd come up through the nose, and they'd tap, tap, tap. It looked basically like an ice pick—that's why they call it an ice pick lobotomy. And they'd run it up into your frontal lobe, and they'd scramble the frontal lobe. Basically, it made the perfect patient. They could bathe themselves, clean themselves, um, communicate, uh—but they had no emotions.
> MAN: What's that noise?
> [Silence, as the group listens intently.]

WOMAN: That's dripping water.

GRAHAM: But anyway, um, later on—late fifties, early sixties, they quit that procedure because, basically, they said they were stealing their souls. Which, basically, they were.[17]

Copperhead's lobotomy history contains a number of similarities to the historical tour, but also some noteworthy differences. On the historical tour, lobotomy is described as a two-to-five-minute procedure; on the paranormal tour, the time is shortened to thirty seconds. On the historical tour, our guide explained that doctors went through the orbital plate; on the paranormal tour, Copperhead includes an additional route through the nose. On the historical tour, Thorazine is presented as the cause of lobotomy's decline; on the paranormal tour, doctors are said to have abandoned the operation because they realized their colleagues were stealing patients' souls. Although the histories of lobotomy presented on the TALA's historical tour and the first paranormal tour do not necessarily match up with medical histories of the procedure, neither presents an egregiously "wrong" history of lobotomy. Even Copperhead's soul-stealing description of lobotomy can be found in medical discourse (Rylander 1948).

Tours are not simply forms of entertainment; many also serve a pedagogical function (Pezzullo 2007). What do we learn about lobotomy on these tours? Each account of lobotomy concludes with a moral, but each moral is the conclusion to a different lesson. The explanation of lobotomy's demise on the paranormal tour casts the lobotomists in a decidedly diabolical role— as stealers of souls—who are stopped when "they" (presumably the medical profession) become wise to the evil actions of their colleagues. In this history of lobotomy, the medical profession is disidentified with procedure, and thus emerges as a hero for putting an end to the practice. Although the atmosphere of the paranormal tour is designed to be frightening, this version of lobotomy's history is oddly comforting, as we are able to clearly distinguish between what happened *then* and what happens *now* and between what happened to *them* and what happens to *us*. The moral from the historical tour, however, which asks visitors to reflect critically on contemporary medical practice, is decidedly *less* comforting than the moral provided on the paranormal tour. In this moral, in which our guide asks us not to judge the lobotomists but to see them in a larger historical context, we are asked to reflect on the limits of contemporary medical knowledge and practice.

The final paranormal tour begins at ten p.m. and lasts for over three hours. Once again, our tour leader is Greg "Copperhead" Graham. Our group of ten is comprised of avid ghost hunters—one is wearing a *Ghost Adventures* t-shirt—and many have brought their own equipment: low-light cameras, voice recorders, dowsing rods, and smart phones with paranormal apps. Based on what I had seen on *Ghost Adventures* and experienced on the lobotomy flashlight tour only three hours earlier, I expected lobotomy to figure prominently on this tour. However, during the three hours, neither Copperhead nor any of my fellow tourists mentioned the operation, perhaps because tours were not allowed in the medical center at night due to its deteriorated condition or perhaps because this tour was designed to be less discursive and more experiential.

On this tour, Copperhead leads our group to various paranormal "hot spots" around the hospital. At each site, he attempts to converse with ghosts he only described on the flashlight lobotomy tour: the murdered patient, two men who committed suicide, Lilly's ghost in the room with the rubber balls. Copperhead begins each conversation by imploring the ghosts to speak to him, and when he begins to offer them candy, the tour starts to feel a little like a visit to a paranormal zoo. In each room we stand and sometimes sit in a circle, eyes fixed on Copperhead's ghost-hunting equipment and unwrapped pieces of candy, nervous chatter giving way to contemplative silence as we invite the ghosts to make themselves known. Yet time and time again, in the darkened rooms and hallways, there is only silence—interrupted by the occasional sound of dripping water and the rapid breathing of the living.

In the room devoted to medical treatments in the TALA's museum, there is a large placard with a photograph and brief biography of Walter Freeman. It outlines his family history, his work in the pathology laboratory at St. Elizabeth's Hospital, the inspiration he received from Egas Moniz, his partnership with James Watts, his development of the transorbital procedure, his involvement in the West Virginia Lobotomy Project, and his failed operation on Rosemary Kennedy. Immediately after the reference to Kennedy, the placard concludes:

> For this and other failures, Freeman was discredited by the medical profession and lost his license to practice in hospitals. He spent the remainder of his life seeking redemption, pathetically traveling around the country trying to locate his former patients whose lives he could prove he improved. He died of colon

cancer in 1972 at the age of 76. Today Freeman is regarded by many as a monster, an American Mengele.

This biography of Freeman offers tourists more than history—it offers a packaged judgment on lobotomy's history and Freeman's role within it, positioning Freeman next to Joseph Mengele, Auschwitz-Birkenau's infamous "Angel of Death." In this brief biography, Freeman is also painted as a tragic figure, seeking "redemption" for the sins he committed against the brains of his fellow Americans.

Yet Freeman saw his cross-country travels not as redemption, but as research, and if he saw himself as a tragic character in his own story, it is because he believed he and the operation he had championed had been misunderstood. In the last pages of his autobiography, Freeman describes his hope that one day the hospitals of West Virginia would stand as a "monument to the success of lobotomy" (1970, 18–30), not as evidence of its failure. Freeman's choice of "monument" to describe his work in West Virginia is revealing, but for reasons he probably did not intend. Although the root of the word "monument" derives from the Latin *monere*, which means "to remind," *monere* also means "to warn." It is this sense of *monere* from which we get the word "monster."

Monsters are more than just embodiments of fear. Like a tour guide, one of the monster's many cultural functions is that of pedagogue, and the story of the monster's origin is invariably a cautionary tale. For example, in Shelley's *Frankenstein*, the archetypal monster story, the monster warns the reader of the perils of scientific hubris. As many teachers of Shelley know, however, Frankenstein and his monster have merged so thoroughly in the cultural imagination that the monster and Frankenstein have become one. For contemporary audiences, Frankenstein is the monster of the story, and his becoming-monster serves as a lesson for those who dare follow in his footsteps. To be remembered as monstrous is the worst kind of punishment—a social death that endures long after the body is gone.

The similarities between monsters and monuments do not end with their common etymology. Both offer lessons that shore up the moral boundaries and social norms of civil society:

The monster . . . is both symptom of civic distress as well as antidote. It represents un-normalcy as well as enacting—and exacting—correctness. It writes fear as well as desire into the social text. As a consequence, while repudiated on one hand, monsters are invariably recuperated as titillating thrill and entertainment on the other—a fascinating reminder that transgression, at least in some form, must be legislated. (Ingebretsen 1998, 29)

As Ingebretsen observes, our fear of the monster comingles with our desire for it. If we did not desire the monstrous lobotomist in some way, we would not continue writing his character into our culture. But this desire is not a desire *for* the monster as much as it is a desire for its punishment, a desire to right what has been wronged, to restore the boundaries that have been crossed. The monster exists in part to be staked, Ingebretsen argues, and the monster's staking entertains us because it offers, like the conclusion of the lobotomy history told on the TALA's paranormal tour, a certain measure of comfort. We take comfort because the lesson Dr. Monster teaches is not necessarily for those of us on the tour. We take comfort because Dr. Monster's lesson is a warning for the medical profession.

EPILOGUE

Haunted History

> To be haunted, to write from that location, to take on the condition of
> what you study, is not a methodology or a consciousness you can simply
> adopt or adapt as a set of rules or an identity; it produces its own insights
> . . . Following the ghosts is about making a contact that changes you and
> refashions the social relations in which you were located.
>
> —AVERY GORDON, *GHOSTLY MATTERS: HAUNTING AND THE*
> *SOCIOLOGICAL IMAGINATION* (2008)

During my first trip to the Freeman and Watts archive at George Washington
University, I immersed myself in Walter Freeman's writings and personal effects:
his memoirs; drafts of articles and presentations; poems about the frontal lobes
and poems about his beard; photographs of the doctor in surgical scrubs, hiking
in the California woods, and smiling with his family. I sifted through several
dozen Christmas cards from Freeman's patients and their families—the same
cards he once dumped on a table at the Langley Porter clinic as evidence of
his success and proof of their gratitude, an event I discuss in chapter 1. Each
card is carefully labeled with the letters "LOB" and what I presume is a number
corresponding to their position in Freeman's operational queue. LOB 29. LOB
48. LOB 201. The cards and letters are overwhelmingly positive and cheerful—in
the many dozens preserved in the archive, only a handful express dissatisfaction
with Freeman or the operation they or their loved ones received. "To my Doctor,"
one patient wrote in neat script on a Valentine's Day card. On the front Freeman
printed: LOB 64. I watched film of the prefrontal surgery and took notes as I
listened to Freeman's deep voice describing the process in detail. I examined the
Freeman family ice pick and felt its cold heft in my hands, running my finger
over the dents in the tip.

Archival work is embodied work. Making contact with artifacts engages the
senses in a way that making contact with digital images does not, or at least

not yet (Turkel 2001). Eve Kosofsky Sedgwick (2003) has described an intimacy between textures and emotions (17), and it may be the act of touching these objects—making physical contact with them with our bare, or white-gloved, hands—that provokes such strong feelings about archival work. Of course, research and writing in general elicit any number of emotions: the wonder and curiosity that drive us forward, the choking fear of failure, the excitement at finding something new. The feelings evoked by archival work, however, are of a different kind: more personal, and somehow more urgent. A number of rhetorical historians have described these complex emotions, such as the guilty pleasure involved in rummaging through someone else's private stuff never meant for public consumption (Bergmann 2010). Although I had prepared for my trip to the archive in many ways and looked forward to the thrill of physically encountering its contents, I found myself utterly unprepared for the particular emotional impact it had on me.

Toward the end of my stay, I noticed a peculiar feeling I couldn't seem to identify—or shake. Back in my hotel room one evening, rereading portions of Freeman's memoir, I was suddenly struck by what it was. At the end of one chapter, Freeman estimated that 10 percent of patients in American hospitals could be helped by the operation he had championed until the end of his life. "But nobody else sees it that way," he wrote, "and it is very doubtful whether I shall ever be given the chance to prove my point" (1970, 14–26). With a shock, I realized that I had been feeling sadness—for Walter Freeman. As someone just starting my career, I was sympathizing with the end of his; touching the traces of Walter Freeman's life, I had humanized a man that so many consider a monster. That is what the power of leaning in and listening to someone's voice, for so many days—really *listening*—can do. To touch is to risk being touched.

A number of rhetorical historians have commented on the "passionate attachments" we develop toward subjects of historical research (Royster 1995; Bizzell 2000). Elizabeth Birmingham (2008) has described this process as "befriending" our subjects, and she describes the rhetorical historian's "sixth sense" not as the ability to see the dead, but "to help the dead, who do not know they are dead, finish their stories, and we do this in the moment that we realize their stories are ours" (144). I imagine this identification must be a positive experience when one's subject is an underappreciated woman architect, in Birmingham's case, or Ida B. Wells, in Jacqueline Jones Royster's case, but what does one do with identification and empathy when one's subject is one of the most reviled figures in American medical history?

I reflected on this uncomfortable feeling for a few moments, and then I kept reading. On the same page where Freeman lamented the loss of his reputation, he extolled his success by pointing to his "adolescents in distress," claiming that six out of seven were out of the hospital and doing well. With a jolt of recognition, I realized that one of those adolescents was Howard Dully. I briefly wondered if Freeman thought Howard was doing well or if he considered him to be the seventh, who wasn't. Then I had a powerful thought: Howard Dully was the seventh, no matter what Walter Freeman might have believed. And at that point, my sadness—and my identification—shifted. I hadn't listened to the NPR documentary since hearing it the first time in 2005, but that night in the hotel I found a copy online, and I listened to Howard Dully's baritone voice again. And then I listened a second time, frequently wiping my eyes. We may not choose our emotions or our attachments, but once we recognize them, we can cultivate them in certain ways.

The summer of my first visit to the archive, I was undergoing psychiatric treatment for depression. Each morning before walking to the DC metro, getting coffee, and making my way to the Special Collections reading room, like millions of other Americans, I took one pill to mitigate my sadness, and each evening before I crawled into bed, I swallowed another to dampen my fear and anxiety. As I read through case histories of Freeman and Watts's patients that week, it was not lost on me that many of their symptoms were identical to my own, but I hadn't given it much thought. I was far too busy recreating Walter Freeman's life in my notebook. After the night above, however, I found myself slowing down and searching for traces of these people, poring over their writing (which, due to privacy restrictions, I am not allowed to reproduce here). I ran my fingers over the raised letters of a Christmas card, the creases of a pencil drawing of John F. Kennedy, and the soft frayed edges of a letter I imagined must have been kept for some time in someone's pocket.

I was particularly drawn to one letter, written by a woman who told Freeman of her intense anxiety and asked for drugs not unlike those flowing through my bloodstream as I read her words. She dug pen into paper with such force that each letter was clearly palpable on the back of the page, a performative braille of desperation. I sat with that letter for a long time. Later, reading one of Freeman's articles, I learned that the woman died of a "barbiturate overdose" just a few years after writing the letter.

In the years since, I have often thought of this woman, as well as Alice Hammatt, Sallie Ellen Ionesco, Rosemary Kennedy, Howard Dully, and the thousands of other unnamed people whose lives were changed by this operation. I thought of them when I told my doctor that the drugs I was taking were making me feel worse rather than better. I thought of them in the empty halls and in the operating room of the former Weston State Hospital. I thought of them while reading descriptions of the "wild" women and emasculated men in the popular press. I thought of them while reading Walter Freeman's claims of success. These women and men continue to haunt me.

To follow ghosts, as Avery Gordon writes, is to "write stories that not only repair representational mistakes, but also strive to understand the conditions under which a memory was produced in the first place, toward a countermemory, for the future" (2008, 22). With this book, I have attempted to understand the conditions in which lobotomy emerged as a medical marvel, and I have explored the impact of that marvelous history. Yet there is something missing in this story and in all histories of lobotomy: tens of thousands of stories that will never be told. Those stories, and the faces, voices, and lives behind them, haunt this story as they haunt all histories. Histories are intrinsically rhetorical. They select and interpret a certain reality for their audiences, and each time something is made present, something is made absent by default.

"Haunting," Gordon writes, "is about how to transform a shadow of a life into an undiminished life whose shadows touch softly in the spirit of a peaceful reconciliation" (2008, 208). While I agree with this impulse, I'm afraid that I cannot—nor would I want to—offer this kind of comforting conclusion. The rhetorical perspective is that of the nomad; rhetoric emerges in uncertainty, and it thrives in flux; rhetoric flourishes in *aporia* and doubt rather than finality; rhetoricians relish conversations that never end (Burke 1941, 110–111). And so while I believe that "wrong" stories about lobotomy have much to teach us about the powerful connections between medicine and the meanings of medicine in the broader culture, I do not disagree with the impulse to shape a different meaning of lobotomy for the future or even the impulse to repair "representational mistakes." After all, our meanings change according to our purposes. Thus far, psychiatrists, neurologists, neurosurgeons, hospital superintendents, politicians, activists, bioethicists, journalists, novelists, filmmakers, historians, and now a rhetorician have had a hand in crafting the meaning of lobotomy. However, I hope it is Howard Dully who shapes lobotomy's meaning in the future and who helps to repair our inevitable representational mistakes—not necessarily because his is a more accurate account than ours but because it is more important.

NOTES

Introduction

1. I use the term "public culture" to refer to public discourse and popular culture: literature, film, poetry, journalism, political discourse, etc. See Hariman and Lucaites 2007, 13–14.

2. Although Moniz was the first to develop the procedure that came to be called "lobotomy" (his preferred term was "leucotomy") others had tread—albeit tentatively—in this area before him, most notably Gottlieb Burckhardt in the nineteenth century. For a detailed history of the early development of psychosurgery, see J. Pressman 1999, 46–147.

3. For example, lobotomy was used to treat actor Warner Baxter's chronic arthritic pain ("Warner Baxter" 1951), and it was recently revealed that Eva Perón was lobotomized a few months before she died of cervical cancer (Nijensohn et al. 2012). But even when lobotomy was used to treat physical pain, the primary objective was the same: to dampen the emotional response to pain, rather than changing the sensation itself (Freeman and Watts 1950, 353–374). For more on lobotomy and pain, see Raz 2009.

4. Exact numbers regarding the extent of lobotomy's use in the United States are difficult to come by. A 1951 survey of psychosurgery in state hospitals (Kramer 1954) estimates the total at roughly twenty thousand, although the number is likely higher than that.

5. Tragically, Jack Pressman died before *Last Resort* was published and never had the chance to see the accolades it rightly received.

6. For more on the cultural meaning of conjoined twins, see Wu 2012 and Samuels 2011.

7. Ambroise Paré's *On Monsters and Marvels,* for example, a sixteenth-century taxonomy of extraordinary humans and animals, interprets bodily difference as a sign from the divine.

8. Although unambiguity is a discursive norm in science writing, its texts do not necessarily function this way. For an illuminating study of how polysemy may be deployed as a rhetorical strategy by scientists writing for a broad audience, see Ceccarelli 2001.

9. Erving Goffman (1963) has described this contagion as "courtesy stigma," in

which the problems faced by stigmatized people affect those they come into contact with "in waves of diminishing intensity" (30).

10. I recognize that not every historian feels this way. Many critically astute historians and historiographers have troubled this very idea.

11. In many ways, my notion of marvel resembles Michael Calvin McGee's (1980) concept of the "ideograph." McGee identifies ideographs, ordinary terms like "rule of law" or "equality" commonly found in political discourse, as the linguistic trace of a dominant ideology (14). McGee is clear that ideographs are terms of "high order abstraction" (15)—phrases like "freedom of speech" and words like "equality." As McGee puts it, "no one has ever seen an 'equality' strutting up the driveway" (10). Although no one has ever seen a surgical procedure strutting anywhere, and although I will discuss the many ways in which lobotomy came to function as metaphor, to call the surgery a "high order" abstraction is a bad fit, and as a constitutive methodology for this book, I find the ideograph's commitment to abstraction and ideological analysis to be too limited in scope.

12. A good example is Kim Nielsen's (2004) political biography of Helen Keller. Although Nielsen is a historian by training, her book explores Keller's biography alongside the many cultural meanings her "many lives" accrued.

13. Baty draws the term "representative character" from the work of Robert Bellah, Richard Madsen, William Sullivan, Ann Swidler, and Steven Tipton (1985). In their definition, the representative character is a "public image that helps define, for a given group of people, just what kinds of personality traits it is good and legitimate to develop. A representative character provides an ideal, a point of reference and focus, that gives living expression to a vision of life" (39).

Chapter 1

1. For a longer account of Hammatt's surgery, see El-Hai 2005, 7–15. Although Alice Hammatt is referred to in the lobotomy literature as "Case 1," she is mentioned by name in Walter Freeman's memoirs as well as El-Hai's biography of Freeman. I have included her full name in this chapter, as well as Sallie Ellen Ionesco's, because their names are public information.

2. The pages in Freeman's unpublished memoir, "Adventures in Lobotomy" (1970), are not numbered in sequence. All in-text citations to this work therefore employ both chapter and page number.

3. In large part, our distrust of emotions emerges from the idea that they are out of our control—we feel that emotions act on us, that they are not *of* us. *Pathein* in Greek means *to suffer*—and while suffering is often characterized as pain or illness, it might also be thought of as an *undergoing*. To have emotion is to be affected, acted on, passive (which also has roots in *pathos*) (Ahmed 2004, 2).

4. In 2007, in a plan that could have been scripted from the oeuvre of Michel

Foucault, the US government proposed to relocate the Department of Homeland Security to the abandoned western campus, a move that has been met with considerable opposition from historical preservationists.

5. Jacobsen later wrote that one of the chimpanzees looked as though it had "joined the happiness cult of the Elder Micheaux, and had placed its burdens on the Lord!" (Jacobsen, Wolf, and Jackson 1935, 10).

6. See J. Pressman for a detailed account of lobotomy's early history (1999, 47–101).

7. After reading about Moniz's initial results, Freeman wrote a letter to Moniz in which he praised his "magnificent researches," particularly his recent work with psychosurgery, and explained that he planned "to recommend a trial of this procedure in certain cases that come under my care." Walter Freeman to Egas Moniz, May 25, 1936, box 5, folder 9, Walter Freeman / James Watts Papers, University Archives, Special Collections Research Center, The George Washington University (hereafter cited as Freeman / Watts Papers).

8. Freeman described Watts's initial attitude toward transorbital lobotomy as "I won't and you shan't," referencing the rift between them on the subject as a dispute over authority (1970, 14–14). He also noted that Watts, in his personal practice, eventually gave up "on the major prefrontal lobotomy except as a secondary operation, and was doing all of them by the transorbital method," even though Watts never published anything on the matter (Freeman 1970, 14–21). The disagreement between Freeman and Watts appears to mirror a larger struggle between neurologists and neurosurgeons over professional territory (Gavrus 2011).

9. According to Eliot Valenstein (1986), Moniz built his theory of psychopathology from Pierre Janet's theory of the *idée fixe*, which Janet argued was the root of hysteria (84).

10. This idea bears resemblance to the contemporary "kindling" theory used to explain the increased frequency, severity, and spontaneity of symptoms in depression, anxiety, and panic disorders (e.g., Post and Weiss 1998).

11. During prefrontal surgeries, Freeman and Watts would frequently converse with their patients, who were asked to say prayers, recite the Pledge of Allegiance, sing patriotic songs, and engage in other oddly ideological tests of orientation and mental acuity. Sometimes, as in the case of the brakeman, the surgical team observed visible changes in their patients after certain cuts were made, such as a lack of self-consciousness "even to the point of being witty. For instance, in an extremely serious-minded individual (Case 53), with a great deal of self-consciousness and feeling of inferiority, the patient was asked: 'What's going through your mind?' After a long pause, he replied: 'A knife'" (Freeman and Watts 1950, 116).

12. Walter Freeman to Egas Moniz, September 21, 1952, box 5, folder 21, Freeman / Watts Papers.

13. For an insightful study of the intersection of disability, dependency,

individualism, medical authority, private and public care, and US literary culture, see Snyder and Mitchell 2006, 37–68.

14. See O'Brien 2004 for a well-articulated critique of this position. O'Brien rightly notes that Rosemary Kennedy would likely have been considered "feebleminded" in the 1920s and 1930s, which would have carried considerable stigma no matter what the underlying diagnosis would have been. Furthermore, feeblemindedness (as opposed to the dominant Freudian theories of psychopathology) was attributed to heredity, which would have further indicted the Kennedy family.

15. Walter Freeman wrote volumes of derogatory comments about psychoanalysis in his personal writing and correspondence. One of the most vivid examples of Freeman's attitude toward psychoanalysis is found in a scathing comment Freeman crossed out of a talk he prepared for the 1967 American Psychiatric Association conference, entitled "Psychiatrists Who Kill themselves: A Study in Suicide":

> [Psychoanalysts] are the most rigid, self-righteous and supercilious of all psychiatrists. They are so sure of their own salvation (outwardly) that they have no patience, only contempt, for those who have not undergone personal analysis. They seal themselves off from other methods of treatment, and pursue their own way little, if at all, influenced by methods developed outside the doctrine. They continue in compulsive fashion to apply analytic procedures in the face of obvious lack of success, and their interpretations either meet with stony resistance on the part of their victims, or succeed only too well in brainwashing their more suggestible patients and reducing them to equally intolerant and rigid individuals who join with others in laudation of their masters, a sort of intellectual and even emotional emasculation (1967,n.p.).

16. Tarumianz explained that Delaware State Hospital would save $351,000 over the course of ten years if he lobotomized 180 patients. Of the 180, he calculated, 10 percent would die and 50 percent would become well enough to leave the hospital (American Medical Association 1941a, 44). "I think this is a matter not only of medicine," Tarumianz stated, "but that the taxpayers should also be considered very seriously, if you are dealing with some 200,000 human beings [in American psychiatric wards] who are hospitalized and who are suffering from chronic serious mental dilapidation, maybe not ipso facto, but they are showing signs of dilapidation. This economic side goes into millions of dollars" (43).

17. Grinker was not wholly opposed to psychosurgery and admitted he saw its "value" in certain cases. During the roundtable discussion, he stated that lobotomy should be viewed as an experimental procedure suitable for some "older patients," "middle-aged housewives," and "people who have no chance whatsoever except to continue in state hospitals" (American Medical Association 1941a, 188).

18. A similar complaint was made by psychiatrist John Whitehorn in the First Research Conference on Psychosurgery, held in 1949. Whitehorn expressed concern about diagnostic classification and its tenuous reliance on words like "dread," which are difficult to generalize yet, as his colleagues insisted, necessary for professional

communication about psychosurgery. "I have no intensimeter to measure psychic pain," explained Whitehorn, "and I am very reluctant to take at face value the words of the patient about it." "We are here not simply to play around with words," insisted organizer and surgeon Fred Mettler in response, describing Whitehorn's concern about language use as an "intense dread of categorization" (Federal Security Agency 1949, 13–14).

19. Freeman continued to perform transorbital lobotomies until 1967, when a patient at Berkeley's Herrick hospital died after the surgery, and Freeman's surgical privileges subsequently were revoked.

20. For a compelling example of how contemporary psychiatry might acknowledge these forces in theory and practice, see Lewis 2006.

Chapter 2

1. Freeman went as far as to chide his colleagues for relying *only* on popular press accounts of lobotomy, complaining that they really ought to "have more of an acquaintance with the situation than is afforded by *The Saturday Evening Post* and *Reader's Digest.*" Walter Freeman to John Caldwell, Nov. 19, 1952, box 1, folder 4, Freeman / Watts Papers.

2. Walter Freeman to James Watts, April 26, 1969, box 23, folder 13, Freeman / Watts Papers.

3. For an excellent study of the use of gender norms to diagnose men, specifically male hysterics, see Micale 2008.

4. There is one notable exception: queer desire. After surgery, one man gave up "an unduly close friendship with a young man of his own age who had been a drinking companion and possibly a homosexual." In this case, sexual desire was rerouted to more acceptable heterosexual channels: sexuality, they concluded, "was no longer a problem" in his life (Freeman and Watts 1950, 177).

5. Other doctors (Strecker, Palmer, and Grant 1942) advised against marriage and childbirth for patients after their operation. After noting that one of their patients "apparently . . . free from symptoms" married and had a baby, they specify that she did so "against our advice" (524).

6. Lobotomy was said to have offered a special benefit to laboring women: after Freeman and Watts (1950) watched one of their patients deliver her second child, they made special note of her "cheerfulness and lack of concern" (217).

7. Later in the article, Hoffman comments that for him, psychosurgery prompted comparisons to the story about the farmer who makes a pact with the devil: "Here, however, it is the surgeon, rather than the patient, who appears to have made the pact, and unfortunately, there is no Daniel Webster to release the patient from his pact" (1949, 235).

8. In a contrasting example, in 1952 a story about a man named Millard Wright attracted the attention of the national press. Like Case 1000, the woman who had been

reformed by lobotomy, Wright had willingly submitted to the operation in order to cure his penchant for burglary. Yet although Case 1000 often was referred to by gender in headlines, Wright was identified only as a "burglar" and "thief." Wright's story has a tragic ending. After his surgery, he returned to a life of crime, and after he was arrested, he hung himself. In his suicide note, he apologized to his doctor ("Surgery Cure Fails" 1952; "Surgery Ends in Suicide" 1952).

9. Thanks to Susan Squier for pointing out the irony in the phrase "the new woman."

10. This "childish" effect also extended to a description of their cultural tastes, which often changed after lobotomy. Some patients who before the operation "were great readers of good literature," Freeman and Watts remarked, "will be interested only in the comic books or in the movie magazines. Men of considerable intellectual achievement will read avidly the sports page" (1943, 803). Other doctors commented on this aspect as well, noting that a number of patients whose tastes were "relatively sophisticated" before surgery seemed to "derive more pleasure from simple things" afterward—such as dogs, horses, ice cream, and movies. After surgery, patients were apt to show "satisfaction in things as they are" (Strecker, Palmer, and Grant 1942, 525–526).

11. Intriguingly, during the period when the cure stories dominated, a similar story broke in Wisconsin about a man named John Milner who had been released from the hospital and later intentionally killed his father while hunting. However, rather than blame lobotomy for her brother's crime, Milner's sister Esther emphasized that the family considered lobotomy a "great triumph of science, and hope that confidence in brain surgery will not be weakened by this tragedy" ("Son Confesses" 1942, 1).

12. Marshall v. Yates, 223 U.S.P.Q (BNA) 453; Copy. L. Rep. (CCH) P25, 594 (1983).

Chapter 3

1. Jonathan Sadowsky (2006) offers a compelling critique of the pendulum metaphor used to discuss the shifts in psychiatry between treatments that focus on psyche and soma, charging that this metaphor obscures the many points of overlap between psychoanalysis and biopsychiatry and also leads to the conclusion that these two treatment paradigms were incommensurable. As a number of historians have argued, the action of somatic treatments like electroconvulsive therapy (Sadowsky 2006), psychopharmacology (Metzl 2003), and psychosurgery (Raz 2008) was often discussed in the psychiatric community using psychoanalytic epistemology and terminology.

2. For an extended analysis of *kairos* in ancient Greece, see Hawhee 2004, 65–85.

3. For a critique of this definition of personhood as it applies to disability, see Johnson 2012.

4. My thanks to Jeff Smith for pointing me to this film.

5. The suggestion that Mindszenty was drugged has been refuted by István Rév (2002, 92n4).

6. One year after Mindszenty's conviction, American businessman Robert Voegler

was arrested and tried by the Hungarian government and delivered a similar confession in a Budapest courtroom. Unlike Mindszenty, Voegler was not suspected of having undergone a personality change, and many believed he was simply performing for the court, a claim that was likely strengthened by Voegler's garish makeup. For a discussion of the Voegler case, see Carruthers 2009, 136–173.

7. Kinkead's title referred to the book's thesis that American soldiers had performed honorably in captivity in every war but Korea, a historical "fact" he used to speculate that something essential had changed in the national character since the Second World War. These figures, as well as Kinkead's argument, were subsequently, and strenuously, refuted (Biderman 1963, 28; Wubben 1970).

8. The Americans comprised a miniscule portion of more than twenty thousand total prisoners who refused repatriation after the war. Most of the nonrepatriates were Chinese and North Korean soldiers who did not wish to return due to fears of political retribution. The United Nations Command, sensing a public relations opportunity, were adamant that the twenty thousand prisoners ought to be able to repatriate to a country of their choosing. For more on Korean War nonrepatriation, see Zweiback 1998.

9. In this chapter, I present the briefest history of each of these examples in order to highlight the fear of personality change common to them. For a history of the Mindszenty case, see Rév 2002; Streatfeild 2007; and Carruthers 2009. For a nuanced description of the Korean POW saga, see Carruthers 2009 and Zweiback 1998. For analyses of the brainwashing phenomenon, see Biderman 1962; Biderman 1963; Marks 1979; Seed 2004; Taylor 2004; and Melley 2008.

10. For a discussion of the Chinese ideographs from which Hunter took his term, see Taylor 2004, 4–5.

11. Thank you to Zhongdang Pan for his assistance in this translation.

12. Before he became the popular expert on psychological warfare, Hunter worked editorial stints for papers like the *Japan Advertiser*, *Hanckow Herald*, and *Peking Leader*.

13. For more on the history of the "artificial slave," see LaGrandeur 2011.

14. I have found no evidence that lobotomy was in use in Nazi Germany, even though the timing would have been right. Even the book *Psychiatrists: The Men behind Hitler*, published by a wing of the Church of Scientology—a vocal critic of psychiatry—admits that lobotomy was not "immediately connected to the Nazi era," though it does conclude that lobotomy shares "a recognizable tradition of barbarism and the psychiatric philosophy of the Third Reich" (Röder, Kubillus, and Burwell 1994, 212).

15 Far right anxieties about mental health programs were rooted in more mainstream conservative critiques of the psychiatric profession as antireligious and leftist, and these concerns were often amplified by many ultraconservatives' nationalist and anti-Semitic beliefs. In testimony against federal mental health legislation, for example, ultraconservative John Kasper, a white nationalist and antifluoridation activist, described psychiatry as "a foreign ideology; it is alien to any kind of American thinking. . . . Its history began with Sigmund Freud who is a Jew. . . . Almost 100% of all

psychiatric therapy . . . and about 80% of the psychiatrists are Jewish. . . . One particular race is administering this particular thing" (quoted in Marmor, Bernard, and Ottenberg 1960, 341). For more on anti-Semitism and critiques of psychiatry, see Frosh 2005.

16. I urge the reader to consider the information that I provide from Kominsky's text—which is one of the only thorough discussions of the Russian textbook in any literature—with a critical eye. Kominsky ran for governor of Rhode Island on the Communist Party ticket in 1938, and he made a name for himself with the book in which *Brain-Washing* is analyzed. The book, *The Hoaxers: Plain Liars, Fancy Liars, and Damned Liars* (1970), the only work Kominsky ever published, is a systematic debunking of anti-Semitic and anticommunist propaganda by the Far Right.

17. According to an editorial in the *American Journal of Psychiatry* (1953), the USSR prohibited lobotomy in 1950 by order of the Soviet Ministry of Health, and the journal's account of the ban reveals more than a little of the ideological leanings of its author: "There was unanimous agreement that foreign theories re psychosurgery were unsound and diametrically opposed to the clear teachings of Pavlov. The dutiful Soviet psychiatrists registered their unswerving adhesion to the official version of Pavlovian doctrine and their emphatic opposition to the reckless, capitalistic surgical adventuring of Western doctors" ("No Psychosurgery" 1953; Laurence 1953); see also Galach'yan 1968; Kiev 1968.

Chapter 4

1. For critiques of the illusory vision of brain imaging, see Waldby 2000; Dumit 2004; Beaulieu 2012; Fitzpatrick 2012.

2. The concept of the limbic system has become a controversial issue in neuroscience, and some prominent researchers on the neuroscience of emotion, like Joseph LeDoux (2002), have even argued that the term should be abandoned due to its vagueness.

3. See also Kennedy 1968, 81–99.

4. See Lombroso 1911. For critical studies of contemporary biological criminology, see Rose 2000; Rose 2007; and Littlefield 2011.

5. For a reflection on "evil" as an explanation for Whitman's actions, see Eberly 2003.

6. Ervin was later sued for medical malpractice in 1979 by the mother of one of the patients whose case was discussed in *Violence and the Brain* (Dietz 1979). For more on the connection of Ervin and Mark's theories to race, see Mason (1973), who wondered in *Ebony* magazine if psychosurgery was a "new threat to blacks."

7. For a rhetorical perspective on Szasz's theory of mental illness, see Vatz and Weinberg 1994. The early 1970s were also a point of tremendous upheaval with regard to the legitimacy of psychiatry as a medical science. In a famous experiment, psychologist David Rosenhan and eight other healthy "pseudopatients" presented themselves to psychiatrists with vaguely psychotic symptoms, and all were diagnosed

with schizophrenia. Rosenhan's experiment, "On Being Sane in Insane Places," published in *Science* in 1974, rocked the field of mental health. Rosenhan concluded:

> based in part on theoretical and anthropological considerations, but also on philosophical, legal, and therapeutic ones, the view has grown that psychological categorization of mental illness is useless at best and downright harmful, misleading, and pejorative at worst. Psychiatric diagnoses, in this view, are in the minds of observers and are not valid summaries of characteristics displayed by the observed. (251)

8. For a history of the shift from psychoanalysis to biological psychiatry, see Healy 1999. For an analysis of the role of rhetoric in this shift, see Kirk and Kutchins 1992.

9. Breggin's public stance has cost him professionally. In 1987, for example, he was brought before Maryland's medical disciplinary board after he stated on *The Oprah Winfrey Show* that patients should judge their psychiatrists on their qualities of empathy and compassion, recommending that patients should leave if offered medication during their first session with a new doctor. Breggin's comments were seen by many to advocate that people with mental illness should refuse medication, a position roundly critiqued by the National Alliance for Mental Illness (NAMI), which filed the complaint. Director Laurie Flynn was especially critical of Breggin's position as a public figure, wondering if "an M.D. who prescribes for all psychiatric patients across America without even having seen these patients should continue to be licensed by the State of Maryland" (Goleman 1987).

10. The CCHR was, and continues to be, the political wing of the Church of Scientology's campaign against psychiatry. Peter Breggin's wife was a member of the church, but he never joined and vociferously denies any connection with the organization ("Interview" 2000).

11. Breggin is not alone in this comparison. See, e.g., Lehmann's (1955) description of Thorazine as a "pharmacological substitute for lobotomy" (91).

12. In chapter 5, I discuss this rhetorical strategy of invoking lobotomy as a point of comparison as an "evolutionary" strategy of memory management.

13. The bill (HR 5371), sponsored by Louis Stokes (D-OH), sought to prohibit psychosurgery in federally connected health care facilities but failed to make it out of the House Committee on Interstate and Foreign Commerce.

14. Although the Oregon statute remains in effect today, I have been unable to find statistics about how often it has been used since 1980.

Chapter 5

1. Although ablative psychosurgery is rare in the United States, in China psychosurgeries are being performed in a number of state-run hospitals at a rate that rivals the peak of lobotomy in the United States (Zamiska 2007, 1).

2. Some scholars, like Foucault (1977) and Nora ([1984] 1989) have suggested that collective memory has been subjugated by history, while others, like Geary (1994) and

Ricouer (2006), have argued that history itself is a kind of collective memory. For an acerbic critique of the new field of memory studies from a historian's perspective, see Klein 2000.

3. For more on how rhetoric, particularly contention and dispute, creates communities, see C. Miller 1993.

4. The classic syllogism "All men are mortal; Socrates is a man; therefore, Socrates is mortal" in the form of an enthymeme becomes "Socrates is a man; therefore, Socrates is a mortal." In this example, the rhetor assumes that the audience already believes "all men are mortal," which then *goes without saying.*

5. This affectively charged, assumed evaluation is illustrated by psychiatrists Kenneth Davis and Daniel Stewart (2008), who write, "if someone today were to suggest a frontal lobotomy as a means of relieving mental anguish, the responses might include sardonic laughter, revulsion, or even outrage" (457).

6. For a compelling critique of neuroethics, see Whitehouse 2012.

7. Although the intent of DBS is not ablation, it is still a risky procedure. It seems prudent to note here that *any* form of neurosurgery runs the risk of intracranial hemorrhage, as Elliot et al. observe (2011, 177).

8. For what it's worth, the *Oxford English Dictionary* does not support the case of many DBS advocates. "Psychosurgery" is defined broadly as "neurosurgery performed to treat mental illness and alter behaviour." If the definitional issue turns on the meaning of "surgery," even this definition does little to clear things up, for "surgery" is defined as "the art or practice of treating injuries, deformities, and other disorders by manual operation or instrumental appliances." What is deep brain stimulation if not the use of an instrumental appliance to treat a disorder?

Chapter 6

1. I draw this reference from Phaedra Pezzullo (2005).

2. Tennessee Williams's sister Rose received a prefrontal lobotomy in 1946, an event that haunted the playwright to the end of his life.

3. For a dramatization of this aspect of Dahmer's crimes, see Joyce Carol Oates's 1996 novella *Zombie.*

4. My thanks to Rick Popp and his book *The Holiday Makers* (2012) for pointing me to Edward Bruner's work.

5. For a careful study of Thomas Kirkbride and the Kirkbride Plan, see Tomes 1984. For critiques of "moral treatment," see Foucault 1988; Scull 1979; Scull 2005; and Rothman [1971] 2009.

6. In 1980, the name was shortened to "Weston Hospital." To avoid confusion, I will refer to the hospital by the names that correspond to each time period. That includes the hospital's current incarnation as the Trans-Allegheny Lunatic Asylum.

7. And indeed, proposals to increase funding encountered resistance, particularly

from the West Virginia Chamber of Commerce, which denounced Armentrout's reporting as mere "clamor" (Morgan 1949).

8. The director of Spencer State Hospital announced his resignation in the midst of the exposé, and Joseph Knapp resigned as the superintendent of Weston State Hospital shortly after the story ran ("Dr. J. L. Knapp Resigns" 1949).

9. In later years, Freeman conducted this follow-up by means of correspondence with patients or their family members, which often came in response to the annual Christmas greetings he sent out to former patients and their families each year. These cards often included a picture of the doctor in recreational mode— in one Freeman is shown with his backpack on, in the midst of a hike in the mountains; in another, he waves at the camera from the driver-side window of his camper.

10. Walter Freeman to Egas Moniz, Sept. 9, 1952, box 5, folder 21, Walter Freeman / James Watts Papers.

11. Although Freeman did not provide statistics on the race of his patients, nor a breakdown of patients by institution, it is reasonable to assume that patients at Lakin constituted a significant number of those in the West Virginia Project, particularly since the state was considering closing the institution (Goodman and Maggio 2008). I will add that the only photograph of an African American lobotomy patient I found in my research illustrates Freeman's *JAMA* article on the West Virginia Lobotomy Project.

12. Walter Freeman to Egas Moniz, Sept. 9, 1952, box 5, folder 21, Walter Freeman / James Watts Papers.

13. The tour guide from the historical tour did not give me permission to use her name. Greg "Copperhead" Graham, my paranormal tour guide, gave his permission.

14. From my research, I am unable to confirm that Weston was the location where Freeman operated on twenty-two patients in just over two hours. However, since Weston was the most populated hospital in West Virginia, it seems reasonable to assume this may have been the case.

15. Recording devices were not permitted on the historical tour. As such, the quotations from our tour guides are reconstructed from my field notes, although the material in quotation marks is verbatim.

16. Knapp had resigned by the time Freeman began the West Virginia lobotomy project ("Dr. J. L. Knapp Resigns" 1949).

17. As noted above, although audiovisual recording is not allowed on the historical tours, it is invited on the paranormal tours. An email sent to ticket holders explains, "You're welcome to bring a flashlight, snacks, and your own investigation equipment such as cameras, voice recorders, K-II meters, dowsing rods, etc. If you have a smart phone, such as Droid or iPhone, there's an app for that: search for keywords such as 'paranormal investigation', 'digital dowsing', 'ghost detector,' etc. NO OUIJA BOARDS!" (email to author, August 12, 2011).

REFERENCES

Aarons, Leroy. 1972. "Brain Surgery Is Tested on Three California Convicts." *Washington Post*, February 25.

Abosch, Aviva, and G. Rees Cosgrove. 2008. "Biological Basis for the Surgical Treatment of Depression." *Neurosurgical Focus* 25: 1–12.

"Actress Frances Farmer Faces Jail Term after 24-Hour Fling." 1943. *Toledo Blade*, January 14.

Ahmed, Sara. 2004. *The Cultural Politics of Emotion*. New York: Routledge.

Alesen, Lewis. 1952a. "The Physician's Responsibility as Leader." *Northwest Medicine* 51, no. 12: 1025–1030.

Alesen, Lewis. 1952b. "Physicians in Politics—as Good Citizens." *California Medicine* 76, no. 6: 367–369.

Alesen, Lewis. 1958. *Mental Robots*. Caldwell, ID: Caxton Printers.

American Medical Association. 1941a. *Neurosurgical Treatment*. TS. Box 16, folder 23. Freeman/Watts Collection. Gelman Library. George Washington University Archives, Washington, DC.

American Medical Association. 1941b. "Neurosurgical Treatment of Certain Abnormal Mental States: Panel Discussion at Cleveland Session." *Journal of the American Medical Association* 117, no. 7: 517–527.

Andersen, Paul K. 1989. "Remarks on the Origin of the Term 'Passive.'" *Lingua* 79: 1–16.

Andy, Orlando. 1966. "Neurosurgical Treatment for Abnormal Behavior." *American Journal of the Medical Sciences* 252, no. 2: 232–238.

Andy, Orlando. 1970. "Thalamotomy in Hyperactive and Aggressive Behavior." *Confinia Neurologica* 32: 322-325.

Aristotle. 1991. *On Rhetoric: A Theory of Civic Discourse*. Translated by George A. Kennedy. New York: Oxford University Press.

Armentrout, Charles R. 1949a. "The Price of Economy—Misery! Mental Patients Doomed to Lives of Neglect, Monotony, Indecency." *Charleston Gazette*, January 23.

Armentrout, Charles R. 1949b. "The Price of Economy—Misery! Inmates at Weston Have to Live in Quarters Unfit for Livestock." *Charleston Gazette*, January 24.

Armentrout, Charles R. 1949c. "The Price of Economy—Misery! 115 Incontinent Women, Scantily Clad, Sit All Day in Smelly Room at Weston." *Charleston Gazette*, January 25.

Armentrout, Charles R. 1949d. "Forsaken and Forgotten: Criminally Insane Roam, Sit—and Plot to Escape." *Charleston Gazette*, January 27.

Armentrout, Charles R. 1949e. "Forsaken and Forgotten: Escape Is Easy at Lakin for Mentally-Ill Negroes." *Charleston Gazette*, January 28.

Armentrout, Charles R. 1949f. "Forsaken and Forgotten: Mentally Sick Children at Lakin Have No Hope." *Charleston Gazette*, November 27.

Armentrout, Charles R. 1952. "Improved but Unwanted: Discharged Mental Patients Find Doors Barred by Their Own Families." *Charleston Gazette*, November 27.

Arnold, William. [1978], 1982. *Shadowland*. New York: Berkley.

Arnot, Charles P. 1955. "Reds May Use Lobotomy to 'Brain-Wash' Foes." *Kannapolis (NC) Daily Independent*, March 29.

Assmann, Jan. 1995. "Collective Memory and Cultural Identity." Translated by John Czaplicka. *New German Critique* 65: 125–133.

Asylum. 2008. Directed by David R. Ellis. Burbank, CA: Hyde Park Entertainment.

Auerback, Alfred. 1963. "The Anti–Mental Health Movement." *American Journal of Psychiatry* 120: 105–111.

Bachelard, Gaston. [1934] 1984. *The New Scientific Spirit*. Boston: Beacon Press.

Ballantine, H. Thomas, Walter L. Cassidy, Norris B. Flanagan, and Raul Marino Jr.. 1967. "Stereotaxic Anterior Cingulotomy for Neuropsychiatric Illness and Intractable Pain." *Journal of Neurosurgery* 26, no. 5: 488–495.

Ballif, Michelle. 2013. "Historiography as Hauntology: Paranormal Investigations into the History of Rhetoric." In *Theorizing Histories of Rhetoric*, edited by Michelle Ballif, 139-153. Carbondale: Southern Illinois University Press.

Barker-Benfield, G. J. 2000. *The Horrors of the Half-Known Life: Male Attitudes toward Women and Sexuality in Nineteenth-Century America*. London: Routledge.

Barton, Ellen. 2001. "Textual Practices of Erasure: Representations of Disability and the Founding of the United Way." In *Embodied Rhetorics: Disability in Language and Culture*, edited by James Wilson and Cynthia Lewiecki-Wilson, 169–199. Carbondale: Southern Illinois University Press.

Barton, William S. 1953. "Brain Surgery Seen as Aid for Christine: Psychiatrists Told of Success with Lobotomy Operation." *Los Angeles Times*, May 6.

Baty, S. Paige. 1995. *American Monroe: The Making of a Body Politic*. Berkeley: University of California Press.

Beaulieu, Anne. 2012. "Fast-Moving Objects and Their Consequences: A Response to the Neuroscientific Turn in Practice." In *The Neuroscientific Turn: Transdisciplinarity in the Age of the Brain*, edited by Melissa Littlefield and Jenell Johnson, 152–159. Ann Arbor: University of Michigan Press.

Bellah, Robert, Richard Madsen, William Sullivan, Ann Swidler, and Steven Tipton. 1985. *Habits of the Heart: Individualism and Commitment in American Life*. Berkeley: University of California Press.

Berkenkotter, Carol. 2008. *Patient Tales: Case Histories and the Uses of Narrative in Psychiatry*. Columbia: University of South Carolina Press.

Berkenkotter, Carol, and Doris Ravotas. 2008. "Psychotherapist as Author: Case Reports, Classification and Categorization." In *Patient Tales: Case Histories and the Uses of Narrative in Psychiatry*, 145–160. Columbia: University of South Carolina Press.

Bergmann, Linda S. 2010. "The Guilty Pleasures of Working with Archives." In *Working in the Archives: Practical Research Methods for Rhetoric and Composition*, edited by Alexis E. Ramsey, Wendy B. Sharer, Barbara L'Eplattenier, and Lisa Mastrangelo, 220–231. Carbondale: Southern Illinois University Press.

Biderman, Albert D. 1962. "The Image of Brainwashing." *Public Opinion Quarterly* 26: 547–563.

Biderman, Albert D. 1963. *March to Calumny: The Story of American POWs in the Korean War*. New York: Macmillan.

Bingham, June. 1951. "What the Public Thinks of Psychiatry." *American Journal of Psychiatry* 107: 599–601.

Birmingham, Elizabeth. 2008. "'I See Dead People': Archive, Crypt, and an Argument for the Researcher's Sixth Sense." In *Beyond the Archives: Research as a Lived Process*, edited by Gesa E. Kirsch and Liz Rohan, 139–46. Carbondale: Southern Illinois State University Press.

Bizzell, Patricia. 2000. "Feminist Methods of Research in the History of Rhetoric: What Difference Do They Make?" *Rhetoric Society Quarterly* 30, no. 4: 5–17.

Boss, Pete. 1986. "Vile Bodies and Bad Medicine." *Screen* 27, no. 1: 14–25.

"Brain Surgery by D.C. Doctors Cures Insane." 1940. *Washington Times-Herald*, September 18.

"Brain Surgery Invoked to Curb Evil Impulses: Outlook Changed, Says Woman Criminal." 1946. *Chicago Daily Tribune*, December 7.

Brain-Washing: A Synthesis of the Russian Textbook on Psychopolitics. 1955. Englewood, CO: Kenneth Goff Publications.

Braslow, Joel. 1997. *Mental Ills and Bodily Cures: Psychiatric Treatment in the First Half of the Twentieth Century*. Berkeley: University of California Press.

Breggin, Peter. 1972a. "Lobotomies: An Alert." *American Journal of Psychiatry* 129: 130.

Breggin, Peter. 1972b. "Lobotomies Are Still Bad Medicine." *Medical Opinion*, March 8, no. 3: 32–36.

Breggin, Peter. 1972c. "The Return of Lobotomy and Psychosurgery." *Congressional Record*, February 24, E1602–E1612.

Breggin, Peter. 1980. "Brain-Disabling Therapies." In *The Psychosurgery Debate*, edited by Eliot Valenstein, 467–505. San Francisco: W. H. Freeman.

Breggin, Peter. 1991. *Toxic Psychiatry*. New York: St. Martin's Press.

Breggin, Peter, and Daniel S. Greenberg. 1972. "Return of the Lobotomy." *Washington Post*, March 12.

Brody, Richard. 2010. "The Mind's Island." *New Yorker Online*, February 25. http://www.newyorker.com/online/blogs/movies/shutter-island.

Brook, Robert H. 2010. "A Physician = Emotion + Passion + Science." *Journal of the American Medical Association* 304, no. 22: 2528–2529.

Brook, Robert H. 2011. "Reflecting Emotion with the Science in Research Article Prose—Reply." *Journal of the American Medical Association* 305, no. 11: 1096.

Brown, M. H., and J. Lighthill. 1968. "Selective Anterior Cingulotomy: A Psychological Evaluation." *Journal of Neurosurgery* 29: 513–519.

Bruner, Edward M. 2005. *Culture on Tour: Ethnographies of Travel.* Chicago: University of Chicago Press.

Bryant, Donald C. 1973. *The Rhetorical Dimensions of Criticism.* Baton Rouge: Louisiana State University Press.

Burckhardt, Gottlieb. 1891. "Über Rindenexcisionen, als Beitrag zur operativen Therapie der Psychosen." *Allgemeine Zeitschrift für Psychiatrie und Psychisch-gerichtliche Medizin* 47: 463–548.

Burdick, Usher. 1957. "Beware of Psychiatrists." *Congressional Record*, June 13, 9060–9061.

Burke, Kenneth. 1941. *The Philosophy of Literary Form.* Berkeley: University of California Press.

Burke, Kenneth. 1951. "Rhetoric—Old and New." *Journal of General Education* 45: 202–209.

Burke, Kenneth. 1966. *Language as Symbolic Action: Essays on Life, Literature, and Method.* Berkeley: University of California Press.

Burke, Kenneth. 1969. *A Rhetoric of Motives.* Berkeley: University of California Press.

Burton, Hal. 1953. "How to Prevent a Murder (Sometimes)." *Newsday*, April 11, 22–23.

Butler, Judith. 1994. "Against Proper Objects." *Differences: A Journal of Feminist Cultural Studies* 6, nos. 2–3: 1–26.

Byers, Thomas B. 1989. "Kissing Becky: Masculine Fears and Misogynist Moments in Science Fiction Films." Arizona Quarterly 45: 77–95.

Cabrera, Cloe. 2010. "'Alone' Haunted House Makes Its Debut at Howl-O-Scream." *TBO Extra*, September 29. http://www2.tboextra.com/lifestyles/tboextra-nightlife/2010/sep/29.

Canby, William C., and Ernest Gellhorn. 1978. "Physician Advertising: The First Amendment and the Sherman Act." *Duke Law Journal, Symposium on the Antitrust Laws and the Health Services Industry* 2: 543–85.

"The Cardinal's Trial." 1949. *Tablet* 193: 118.

Carruthers, Susan L. 2009. *Cold War Captives: Imprisonment, Escape, and Brainwashing.* Berkeley: University of California Press.

Ceccarelli, Leah. 2001. *Shaping Science with Rhetoric: The Cases of Dobzhansky, Schrodinger, and Wilson.* Chicago: University of Chicago Press.

Chambers, Tod. 2009. "The Virtue of Incongruity in the Medical Humanities." *Journal of the Medical Humanities* 30, no. 3: 151–154.

Chesler, Phyllis. 1972. *Women and Madness.* New York: Palgrave Macmillan.

Cho, Der-Yang, Wen-Yuan Lee, and Chun-Chung Chen. 2008. "Limbic Leukotomy for Intractable Major Affective Disorders: A 7-Year Follow-Up Study Using Nine

Comprehensive Psychiatric Test Evaluations." *Journal of Clinical Neuroscience:* 15, no. 2: 138–142.

Clymer, R. Swineburne. 1958. *The Age of Treason.* Quakertown, PA: Humanitarian Press.

Cohen, Jeffrey. 1996. *Monster Theory: Reading Culture.* Minneapolis: University of Minnesota Press.

Cohen, Lucille. 1947. "Surgery May Free 9 Mental Patients." *Seattle Post-Intelligencer,* August 27.

"Confessions to Reds Are Laid to Surgery." 1950. *New York Times*, September 2.

Countian, Kanawha. 1949. "House of Delegates Votes Consent That State Seek Hospital at Martinsburg." *Charleston Gazette*, February 9.

Corrigan, Maureen. 2011. "The Sad Lesson of 'Body Snatchers': People Change." *Fresh Air*, October 17. National Public Radio.

Corydon, Bent, and Ron DeWolfe. 1987. *L. Ron Hubbard: Messiah or Madman?* Secaucus, NJ: Lyle Stuart Books.

Cuordileone, K. A. 2000. "Politics in an Age of Anxiety: Cold War Political Culture and the Crisis in American Masculinity, 1949-1960." *Journal of American History* 87, no. 2: 515–545.

Crichton, Michael. 1972. *The Terminal Man.* New York: Avon.

"Dahmer Lobotomies Were Trial and Error." 1992. *Ocala (FL) Star Banner*.

Dain, Norman. 1994. "Psychiatry and Anti-Psychiatry in the United States." In *Discovering the History of Psychiatry*, edited by Mark S. Micale and Roy Porter, 415–444. New York and Oxford: Oxford University Press.

Damasio, Antonio. 1999. *The Feeling of What Happens: Body and Emotion in the Making of Consciousness.* New York: Mariner Books.

Davis, Kenneth, and Daniel Stewart. 2008. "Review of 'The Lobotomist.'" *American Journal of Psychiatry* 165: 457–458.

"Debate over Psychosurgery Continues." 1972. Science News 101, no. 12: 182.

Delgado, Jose. 1969. *Physical Control of the Mind: Toward a Psychocivilized Society.* New York: Harper & Row.

Deutsch, Albert. 1948. *The Shame of the States.* New York: Ayer Company.

Diefenbach, Gretchen J., Donald Diefenbach, Alan Baumeister, and M. West. 1999. "Portrayal of Lobotomy in the Popular Press: 1935–1960." *Journal of the History of the Neurosciences* 8: 60–69.

Dietz, Jean. 1979. "Psychosurgery on Trial: Is It Right to Cut?" *Chicago Tribune*, February 11.

Doyle, Richard. 1997. *On Beyond Living: Rhetorical Transformations of the Life Sciences.* Stanford, CA: Stanford University Press.

"Dr. J. L. Knapp Resigns as Weston Superintendent." 1949. *Charleston Gazette* March 24.

Dully, Howard. 2005. Interview. "Howard Dully Talks about 'My Lobotomy.'" *Talk of the Nation*, November 17. National Public Radio.

Dully, Howard, and Charles Fleming. 2007. *My Lobotomy: A Memoir.* New York: Crown Publishers.

Dumit, Joseph. 2004. *Picturing Personhood: Brain Scans and Biomedical Identity*. Princeton, NJ: Princeton University Press.

Eberly, Rosa A. 2003. "Deliver Ourselves from 'Evil.'" *Rhetoric and Public Affairs* 6, no. 3: 551–553.

Einsiedel, Edna. 2007. "Of Publics and Science." *Public Understanding of Science* 16, no. 1: 5–6.

El-Hai, Jack. 2005. *The Lobotomist: A Maverick Medical Genius and His Tragic Quest to Rid the World of Mental Illness*. Hoboken, NJ: John Wiley & Sons.

Elliot, Cameron, Maryana Duchcherer, Tejas Sankar, Glen B. Baker, and Serdar M. Dursun. 2011. "The Neurosurgical Treatment of Depression: Can It Supersede Psychopharmacology?" *Bulletin of Clinical Psychopharmacology* 21, no. 3: 175–178.

"Ex-Army Private, Captured in Korea, Is Well in China and Quoting Mao." 1981. *Norwalk (CT) Hour*, December 11.

"Eyewitness at the Trial." 1949. *Catholic Herald*, February 25.

Fahnestock, Jeanne. 1998. "Accommodating Science: The Rhetorical Life of Scientific Facts." *Written Communication* 15, no. 3: 330–350.

"Families Shocked by GIs Turned Red: Many Refuse to Believe It while Others Think Decision Was Forced." 1953. *Los Angeles Times*, September 25.

Federal Security Agency. 1949. *Proceedings of the First Research Conference on Psychosurgery*, edited by Newton Bigelow. Public Health Service Publication No. 16. Washington, DC: US Government Printing Office.

Feldman, Robert P., and James T. Goodrich. 2001. "Psychosurgery: A Historical Overview." *Neurosurgery* 48: 647–657.

Fine, Sidney. 1989. *Violence in the Model City: The Cavanagh Administration, Race Relations, and the Detroit Riot of 1967*. Ann Arbor: University of Michigan Press.

Finn, Scott. 2008. "'Trans-Allegheny Lunatic Asylum' Offends Some Disability Advocates." *West Virginia Public Radio*, March 3. http://wvpubcastnews.files.wordpress.com/2008/03/lunaticasylum0319.pdf

Finney, Jack. 1954. *The Invasion of the Body Snatchers*. New York: Award Books.

Fins, Joseph J. 2009. "Deep Brain Stimulation, Deontology and Duty: The Moral Obligation of Non-Abandonment at the Neural Interface." *Journal of Neural Engineering* 6, no. 5: 1–4.

Fins, Joseph J., Ali R. Rezai, and Benjamin D. Greenberg. 2006. "Psychosurgery: Avoiding an Ethical Redux while Advancing a Therapeutic Future." *Neurosurgery* 59, no. 4: 713–716.

Fishbein, Morris. 1925. *The Medical Follies: An Analysis of the Foibles of Some Healing Cults, Including Osteopathy, Homeopathy, Chiropractic, and the Electronic Reactions of Abrams, with Essays on the Anti-Vivisectionists, Health Legislation, Physical Culture, Birth Control, and Rejuvenation*. New York: Boni & Liveright.

Fishbein, Morris. 1928. "Medical Journalism in the United States." *Canadian Medical Association Journal* 18, no. 4: 442–446.

Fishbein, Morris. 1941. "Frontal Lobotomy." *Journal of the American Medical Association* 117, no. 7: 534–35.

Fitzpatrick, Susan. 2012. "Functional Brain Imaging: Neuro-Turn or Wrong Turn?" In *The Neuroscientific Turn: Transdisciplinarity in the Age of the Brain*, edited by Melissa Littlefield and Jenell Johnson, 180–198. Ann Arbor: University of Michigan Press.

Fleck, Ludwik. 1979. *Genesis and Development of a Scientific Fact.* Chicago: University of Chicago Press.

Fleming, George W. 1944. "Prefrontal Leucotomy." *Journal of Mental Science* 90: 491–500.

Foucault, Michel. 1972. *Archaeology of Knowledge.* Translated by A. M. Sheridan Smith. New York: Pantheon.

Foucault, Michel. 1977. *Language, Counter-Memory, Practice: Selected Essays and Interviews by Michel Foucault.* Edited by Donald F. Bouchard. Ithaca, NY: Cornell University Press.

Foucault, Michel. 1988. *Madness and Civilization: A History of Insanity in the Age of Reason.* New York: Vintage Books.

Foucault, Michel. 2001. *Fearless Speech.* Edited by Joseph Pearson. Los Angeles: Semiotext(e).

"Frances Farmer, Actress, Jailed." 1943. *St. Petersburg Times*, January 14.

"Frances Farmer to Serve Six Months in Jail." 1943. Biloxi Herald, January 15.

Freeman, Walter. c. 1970. "Adventures in Lobotomy." MS. Box 8, folders 14 and 17. Freeman/Watts Collection. Gelman Library, George Washington University Archives, Washington, DC.

Freeman, Walter. 1948. "Transorbital Lobotomy: Preliminary Report of Ten Cases." *Medical Annals of the District of Columbia* 27, no. 5: 257–261.

Freeman, Walter. 1950. "Transorbital Lobotomy." In *Psychosurgery: In the Treatment of Mental Disorders and Intractable Pain*, 50-58. Springfield, IL: Charles C. Thomas.

Freeman, Walter. 1953. "Level of Achievement after Lobotomy: A Study of One Thousand Cases." *American Journal of Psychiatry* 110: 269–276.

Freeman, Walter. 1955. "Psychosurgery." *American Journal of Psychiatry* 111: 518–520.

Freeman, Walter. 1958a. "Head-and-Shoulder Hunting in the Americas: Photographic Follow-up Studies in Lobotomy." *Medical Annals of the District of Columbia* 27, no. 7: 336–345.

Freeman, Walter. 1958b. "Psychosurgery: Present Indications and Future Prospects." *California Medicine* 88, no. 6 (June): 429–434.

Freeman, Walter. 1961. "Adolescents in Distress: Therapeutic Possibilities of Lobotomy." *Diseases of the Nervous System* 10: 555–558.

Freeman, Walter. 1967. "Psychiatrists Who Kill Themselves: A Study in Suicide." Presented to the American Psychiatric Association, Detroit. Typescript, Freeman Watts Collection, Gelman Library, George Washington University Archives. Washington, DC.

Freeman, Walter. 1972. "Lobotomy in Limbo?" Letter. *American Journal of Psychiatry* 128: 1315–1316.

Freeman, Walter, H. W. Davis, I. C. East, H. D. Tait, S. O. Johnson, and W. B. Rogers. 1954. "West Virginia Lobotomy Project." *Journal of the American Medical Association* 156, no. 10: 939–943.

Freeman, Walter, and James W. Watts. 1937. "Prefrontal Lobotomy in the Treatment of Mental Disorders." *Southern Medical Journal* 30, no. 1: 23–31.

Freeman, Walter, and James W. Watts. 1942. *Psychosurgery: Intelligence, Emotion and Social Behavior Following Prefrontal Lobotomy for Mental Disorders.* Springfield, IL: Charles C. Thomas.

Freeman, Walter, and James W. Watts. 1943. "Prefrontal Lobotomy: Convalescent Care and Aids to Rehabilitation." *American Journal of Psychiatry* 99: 798–806.

Freeman, Walter, and James W. Watts. 1944a. "Behavior and the Frontal Lobes." *Transactions of the New York Academy of Sciences,* series 2, 6: 284–310.

Freeman, Walter, and James W. Watts. 1944b. "Physiological Psychology." *Annual Review of Physiology* 6: 517–542.

Freeman, Walter, and James W. Watts. 1945. "Prefrontal Lobotomy: The Problem of Schizophrenia." *American Journal of Psychiatry* 101: 739–748.

Freeman, Walter, and James W. Watts. 1950. *Psychosurgery: In the Treatment of Mental Disorders and Intractable Pain.* 2nd edition. Springfield, IL: Charles C. Thomas.

Freeman, Walter, and James W. Watts. 1952. "Psychosurgery." *Progress in Neurology and Psychiatry* 7: 374–84.

Freud, Sigmund. [1919] 2003. *The Uncanny.* Translated by David McLintock. New York: Penguin Classics.

Freyhan, F. 1955. "The Immediate and Long Range Effects of Chlorpromazine on the Mental Hospital." In *Chlorpromazine and Mental Health: Proceedings of the Symposium Held under the Auspices of Smith, Kline & French Laboratories,* 71–98. Philadelphia: Lea & Febiger.

Friedman, Lester. 2004. "Introduction: Through the Looking Glass." In *Cultural Sutures: Medicine and Media,* edited by Lester Friedman, 1–15. Durham, NC: Duke University Press.

Frosh, Stephen. 2005. *Hate and the "Jewish Science": Anti-Semitism, Nazism, and Psychoanalysis.* New York: Palgrave MacMillan.

"Fruits of Brainwashing." 1954. *New York Times,* January 28.

Galach'yan, A. G. 1968. "Soviet Psychiatry." In *Psychiatry in the Communist World,* edited by Ari Kiev, 29–50. New York: Science House.

Garland-Thomson, Rosemarie. 2009. *Staring: How We Look.* Oxford and New York: Oxford University Press.

Gavrus, Delia. 2011. "Men of Dreams and Men of Action: Neurologists, Neurosurgeons, and the Performance of Professional Identity, 1920–1950." *Bulletin of the History of Medicine* 85, no. 1: 57–92.

Geary, Patrick. 1994. *Phantoms of Remembrance: Memory and Oblivion at the End of the First Millennium*. Princeton, NJ: Princeton University Press.

Gelman, Sheldon. 1999. *Medicating Schizophrenia: A History*. New Brunswick, NJ: Rutgers University Press.

Gibson, Barbara and Ted Schwartz. 1995. *Rose Kennedy and Her Family: The Best and Worst of Their Lives and Times*. Secaucus, NJ: Carol Pub. Group.

Gieryn, Thomas F. 1983. "Boundary-Work and the Demarcation of Science from Non-Science: Strains and Interests in Professional Ideologies of Scientists." *American Sociological Review* 48, no. 6: 781–795.

Gilbert, Frédéric, and Daniela Ovadia. 2011. "Deep Brain Stimulation in the Media: Over-Optimistic Portrayals Call for a New Strategy Involving Journalists and Scientists in Ethical Debates." *Frontiers in Integrative Neuroscience* 5: 1–6.

Gildenberg, Philip L. 1988. "Stereotactic Neurosurgery: Present and Past." In *Stereotactic Neurosurgery. Volume 2, Concepts in Neurosurgery*, edited by M. Peter Heilbrun, 1–16. Baltimore: Williams & Wilkins.

Goffman, Irving. 1963. *Stigma: Notes on the Management of Spoiled Identity*. New York: Simon and Schuster.

Goldstein, Kurt. 1950. "Prefrontal Lobotomy: Analysis and Warning." *Scientific American* 182, no. 2: 44-47.

Goleman, Daniel. 1987. "Free Expression or Irresponsibility? Psychiatrist Faces Hearing Today." *New York Times*, September 22. http://www.nytimes.com/1987/09/22/.

Goodman, Barak, and John Maggio, directors. 2008. *The Lobotomist*. *The American Experience*. National Public Television.

Goodman, Wayne K. and Thomas R. Insel. 2009. "Deep Brain Stimulation in Psychiatry: Concentrating on the Road Ahead." *Biological Psychiatry* 65, no. 4: 263–266.

Goodnight, G. Thomas. 1982. "The Personal, Technical, and Public Spheres of Argument." *Journal of the American Forensics Association* 18: 214–227.

Gordon, Avery. 2008. *Ghostly Matters: Haunting and the Sociological Imagination*. Minneapolis: University of Minnesota Press.

Gorman, Christine. 1994. "Prozac's Worst Enemy." *Time*, October 10, 64–65.

Gould, Stephen Jay. 1977. *Ontogeny and Phylogeny*. Cambridge, MA: Harvard University Press.

Governor's Select Commission on Civil Disorders. 1968. *Report for Action: An Investigation Into the Causes and Events of the 1967 Newark Race Riots*. New York: Lemma Publishing Corporation.

Graber, Doris. 1976. *Verbal Behavior and Politics*. Urbana: University of Illinois Press.

Graham, Marty. 2007. "Brain 'Pacemaker' Tickles Your Happy Nerve." *Wired*, May 23. http://www.wired.com/science/discoveries/news/2007/05/nerve.

Grimm, Robert J. 1980. "Regulation of Psychosurgery." In *The Psychosurgery Debate*, edited by Elliot Valenstein, 421-438. San Francisco: W. H. Freeman.

Gronbeck, Bruce. 2003. "The Rhetorics of the Past: History, Argument, and Collective

Memory." In *Doing Rhetorical History: Concepts and Cases*, edited by Kathleen Turner, 47–60. Tuscaloosa and London: University of Alabama Press.

Guilty of Treason. 1950. Directed by Felix E. Feist. Freedom Productions, Inc.

Gunn, Joshua, and Shaun Treat. 2005. "Zombie Trouble: A Propaedeutic on Ideological Subjectification and the Unconscious." *Quarterly Journal of Speech* 91, no. 2: 144–174.

Hacking, Ian. 1995. *Rewriting the Soul: Multiple Personality and the Sciences of Memory*. Princeton, NJ: Princeton University Press.

Haga, Kai Yin Allison. 2012. "Rising to the Occasion: The Role of American Missionaries and Korean Pastors in Resisting Communism Throughout the Korean War." In *Religion and the Cold War: A Global Perspective*, edited by Philip E. Muehlenbeck, 88–112. Nashville: Vanderbilt University Press.

Halbwachs, Maurice. [1925] 1980. *The Collective Memory*. New York and London: Harper and Row.

Hall, Stephen S. 2001. "Brain Pacemakers." MIT *Technology Review, September 1*. http://www.technologyreview.com/biomedicine/12553.

Hall, Stuart. [1973] 1999. "Encoding/Decoding." In *The Cultural Studies Reader*, edited by Simon During, 507–517. London: Routledge.

Haraway, Donna. 1988. "Situated Knowledges: The Science Question in Feminism and the Privilege of Partial Perspective." *Feminist Studies* 14, no. 3: 575–599.

Haraway, Donna. 1997. *Modest_Witness@Second_Millenium. FemaleMan_Meets_Oncomouse: Feminism and Technoscience*. New York: Routledge.

Hardesty, David E., and Harold A. Sackheim. 2007. "Deep Brain Stimulation in Movement and Psychiatric Disorders." *Biological Psychiatry* 61, no. 7: 831–835.

Hariman, Robert, and John Louis Lucaites. 2007. *No Caption Needed: Iconic Photographs, Public Culture, and Liberal Democracy*. Chicago: University of Chicago Press.

Hawhee, Debra. 2004. *Bodily Arts: Rhetoric and Athletics in Ancient Greece*. Austin: University of Texas Press.

Healy, David. 1999. *The Antidepressant Era*. Cambridge, MA: Harvard University Press.

Heath, Robert G. 1972. "Right to Be Wrong." Letter. *Medical Opinion*, April 17, 13.

Heimburger, Robert F., C. Courtney Whitlock, and John E. Kalsbeck. 1966. "Stereotaxic Amygdalotomy for Epilepsy with Aggressive Behavior." *Journal of the American Medical Association* 198, no. 7: 741–745.

Heinze, Andrew. 2003. "Schizophrenia Americana: Aliens, Alienists, and the 'Personality Shift' of Twentieth-Century Culture." *American Quarterly* 55, no. 2: 227–256.

Hendershot, Cyndy. 2001. *I Was A Cold War Monster: Horror Films, Eroticism, and the Cold War Imagination*. Bowling Green: Bowling Green University Press.

Henry, Thomas. 1936. "Brain Operation by D.C. Doctors Aids Mental Ills." *Washington Evening Star*, November 20.

Hoffer, Eric. [1951] 2003. *The True Believer: Thoughts on the Nature of Mass Movements*. New York: Harper Perennial Modern Classics.

Hoffman, Jay. 1949. "Clinical Observations Concerning Schizophrenic Patients Treated by Prefrontal Leukotomy." *New England Journal of Medicine* 249, no. 6: 233–236.

Holen, T., and C. V. Mobbs. 2004."Lobotomy of Genes: Use of RNA Interference in Neuroscience." *Neuroscience* 126, no. 1: 1–7.

Holley, Joe. 2007. "Tussle over St. Elizabeth's: Preservationists Set Their Sights on What Could Become Department of Homeland Security Headquarters." *Washington Post*, June 17. http://washingtonpost.com.

Hoover, J. Edgar. 1947. "Speech before the House Committee on Un-American Activities." March 26. Voices of Democracy: The U.S. Oratory Project. http://voicesofdemocracy. umd.edu.

Hopkins, Keith. 1993. "Novel Evidence for Roman Slavery." *Past and Present* 138.1: 3–27. doi:10.1093/past/138.1.3

Hunt, Morton M. 1999. *The New Know-Nothings: The Political Foes of the Scientific Study of Human Nature.* New Brunswick, NJ: Transaction Publishers.

Hunter, Edward. 1950. "'Brain-Washing' Tactics Force Chinese into Ranks of Communist Party." *Miami News*, September 24.

Hunter, Edward. 1951. *Brain-Washing in Red China: The Calculated Destruction of Men's Minds.* New York: Vanguard Press.

Hunter, Edward. 1956. *Brainwashing: The Story of the Men Who Defied It.* New York: Farrar, Straus and Cudahy.

Hunter, Kathryn Montgomery. 1992. "Remaking the Case." *Literature and Medicine* 11, no. 1: 163–179.

Ingebretsen, Edward. 1998. "*Monster*-Making: A Politics of Persuasion." *Journal of American Culture* 21, no. 2: 25–34.

"Interview: Peter Breggin." 2000. Frontline, May 3. http://www.pbs.org/wgbh/pages/ frontline/shows/medicating/interviews/breggin.html

Introvigne, Massimo. 2005. "L. Ron Hubbard, Kenneth Goff, and the 'Brain-Washing Manual' of 1955." *Cesnur: Centro Studi sulle Nuove Religioni.* http://www.cesnur. org/2005/brainwash_13.htm.

Invasion of the Body Snatchers. 1956. Directed by Don Siegel. Allied Artists.

Jacobsen, Carlyle F., J. B. Wolf, and T. A. Jackson. 1935. "An Experimental Analysis of the Functions of the Frontal Association Areas in Primates." *Journal of Nervous and Mental Disease* 92: 1–14.

Jacks, Kim. 2008. "Weston State Hospital." MA thesis, West Virginia State University.

Jasinski, James. 2001. *Sourcebook on Rhetoric: Key Concepts in Contemporary Rhetorical Studies.* London: Sage Publications.

Jenkins, Keith. 2003. *Refiguring History: New Thoughts on an Old Discipline.* London: Routledge.

Johnson, Jenell. 2012. "Disability, Animals, and the Rhetorical Boundaries of Personhood." *jac* 32, no. 1–2: 372–381.

Johnston, Ruth D. 1993. "Committed: Feminist Spectatorship and the Logic of the Supplement." *Journal of Film and Video* 45, no. 4: 22–39.

Jones, Robert A. 2004. "Science in National Cultures: The Message of Postage Stamps." *Public Understanding of Science* 13, no. 1: 75–81.

Jones, Timothy S., and David A. Sprunger. 2002. *Marvels, Monsters, and Miracles: Studies in the Medieval and Early Modern Imagination*. Kalamazoo, MI: Medieval Institute.

Kaimowitz, Gabe. 1980. "My Case against Psychosurgery." In *The Psychosurgery Debate*, edited by Elliot Valenstein, 506–519. San Francisco: W. H. Freeman.

Kaempffert, Walter. 1941. "Turning the Mind Inside Out." *Saturday Evening Post*, May 24, 18.

Kaplan, Jeffrey. 2000. "Kenneth Goff." In *Encyclopedia of White Power: A Sourcebook on the Radical Racist Right*, edited by Jeffrey Kaplan, 120–122. New York: Altamira Press.

Kauffman, Jeffrey. 2004. "Frances Farmer: Shedding Light on *Shadowland*." http://jeffreykauffman.net/francesfarmer/sheddinglight.html. Accessed April 9, 2013.

Kennan, George. 1946. "Long Telegram." National Security Archive. The George Washington University. http://www.gwu.edu/~nsarchiv/coldwar/documents/episode-1/kennan.htm.

Kennedy, Edward M. 1968. *Decisions for a Decade: Policies and Programs for the 1970s*. Garden City, NY: Doubleday & Company.

Kennedy, Edward M. 1972. In *A People of Compassion: The Concerns of Edward Kennedy*. Edited by Thomas P. Collins and Louis M. Savary, 1–23. New York: Regina Press.

Kesey, Ken. [1962] 1999. *One Flew over the Cuckoo's Nest*. New York: Penguin Books.

Kessler, Ronald. 1996. *Sins of the Father: Joseph P. Kennedy and the Dynasty He Founded*. New York: Time Warner Books.

Kiev, Ari. 1968. "Introduction." In *Psychiatry in the Communist World*, edited by Ari Kiev, 1–17. New York: Science House.

"Kill or Cure." 1946. *Time*, December 23, 66–67.

Kinkead, Eugene. 1959. *In Every War but One*. New York: Greenwood Press.

Kirk, Stuart, and Herb Kutchins. 1992. *The Selling of DSM: The Rhetoric of Science in Psychiatry*. New York: Aldine de Gruyter.

Kirkbride, Thomas Story. 1854. *On the Construction, Organization, and General Arrangements of Hospitals for the Insane*. Philadelphia: Lindsay & Blakston.

Klein, Kerwin L. 2000. "On the Emergence of Memory in Historical Discourse." *Representations* 69: 127–150.

Kominsky, Morris. 1970. *The Hoaxers: Plain Liars, Fancy Liars, and Damned Liars*. Boston: Branden Press.

Koppell, Brian Harris, Andre G. Machado, and Ali R. Rezai. 2005. "Not Your Father's Lobotomy: Psychiatric Surgery Revisited." *Clinical Neurosurgery* 52: 192–195. http://book2.neurosurgeon.org.

Koppell, Brian Harris, and Ali R. Rezai. 2003. "Psychiatric Neurosurgery: A Historical Perspective." In *Neurosurgery Clinics of North America—Surgery for Psychiatric Disorders*, edited by A. R. Rezai, S. A. Rasmussen, and B. D. Greenberg, 181–197. Philadelphia: Saunders.

Kragh, Jesper Vaczy. 2010. *Det hvide snit: Psykokirurgi og dansk psykiatri 1922–1983*. Odense: University of Southern Denmark Press.

Kramer, Morten. 1954. "The 1951 Survey of the Use of Psychosurgery." In *Proceedings of the Third Research Conference on Psychosurgery*, edited by F. A. Mettler and W Overholser, 159–173. Washington, DC: US Government Printing Office.

Kuhn, Thomas S. 1970. *The Structure of Scientific Revolutions*. 2nd edition. Chicago: University of Chicago Press.

LaGrandeur, Kevin. 2011. "The Persistent Peril of the Artificial Slave." *Science Fiction Studies* 38, no. 2: 232–252.

Laing, R. D. 1960. *The Divided Self: An Existential Study in Sanity and Madness*. Harmondsworth: Penguin.

Lal, G. B. 1947. "Reformed by Brain Surgery." *American Weekly*, March 9, 24.

Lamb, Peter. 1956. "Lobotomy: Commies' Secret for World Domination." *Suppressed* 3: 5.

Larson, Paul 2008. "Deep Brain Stimulation for Psychiatric Disorders." *Journal of the American Society for Experimental NeuroTherapeutics* 5, no. 1: 50–58.

Laurence, William L. 1937. "Surgery Used on the Soul-Sick Relief of Obsessions Is Reported." *New York Times*, June 7.

Laurence, William L. 1953. "Lobotomy Banned in Soviet as Cruel." *New York Times*, August 22.

Leamer, Laurence. 1994. *The Kennedy Women: The Saga of an American Family*. New York: Villard Books.

Leavitt, Judith W. 1986. *Brought to Bed: Childbearing in America 1750–1950*. New York: Oxford University Press.

LeDoux, Joseph E. 2002. *The Synaptic Self: How Our Brains Become Who We Are*. New York: Viking.

Lee, Gregory P., Antoine Bechara, Ralph Adolphs, John Arena, Kimford J. Meador, David W. Loring, and Joseph R. Smith. 1998. "Clinical and Physiological Effects of Stereotaxic Bilateral Amygdalotomy for Intractable Aggression." *Journal of Neuropsychiatry and Clinical Neurosciences* 10, no. 4: 413–420.

Lehmann, H. E. 1955. "Therapeutic Results with Chlorpromazine (Largactil) in Psychiatric Conditions." *Journal of the Canadian Medical Association* 72: 91–99.

Lehmann, H. E. 1989. "The Introduction of Chlorpromazine to North America." *Psychiatric Journal of the University of Ottawa* 14, no. 1: 263–265.

Leshner, Alan I. 2003. "Public Engagement with Science." *Science* 299: 977.

Leviero, Anthony. 1956. "Thinking to Order." *New York Times*, May 20.

Lewis, Bradley. 2006. *Moving Beyond Prozac, DSM, and the New Psychiatry: The Birth of Postpsychiatry*. Ann Arbor: University of Michigan Press.

Lifton, Robert Jay. [1961] 1989. *Thought Reform and the Psychology of Totalism: A Study of Brainwashing in China*. Chapel Hill: University of North Carolina Press.

Lindstrom, Petter A. 1972. "A Flawed Judgment." Letter. *Medical Opinion*, April 17, 464.

Lipsitz, George. 1990. *Time Passages: Collective Memory and American Popular Culture*. Minneapolis: University of Minnesota Press.

Lipsman, Nir, A. Meyerson, and Andres M. Lozano. 2012. "A Narrative History of the

International Society for Psychiatric Surgery: 1970–1983." *Sterotactic and Functional Neurosurgery* 12: 347–355.

Littlefield, Melissa M. 2011. *The Lying Brain: Lie Detection in Science and Science Fiction.* Ann Arbor: University of Michigan Press. "Lobotomy Called No Mental Cure by Psychiatrist." 1957. *Chicago Daily Tribune*, September 4.

"Lobotomy Disappointment." 1949. *Newsweek*, December 12, 51.

Locke, John. [1694] 1975. *An Essay Concerning Human Understanding.* Edited by Peter Nidditch. Oxford: Clarendon Press.

Locke, Simon. 2005. "Fantastically Reasonable: Ambivalence in the Representation of Science and Technology in Super-Hero Comics." *Public Understanding of Science* 14, no. 1: 25–46.

Lombroso, Cesare. 1911. *Crime: Its Causes and Remedies.* Translated by Henry P. Horton. Boston: Little, Brown, and Company.

"Medicine: Losing Nerves." 1947. *Time*, June 30. http://www.time.com/time/magazine/article/0,9171,854753,00.html.

MacCannell, Dean. 1999. *The Tourist: A New Theory of the Leisure Class.* Berkeley: University of California Press.

MacGregor, Greg. 1953. "Sympathy Wanes for Red-Led G.I.'s." *New York Times*, October 20.

MacLean, Paul. 1949. "Psychosomatic Disease and the 'Visceral Brain': Recent Developments Bearing on the Papez Theory of Emotion." *Pscyhosomatic Medicine* 11, no. 6: 338–353.

Makow, Henry. 2004. "John Kerry and the Art of Brainwashing." *Rense.com*, August 1. http://rense.com/general56/ubfit.htm.

Maltin, Leonard. 2012. "Rev. of Guilty of Treason." Turner Classic Movies. http://www.tcm.com/tcmdb/title/77067/Guilty-of-Treason.

The Manchurian Candidate. 1962. Directed by John Frankenheimer. United Artists.

Mann, Katrina. 2004. "'You're Next!': Postwar Hegemony Besieged in Invasion of the Body Snatchers." *Cinema Journal* 44, no. 1: 49–68.

Mark, Vernon H., and Frank Ervin. 1970. *Violence and the Brain.* New York: Harper Collins.

Mark, Vernon H., William Sweet, and Frank Ervin. 1967. "The Role of Brain Disease in Riots and Urban Violence." *Journal of the American Medical Association* 201, no. 11: 895.

Marks, John. 1979. *The Search for the "Manchurian Candidate": The CIA and Mind Control.* New York: McGraw-Hill.

Marmor, Judd, Viola W. Bernard, and Perry Ottenberg. 1960. "Psychodynamics of Group Opposition of Health Programs." *American Journal of Orthopsychiatry* 30, no. 2: 330–341.

Mashour, George A., Erin E. Walker, and Robert L. Martuza. 2004. "Psychosurgery: Past, Present, and Future." *Brain Research Reviews* 48: 409–419.

Mason, B. J. 1973. "New Threat to Blacks: Brain Surgery to Control Behavior." *Ebony*, February, 63–72.

Mayberg, Helen S., Andres M. Lozano, Valerie Voon, Heather E. McNeely, David Seminowicz, Clement Hamani, Jason M. Schwalb, and Sidney H. Kennedy. 2005. "Deep Brain Stimulation for Treatment-Resistant Depression." *Neuron* 45: 651–660.

McGee, Michael Calvin. 1980. "The 'Ideograph': A Link between Rhetoric and Ideology." *Quarterly Journal of Speech* 66, no. 1: 1–16.

McGirr, Lisa. 2002. *Suburban Warriors: The Origins of the New American Right*. Princeton, NJ: Princeton University Press.

"Medicine's Golden Era." 1944. *Baltimore Evening Sun*, May 22.

Meerloo, Joost. 1951. "The Crime of Menticide." *American Journal of Psychiatry* 107 (February): 594–598.

Meerloo, Joost. 1956. *The Rape of the Mind: The Psychology of Thought Control, Menticide, and Brainwashing*. Cleveland: World Publishing Company.

Melley, Timothy. 2000. *Empire of Conspiracy: The Culture of Paranoia in Postwar America*. Ithaca, NY: Cornell University Press.

Melley, Timothy. 2008. "Brainwashed! Conspiracy Theory and Ideology in the Postwar United States." *New German Critique* 35, no. 1: 145–164.

Merton, Robert K. 1973. *The Sociology of Science: Theoretical and Empirical Investigations*. Chicago: University of Chicago Press.

Metzl, Jonathan. 2003. *Prozac on the Couch: Prescribing Gender in the Era of Wonder Drugs*. Durham, NC: Duke University Press.

Micale, Mark. 2008. *Hysterical Men: The Hidden History of Male Nervous Illness*. Cambridge, MA: Harvard University Press.Micale, Mark, and Roy Porter. 1994. "Introduction: Reflections on Psychiatry and its Histories." In *Discovering the History of Psychiatry*, edited by Mark S. Micale and Roy Porter, 3–38. New York and Oxford: Oxford University Press.

Miller, Carolyn R. 1992. "*Kairos* in the Rhetoric of Science." In *A Rhetoric of Doing: Essays on Written Discourse in Honor of James Kinneavy*, edited by Stephen P. Witte, Neil Nakadate, and Roger D. Cherry, 310–327. Carbondale: Southern Illinois University Press.

Miller, Carolyn R. 1993. "The Polis as Rhetorical Community." *Rhetorica: A Journal of the History of Rhetoric* 11, no. 3: 211–240.

Miller, Steve. 2001. "Public Understanding of Science at the Crossroads." *Public Understanding of Science* 10, no. 1: 115–120.

Mindszenty, József. 1974. *Memoirs*. New York: Macmillan Publishing Company.

"Mindszenty Upheld by City Paraders." 1949. *New York Times*, February 14.

Moffitt, Jack. 1956. Review of *Invasion of the Body Snatchers*, directed by Don Siegel. *Hollywood Reporter*, February 2, 13.

Moniz, Egas. [1936] 1964. "Attempt at Surgical Treatment of Certain Psychoses." Translated by Robert H. Wilkins. *Journal of Neurosurgery* 21: 1110–1114.

Moran, Mark. 2004. "Psychosurgery Evolves into New Neurosurgery Approaches." *Psychiatric News* 39 (January 2): 28.

Morgan, John G. 1949. "Chairman Backs Exposé Articles." *Charleston Gazette*, February 1.

"My Lobotomy: Howard Dully's Journey." 2005. Produced by Piya Kochhar and Dave Isay. *Sound Portraits*, November 16. National Public Radio.

Nealon, Jeffrey T. 2008. *Foucault beyond Foucault: Power and its Intensifications After 1984*. Stanford, CA: Stanford University Press.

Neergaard, L. 2008. "Brain Pacemakers Tackle Depression." *Discovery Channel News, May 21*. http://dsc.discovery.com/news/2008/05/27/depression-pacemaker.html.

Nickerson, Michelle M. 2004. "The Lunatic Fringe Strikes Back: Conservative Opposition to the Alaska Mental Health Bill of 1956." In *The Politics of Healing: Histories of Alternative Medicine in Twentieth-Century North America*, edited by Robert D. Johnston, 117–152. London: Routledge.

Nielsen, Kim. 2004. *The Radical Lives of Helen Keller*. New York: New York University Press.

Nietzsche, Friedrich. [1886] 2001. *Beyond Good and Evil: Prelude to a Philosophy of the Future*. Edited by Rolf-Peter Horstmann. Translated by Judith Norman. Cambridge: Cambridge University Press.

Nijensohn, D. E., L. E. Savastano, A. D. Kaplan, and E. R. Laws Jr. 2012. "New Evidence of Prefrontal Lobotomy in the Last Months of the Illness of Eva Perón." *World Neurosurgery* 77, no. 3: 583–590.

"No Psychosurgery in the U.S.S.R." 1953. *American Journal of Psychiatry* 110: 470.

Nora, Pierre. [1984] 1989. "Between Memory and History: *Les lieux de mémoire*." *Representations* 26: 7–25.

"Noted 'Ice Pick' Operation Done at Lakin State." 1950. *Charleston Gazette*, July 6.

Oates, Joyce Carol. 1995. *Zombie*. New York: HarperCollins.

O'Brien, Gerald. 2004. "Rosemary Kennedy: The Importance of a Historical Footnote." *Journal of Family History* 29, no. 3: 225–236.

O'Leary, J. Patrick. 2004. "Marion Sims: A Defense of the Father of Gynecology." *Southern Medical Journal* 97, no. 5: 427–429.

Oltman, Jane E., Bernard S. Brody, Samuel Friedman, and William Green. 1949. "Frontal Lobotomy: Clinical Experience with 107 Cases in a State Hospital." *American Journal of Psychiatry* 105, no. 10: 742–751.

One Flew over the Cuckoo's Nest. 1975. Directed by Milos Forman. United Artists.

"Operate on Brain to Reform Woman." 1946. *New York Times*, December 7.

Oregon Senate. 1973. Oregon Psychosurgery Bill (SB) 298. Portland: Oregon Legislative Assembly.

Parry-Giles, Shawn J. 1994. "Propaganda, Effect, and the Cold War: Gauging the Status of America's 'War of Words.'" *Political Communication* 11, no. 2: 203–213.

Pasley, Virginia. 1955. *21 Stayed*. New York: Farrar, Straus and Cudahy.

Perelman, Chaïm. 1982. *The Realm of Rhetoric*. Notre Dame: University of Notre Dame Press.

Pezzullo, Phaedra. 2007. *Toxic Tourism: Rhetorics of Pollution, Travel, and Environmental Justice*. Tuscaloosa: University of Alabama Press.

Planet of the Apes. 1968. Directed by Franklin J. Schaffner. Twentieth Century-Fox.

Plumb, Robert. 1949. "Wider Data Urged in Brain Surgery." *New York Times*, May 7.

Popp, Richard. 2010. "Domesticating Vacations: Gender, Travel, and Consumption in Post-War Magazines." *Journalism History* 36, no. 3: 126–137.

Popp, Richard. 2012. *The Holiday Makers: Magazines, Advertising, and Mass Tourism in Postwar America*. Baton Rouge: Louisiana State University Press.

Portelli, Alessandro. 1991. *The Death of Luigi Trastulli and Other Stories*. New York: State University of New York Press.

Post, Robert M. and Susan R.B. Weiss. 1998. "Sensitization and Kindling Phenomena in Mood, Anxiety, and Obsessive-Compulsive Disorders: The Role of Serotonergic Mechanisms in Illness Progression." *Biological Psychiatry* 44, no. 3: 193-206.

Potter, Robert D. 1946. "Miracles of Brain Surgery." *American Weekly*, May 19, 11.

Pressman, Gabriel. 1949. "Eye-Witness Account of Cardinal's Trial, Sent from Outside Hungary, Depicts Cynical Travesty on Justice." *North Country Catholic Edition of Our Sunday Visitor*, February 27.

Pressman, Jack D. 1999. *Last Resort: Psychosurgery and the Limits of Medicine*. New York: Cambridge University Press.

Price, Margaret. 2011. *Mad at School: Rhetorics of Mental Disability and Academic Life*. Ann Arbor: University of Michigan Press.

"Probers Made Ill By Weston Visit." 1949. *Charleston Gazette*, January 30.

"Proposal for Surgery on Convicts Rejected." 1971. *Los Angeles Times*, December 26.

Psychosurgery Review Board (Australia). http://www.prb.vic.gov.au. Accessed April 11, 2009.

"Push Button People." 1967. *New York Times*, April 10.

Racine, Eric, Ofek Bar-Ilan, and Judy Illes. 2005. "fMRI in the Public Eye." *Nature Reviews Neuroscience* 6, no. 2: 159–164.

Raz, Mical. 2008. "Between the Ego and the Icepick: Psychosurgery, Psychoanalysis, and Psychiatric Discourse." *Bulletin of the History of Medicine* 82, no. 2: 387–420.

Raz, Mical. 2009. "The Painless Brain: Lobotomy, Psychiatry, and the Treatment of Chronic Pain and Terminal Illness." *Perspectives in Biology and Medicine* 52, no. 4: 555–565.

Raz, Mical. 2010. "Psychosurgery, Industry and Personal Responsibility, 1940–1965." *Social History of Medicine* 23, no. 1: 116–133.

Rév, István. 2002. "The Suggestion." *Representations* 80, no. 1: 62–98.

Reverby, Susan M. 2001. "More Than Fact and Fiction: Cultural Memory and the Tuskegee Study." *Hastings Center Report* 31: 22–28.

Richards, S. E. 2008. "Neurostimulation: Is It a Good Idea to Drill Holes in People's Heads to Treat Them for Depression?" *Slate.com*, February 19. http://www.slate.com/id/2184699/pagenum/all.

Ricouer, Paul. 2006. *Memory, History, Forgetting.* Translated by K. Blamey and D. Pellauer. Chicago: University of Chicago Press.

Robison, Donald. 1965. "The Far Right's Fight against Mental Health." *Look*, January 26.

Röder, Thomas, Volker Kubillus, and Anthony Burwell. 1994. *Psychiatrists: The Men behind Hitler.* Los Angeles: Freedom Press.

Rose, Nikolas. 2000. "The Biology of Culpability: Pathological Identity and Crime Control in a Biological Culture." *Theoretical Criminology* 4, no. 1: 5–34.

Rose, Nikolas. 2007. *The Politics of Life Itself: Biomedicine, Power, and Subjectivity in the Twenty First Century.* Princeton, NJ: Princeton University Press.

Rosenfeld, J. V., and J. H. Lloyd. 1999. "Contemporary Psychosurgery." *Journal of Clinical Neuroscience* 6, no. 2: 106–112.

Roskies, Adina. 2002. "Neuroethics for the New Millennium." *Neuron* 35, no. 1: 21–23.

Rosenhan, David. 1974. "On Being Sane in Insane Places." *Science* 179: 250–258.

Rothman, David J. [1971] 2009. *The Discovery of the Asylum: Social Order and Disorder in the New Republic.* Piscataway, NJ: Aldine Transaction.

Royster, Jacqueline Jones. 1995. "To Call a Thing by Its True Name: The Rhetoric of Ida B. Wells." *Reclaiming Rhetorica: Women in the Rhetorical Tradition*, edited by Andrea A. Lunsford, 167–184. Pittsburgh: University of Pittsburgh Press.

Ruch, Walter W. 1946. "Operate on Brain to Reform Woman." *New York Times*, December 7.

Rylander, Gosta. 1948. "Personality Analysis Before and After Frontal Lobotomy." *Association for Research in Nervous and Mental Disease* 27: 691–705.

Sachdev, Perminder. 2007. "Is Deep Brain Stimulation a Form of Psychosurgery?" *Australasian Psychiatry* 15, no. 2: 97–99.

Sachdev, Perminder, and Xiaohua Chen. 2008. "Neurosurgical Treatment of Mood Disorders: Traditional Psychosurgery and the Advent of Deep Brain Stimulation." *Current Opinion in Psychiatry* 22: 25–31.

Sadowsky, Jonathan. 2006. "Beyond the Metaphor of the Pendulum: Electroconvulsive Therapy, Psychoanalysis, and the Styles of American Psychiatry." *Journal of the History of Medicine and Allied Sciences* 61, no. 1: 1–25.

Safire, William. 2002. "The But-What-If Factor." *New York Times*, May 16. http://www.nytimes.com/2002/05/16/opinion/16SAFI.html.

Samuels, Ellen. 2011. "Examining Millie and Christine McKoy: Where Enslavement and Enfreakment Meet." *Signs* 37, no. 1: 53–81. doi:10.1086/660176.

Samuels, Stuart. 1979. "The Age of Conspiracy and Conformity: Invasion of the Body Snatchers." In American History/American Film: Interpreting the Hollywood Image, edited by John E. O'Connor and Martin A. Jackson, 203-217. New York: Ungar Publishing Company.

San Fernando Valley Doctors Committee on Mental Health. [1961?] *The Doctors Speak Up: An Answer to Irresponsible Attacks on the Mental Health Program.* Self published.

Agency and Miscellaneous Papers, San Fernando Valley Doctors' Committee on Mental Health Folder, Social Welfare Archives, University of Southern California, Los Angeles.

Sartin, J. S. 2004. "J. Marion Sims, the Father of Gynecology: Hero or Villain?" *Southern Medical Journal* 97, no. 5: 500–504.

"Scalpel Brain-Washing." 1955. *Kannapolis (NC) Daily Independent*, March 29.

Schanda, Balázs. 2011. *Religion and Law in Hungary*. Frederick, MD: Kluwer Law International.

Schiappa, Edward. 2003. *Defining Reality: Definitions and the Politics of Meaning*. Carbondale: Southern Illinois University Press.

Scoville, William Beecher. 1972. "In Defense of Psychosurgery." Letter. *Medical Opinion*, April 17, 13.

Scull, Andrew. 1979. *Museums of Madness: The Social Organization of Insanity in Nineteenth-Century England*. London: Allen Lane.

Scull, Andrew. 2005. *Madhouse: A Tragic Tale of Megalomania and Modern Medicine*. New Haven: Yale University Press.

Sedgwick, Eve Kosofsky. 2003. *Touching Feeling: Affect, Pedagogy, Performativity*. Durham, NC: Duke University Press.

Seed, David. 2004. *Brainwashing: The Fictions of Mind Control: A Study of Novels and Films Since World War II*. Kent, OH: Kent State University Press.

Segal, Judy Z. 2005. *Health and the Rhetoric of Medicine*. Carbondale: Southern Illinois State University Press.

Sheth, Sameer A., Jonathan Neal, Frances Tangherlini, Matthew K. Mian, Andre Gentil, G. Rees Cosgrove, Emad N. Eskandar, and Darin D. Dougherty. 2012. "Limbic System Surgery for Treatment-Refractory Obsessive-Compulsive Disorder: A Prospective Long-Term Follow-up of 64 Patients." *Journal of Neurosurgery* 118: 491–497.

Shorter, Edward. 1997. *A History of Psychiatry: From the Era of the Asylum to the Age of Prozac*. New York: John Wiley & Sons.

Shouse, Eric. 2005. "Feeling, Emotion, Affect." *M/C Journal* 8. http://journal.media-culture.org.au/0512/03-shouse.php.

Showalter, Elaine. 1985. *The Female Malady: Women, Madness, and English Culture, 1830–1980*. New York: Penguin Books.

Shuman, Samuel I. 1980. "The Concept of Informed Consent." In *The Psychosurgery Debate: Scientific, Legal, and Ethical Perspectives*, edited by Elliot S. Valenstein, 439–463. San Francisco: W. H. Freeman and Company.

Small, Sidney Herschel. 1955. "The Brainwashed Pilot." *Saturday Evening Post*, March 19, 31+.

Smith, John E. 1986. "Time and Qualitative Time." *Review of Metaphysics* 40, no. 1: 3–16.

Smith, J. Sydney, and L. G. Kiloh. 1974. *Psychosurgery and Society*. London: Pergamon Press.

Snyder, Sharon, and David Mitchell. 2006. *Cultural Locations of Disability*. Chicago and London: University of Chicago Press.

"Son Confesses Slaying Father While Hunting." 1942. *Wisconsin Rapids Daily Tribune*, October 19.

Song, Sora. 2006. "How Deep Brain Stimulation Works." *Time*, July 16. http://www.time.com/time/magazine/article/0,9171,1214939,00.html.

Squier, Susan. 2004. *Liminal Lives: Imagining the Human at the Frontiers of Biomedicine*. Durham, NC, and London: Duke University Press.

Stein, Rob. 2004. "The Potential of 'Brain Pacemakers': Implanted Devices May Alter Treatment of Many Disorders." *Washington Post*, March 6.

Sterling, Peter. 1978. "Ethics and Effectiveness of Psychosurgery." In *Controversy in Psychiatry*, edited by John Paul Bradie and H. Keith H. Brodie, 126–160. Philadelphia: W. B. Saunders Company.

Stone, A. A. 2008. "Psychosurgery: Old and New." *Psychiatric Times* 25. http://www.psychiatrictimes.com/display/article/10168/1163539?pageNumber=2.

Streatfeild, Dominic. 2007. *Brainwash: The Secret History of Mind Control*. New York: Thomas Dunne Books.

Steffen-Fluhr, Nancy. 1984. "Women and the Inner Game of Don Siegel's 'Invasion of the Body Snatchers.'" *Science Fiction Studies* 11, no. 2: 139-153.

Strecker, Edward A., Harold D. Palmer, and Francis C. Grant. 1942. "A Study of Frontal Lobotomy: Neurosurgical and Psychiatric Features and Results in 22 Cases with a Detailed Report on 5 Chronic Schizophrenics." *American Journal of Psychiatry* 98: 524–532.

Sugrue, Thomas. 1996. *The Origins of the Urban Crisis: Race and Inequality in Post-War Detroit*. Princeton, NJ: Princeton University Press.

"Suicide Note." 2006. *News 8 Austin*. July 24. http://www.news8austin.com/content/news_8_explores/ut_tower_shooting.

Sullivan, Tom. 1961. *Mental Health*? Self published.

Sullivan, Walter. 1966. "Effects of a Tumor on the Brain Can Cause Antisocial Behavior." *New York Times*, August 3.

"Surgeons Hope Brain Operation Will Make Woman Criminal 'Good.'" 1946. *Charleston Gazette*, December 7, 1.

"Surgery Cure Fails, Burglar Hangs Himself." 1952. *Chicago Daily Tribune*, June 30.

"Surgery Ends in Suicide." 1952. *New York Times*, June 30.

"Surgery Is Tried in Morals Case: Part of Degenerate's Brain Cut to Aid Her Character." 1946. *Baltimore Sun*, December 7.

"Surgical Brainwash." 1955. *Kannapolis (NC) Daily Independent*, March 29.

Susman, Warren. 1984. "'Personality' and the Making of Twentieth-Century Culture." In *Culture as History: The Transformation of American Society in the Twentieth Century*, 271–285. New York: Pantheon.

Synofzik, Mathhis, and Thomas E. Schlaepfer. 2008. "Stimulating Personality: Ethical Criteria for Deep Brain Stimulation in Psychiatric Patients and for Enhancement Purposes." *Biotechnology Journal* 3, no. 12: 1511–1520.

Szasz, Thomas. 1961. *The Myth of Mental Illness*. New York: Harper & Row.

Taylor, Kathleen. 2004. *Brainwashing: The Science of Thought Control*. Oxford: Oxford University Press.

Taylor, Charles A. 1996. *Defining Science: A Rhetoric of Demarcation*. Madison: University of Wisconsin Press.

"Their Tongues Cut Off." 1949. *Time*, February 14, 28–32.

Tomes, Nancy. 1984. *A Generous Confidence: Thomas Story Kirkbride and the Art of Asylum-Keeping, 1840–1883*. Cambridge: Cambridge University Press.

Turner, Kathleen J. 2003. "Introduction: Rhetorical History as Social Construction." In *Doing Rhetorical History: Concepts and Cases*, edited by Kathleen Turner, 1–16. Tuscaloosa and London: University of Alabama Press.

Trotter, Robert. 1972. "A Clockwork Orange in a California Prison." *Science News* March 11, 174–175.

Turkel, William J. "Intervention: Hacking History, From Analogue to Digital and Back Again." *Rethinking History* 15, no. 2 (2011): 287–296.

Umbarger, Carter, James Dalsimer, Andrew Morrison, and Peter Breggin. 1962. *College Students in a Mental Hospital: Contribution to the Social Rehabilitation of the Mentally Ill*. New York: Grune & Stratton.

"The Upper South: Tour by Two Soviet Ex-Pilots Evokes a Mixed Reaction." 1949. *New York Times*, February 14.

US Congress. Senate. 1956. *Alaska Mental Health*. Subcommittee on Territories and Insular Affairs, Committee on Interior and Insular Affairs. 84th Congress, 2nd session, February 20–21, March 5. Washington, DC.

US Congress. Senate. 1973. Subcommittee on Health. Committee on Labor and Public Welfare. *Quality of Health Care—Human Experimentation, Part 2*. 93rd Congress, 1st session, March 6. Washington, DC.

US National Commission for the Protection of Human Subjects of Biomedical and Behavioral Research. 1977. *Psychosurgery: Report and Recommendations*. Washington, DC: US Government Printing Office. DHEW publication (OS) 77–0001.

Ussher, Jane M. 2011. *The Madness of Women: Myth and Experience*. London: Routledge.

Vaernet, K., and Anna Madsen. 1970. "Stereotaxic Amygdalotomy and Basofrontal Tractotomy in Psychotics with Aggressive Behavior." *Journal of Neurology, Neurosurgery, and Psychiatry* 33, no. 6: 858–863.

Valenstein, Elliot S. 1973. *Brain Control*. New York: Wiley.

Valenstein, Elliot S. 1986. *Great and Desperate Cures: The Rise and Decline of Psychosurgery and Other Radical Treatments for Mental Illness*. New York: Basic Books.

Vatz, Richard, and Lee S. Weinberg. 1994. "The Rhetorical Paradigm in Psychiatric History: Thomas Szasz and the Myth of Mental Illness." In *Discovering the History of Psychiatry*, edited by Mark S. Micale and Roy Porter, 311–330. New York and Oxford: Oxford University Press.

Vidal, Fernando. 2009. "Brainhood, Anthropological Figure of Modernity." *History of the Human Sciences* 22, no. 1: 5–36.

Waddell, Craig. 1990. "The Role of Pathos in the Decision-Making Process: A Study in the Rhetoric of Science Policy." *Quarterly Journal of Speech* 76: 381–400.

Waldby, Catherine. 1996. *AIDS and the Body Politic: Biomedicine and Sexual Difference*. New York: Routledge.

Waldby, Catherine. 2000. *The Visible Human Project: Informatic Bodies and Posthuman Medicine*. New York: Routledge.

Walker, Jeffrey. 1994. "The Body of Persuasion: A Theory of the Enthymeme." *College English* 56, no. 1: 46–65.

Wall, Lewis L. 2006. "The Medical Ethics of Dr. J. Marion Sims: A Fresh Look at the Historical Record." *Journal of Medical Ethics* 32, no. 6: 346–350.

Wallace, Irving. 1951. "The Operation of Last Resort." *Saturday Evening Post*, October 20, 24+.

Walton, Douglas. 2001. "Persuasive Definitions and Public Policy Arguments." *Argumentation and Advocacy* 37: 117–132.

"Warner Baxter, 59, Film Star, Is Dead." 1951. *New York Times*, May 8. *ProQuest Historical Newspapers*.

Washington, Harriet. 2008. *Medical Apartheid: The Dark History of Medical Experimentation on Black Americans from Colonial Times to the Present*. New York: Anchor.

Washuk, Bonnie. 2011. "Fright Night in Auburn." *Auburn (ME) Sun Journal*, October 15. http://www.sunjournal.com/hauntedhouse.

Weaver, Richard. 1970. "Language Is Sermonic." In *Language Is Sermonic: Richard M. Weaver on the Nature of Rhetoric*, edited by Richard L. Johannesen, Rennard Strickland, and Ralph T. Eubanks, 201–225. Baton Rouge: Louisiana State University Press.

Wells, Sandy. 2009. "Ex–Mental Health Worker Recalls Time of Lobotomies." *Charleston Sunday Gazette Mail*, March 1.

Wertz, D. C. 2002. "Embryo and Stem Cell Research in the United States: History and Politics." *Gene Therapy* 9, no. 11: 674–678.

Whitaker, Robert. 2002. *Mad in America: Bad Science, Bad Medicine, and the Enduring Mistreatment of the Mentally Ill*. New York: Perseus Books.

Whitehouse, Peter. 2012. "A Clinical Neuroscientist Looks Neuroskeptically at Neuroethics in the Neuroworld." In *The Neuroscientific Turn: Transdisciplinarity in the Age of the Brain*, edited by Melissa M. Littlefield and Jenell M. Johnson, 199–215. Ann Arbor: University of Michigan Press.

Wickline, John. 2008. "Picketers to Protest at Weston Hospital." *InterMountain.com*, June 13. http://www.theintermountain.com/page/content.detail/id/507872/Picketers-To-Protest-At-Weston-Hospital.html

Williams, Stephanie. 1957. "Lobotomy Is a Dangerous Weapon." *American Mercury*, August, 141–144.

Williams, Tennessee. [1958] 1998. *Suddenly, Last Summer*. New York: Dramatists Play Service, Inc.

Wilson, Elizabeth A. 1998. *Neural Geographies: Feminism and the Microstructure of Cognition*. New York: Routledge.

Wind, J. J., and D. E. Anderson. 2008. "From Prefrontal Leukotomy to Deep Brain Stimulation: The Historical Transformation of Psychosurgery and the Emergence of Neuroethics." *Neurosurgical Focus* 25, no. 1: 1–5.

Winter, Jay. 2000. "The Generation of Memory: Reflections on the Memory Boom in Contemporary Historical Studies." *Bulletin of the German Historical Institute* 27: 69–92.

Wright, Dale. 1953. "Can Surgery Cure Evil Women?" *Jet*, August 20, 25–27.

Wu, Cynthia. 2012. *Chang and Eng Reconnected: The Original Siamese Twins in American Culture*. Philadelphia: Temple University Press.

Wubben, H. H. 1970. "American Prisoners of War in Korea: A Second Look at the 'Something New in History' Theme." *American Quarterly* 22, no. 1: 3–19.

Yudofsky, Stuart C. 2008. Editorial. "Changing Tides in Neurosurgical Interventions for Treatment-Resistant Depression." *American Journal of Psychiatry* 165, no. 6: 671–674.

Yudofsky, Stuart, and Fred Ovsiew. 1990. Editorial. "Neurosurgical and Related Interventions for the Treatment of Patients with Psychiatric Disorders." *Journal of Neuropsychiatry* 2, no. 3: 253–255.

Zamiska, Nicholas. 2007. "In China, Brain Surgery Is Pushed on the Mentally Ill." *Wall Street Journal*, November 2. http://online.wsj.com.

Zarefsky, David. 2003. "Four Senses of Rhetorical History." In *Doing Rhetorical History: Concepts and Cases*, edited by Kathleen Turner, 19–32. Tuscaloosa and London: University of Alabama Press.

Zola, Irving. 1972. "Medicine as an Institution of Social Control." *Sociological Review* 20, no. 4: 487–504.

Zweiback, Adam. 1998. "'Turncoat GIs': Nonrepatriations and the Political Culture of the Korean War." *Historian* 60, no. 2: 345–362.

INDEX